VISITO.
W.

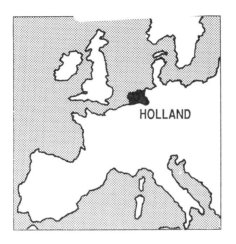

HOLLAND

NORTH SEA

AMELAND
SCHIERMONNIKOOG
TERSCHELLING
VLIELAND
CHAPTER 8
GRONINGEN
LEEUWARDEN
TEXEL
CHAPTER 7
ASSEN
CHAPTER 9
CHAPTER 5
CHAPTER 6
ALKMAAR
CHAPTER 12
ZWOLLE
CHAPTER 13
AMSTERDAM
CHAPTER 4
APELDOORN
ENSCHEDE
DEN HAAG
(THE HAGUE)
CHAPTER 10
AMERSFOORT
CHAPTER 3
CHAPTER 11
UTRECHT
CHAPTER 2
NIJMEGEN
ROTTERDAM
CHAPTER 14
CHAPTER 1
CHAPTER 16
BREDA
CHAPTER 15
MIDDELBURG
EINDHOVEN
VENLO
GERMANY
CHAPTER 17
BELGIUM

0 10 20 30 40 50
kilometres

N

HOLLAND

MAASTRICHT

Contents

Key to Symbols

⛪	Church/Ecclesiastical site	❊	Other place of interest
♣	Parkland	🚶	Recommended walk
Π	Archaeological site	⊞	Building of interest
⚘	Beautiful view/Scenery, Natural phenomenon	🏰	Castle/Fortification
🏛	Museum/Art gallery	🗙	Windmill
		🐦	Birdlife

Key to Maps

●🔺	Town/City	Rivers	
══════	Motorway	Lakes	
—·—·—	National boundary		

How To Use This Guide

This MPC Visitor's Guide has been designed to be as easy to use as possible. Each chapter covers a region or itinerary in a natural progression which gives all the background information to help you enjoy your visit. MPC's distinctive margin symbols, the important places printed in bold, and a comprehensive index enable the reader to find the most interesting places to visit with ease.

At the end of each chapter an Additional Information section gives specific details such as addresses and opening times, making this guide a complete sightseeing companion.

At the back of the guide the Fact File, arranged in alphabetical order, gives practical information and useful tips to help you plan your holiday — before you go and while you are there.

The maps of each region show the main towns, villages, roads and places of interest, but are not designed as route maps and motorists should always use a good recommended road atlas.

The routes are intended as a guide and should not necessarily be attempted in one day.

Placed marked * in the Additional Information are in the museum card scheme. See Fact File for details.

GLOSSARY OF USEFUL WORDS

The visitor to Holland will come across many Dutch words, especially on signs. Many of these are explained in the text, others are fairly obvious but to avoid unnecessary repetition the important ones are listed below.

Bezoekerscentrum	Visitor Centre
Binnen	Indoor, inside (eg Binnenmuseum)
Borg	Fortified manor house (Groningen)
Brink	Village green, or town centre formerly a village green (Derenthe)
Brug	Bridge
Buiten	Outdoors, outside (eg Buitenmuseum)
Dijk	Dyke (In Holland this refers to a bank, not a drainage ditch)
Gebouw	Building (eg Concertgebouw = concert hall)
Gemeente	Municipality
Gemeentehuis	Council Offices
Grote	Big (eg Grotekerk, Grote Markt)
Hof	Court
Hofje	Almshouses (literally 'little court')
Huis	House (sometimes refers to stately home)
Kanaal	Canal
Kasteel	Castle or stately home
Kerk	Church
Klein(e)	Small, little
Klokkenstoel	Wooden belfry, normally isolated from church
Klooster	Monastery or nunnery
Landgoed	Country estate
Markt	Market (square)
Molen	Mill
Openluchtmuseum	Open-air museum
Oudheidkamer	Museum of antiquities
Plein	Square
Poort	Town gate

Ruine	Historical ruin
Rijks-	National or State (eg Rijksmuseum)
Slot	Castle (usually fortified)
Staats-	Government or State (eg Staatsbosbeheer)
Staatsbosbeheer	State Forest Service or Forestry Commission
Stadswandeling	Town walk
Stadhuis	Town hall
Stedelijk	Municipal
Straat	Street
Terp	Artificial mound on which village was built to protect from flooding
Toren	Tower
Vesting	Fortress (historic fortress town centres are usually signed thus)
Waag	Weigh-house
Weeshuis	Orphanage
Wierd	Artificial mound like a *Terp* (In Groningen)
Wipmolen	Small hollow post-mill for pumping water, most common in Zuid-Holland

Note: The letter Y does not normally appear in Dutch, usually being written as IJ. It appears in indexes in the same position as an English Y. For example IJsselstein may sometimes be written as Ysselstein. Also Vollenhove would appear before Vijhuis in a gazetteer, and Workum appears before Wijns. Proper names beginning with these letter are written with them both in capitals, eg IJssel.

INTRODUCTION

Holland is a small country, with an area of about 40,000sqkm of which more than 25 percent has been reclaimed from the sea. This figure increases as yet more land is reclaimed. Two-fifths of the country is below sea level and, without the protection of the man-made dykes, this would be covered by water at high tide. Except for the southernmost parts of the country, where the ground rises to a height of about 300m above sea level, hilly ground is almost unknown, and there are few places where the land exceeds 50m in height. The notion that, because it is flat, the country must be uninteresting, is simply not true. The ever-present water gives a quality of light which the Dutch landscape artists recognised.

Central Holland consists of the three great river plains, which are protected from flooding by a system of dykes, dams, locks and canals. Further south, in Brabant and North Limburg, there is bog peat and heathland, which is also found in Friesland and parts of Utrecht province. Here, great lakes have been formed by the flooding of peat workings. The area known as the Veluwe is one great heathland, stretching from the shores of the IJsselmeer in the north to Arnhem in the south. The east and far south of the country is 'old land' — more hilly and wooded, and where most of the traces of early civilisations are to be found.

As early as the seventh century AD, dykes were constructed to hold back the sea, but the first real development of the polders — land reclaimed from the sea — came in the sixteenth century with the development of windmills for pumping, which enabled the land cut off from the sea by dykes to be drained and used for agriculture.

The draining of the Zuiderzee was contemplated as early as the seventeenth century, but this was not feasible for another 200 years. Work started in 1919, since when more than 1.5 million hectares (6 million acres) have been reclaimed in that area alone. The scale of these engineering feats has to be seen to be believed, and the Dutch are very proud of their achievements. By the time the present plans are completed, the coastline of the Netherlands will have been reduced by approximately 1,550km, of which more than 1,000km is in the 'delta' area around the former islands of the south-west. Although the original plans were intended to provide good defences against the sea and give more agricultural land, the works have done far more than this. Drinking water supplies have been greatly improved, and large areas for recreation have been created. In addition, in the Flevo-polders, two new cities have been built to allow people to move from overcrowded cities to pleasant new environments.

Flora and Fauna

There are many beautiful areas of Holland which abound with plants, birds and animals. The dunes in the west are particularly beautiful, with thorn bushes, brambles and roses growing in profusion beside winding paths, giving colour all year round. Tall pines and delicate silver birches offer restful shade for human and animal population alike, for the area abounds with small mammmals, lizards, pheasants and sea birds. Within the dunes are small lakes, offering safe breeding grounds for a variety of water birds, including spoonbills. Due to the effect of the sea breaking through in bygone days, great deposits of clay have built up and mixed with the sand. This has left large fertile areas which are ideal for growing bulbs and other market garden produce. The whole area from Den Haag in the south to Den Helder in the north is full of colour when the bulbfields are in bloom. South of Den Haag is the area known as Westland, famous for its greenhouses and products such as tomatoes, lettuces and grapes.

Small animals are also to be found in the many new forestry and nature areas of the Flevoland, even deer in a few places. Many migrating birds are found here also, and at the end of May the whole area is ablaze with yellow rape-seed flowers. These flowers also attract the bees, so hives are put out and honey is produced. Beehives can also be found beside the many paths which wind across the heathlands of the Veluwe, Drenthe and parts of Twente and Achterhoek, where deer, foxes, badgers and wild pigs may be seen. There are probably more nature reserves in Drenthe than in any other province and, despite its distance from the coast, the area is well known for the breeding grounds of seagulls. Central Holland, along the three great rivers, is the main fruit-growing area, and it is a treat to visit the region when the apple, pear and cherry trees are in bloom.

The People and the Language

Holland has the highest population density of any other European country, averaging more than 2,000 people per square kilometre of land. More than 14 million people live in the six major cities, and by far the largest part of the population lives within North and South Holland and Utrecht. Although these provinces cover only about one-fifth of the total land area of Holland, almost half of the country's population lives there.

At first the Dutch appear to be rather staid and formal; however, they are most friendly and welcoming. As in many other countries of continental Europe, a handshake should precede any conversation: a Dutchman will shake hands and say his name by way of introduction, and the visitor should do likewise. Many Dutch people speak English very well, although in country villages it is not so widely spoken, particularly by the older folk. Most have a great regard for the British and their allies who played such a large part in the liberation of Holland at the end of World War II. The effort to learn some basic phrases of the language will be much appreciated. In Friesland, the old Fries language is spoken by many people, and in the south of Limburg, French and German may be used. Once you get the idea of the language, it is not too difficult to work out the meaning of some of the words, for many sound similar to the English equivalent, even though the spelling is somewhat different. For example, *huis* in Dutch sounds similar to house in English, and means the same. Most words which are spelt with 'ui' together sound much the same as the 'ou' sound in house. *Uit* means out, or exit. *Boot* in Dutch sounds very similar to boat in English, and means the same. The Dutch 'oo' sound almost always sounds like the English 'oa'. When it is followed by an 'r' it sounds more like 'oor' as in 'door' eg *Spoorweg* (meaning railway).

Visitors should remember that in some of the more traditional villages

Lifting bridges — like this one near the Haringvliet Sluizen — are a common hazard for motorists in Holland

— such as Staphorst, Huizen, and the former islands of Urk and Marken — taking photographs may cause offence. In any case, do not take photographs of local people without first asking, and never do so on a Sunday. In Staphorst, a local bye-law prohibits photography of the inhabitants.

History

The Kingdom of the Netherlands — the correct name of the country, although 'Holland' is becoming more widely used even in official circles and by the Dutch themselves, even though it strictly only applies to the provinces of South and North Holland — was established in 1815 after a long period of conquest by many countries. Evidence for early settlement can be found in the form of huge megalithic monuments, ancient *terps* and dykes, and Roman remains. Because of flooding and the natural division of the country into two halves by the great rivers, the south of the country developed at a much faster rate. Fortunes changed with the development of the windmill for pumping, which enabled the land behind the dykes to be drained, and with the growth of international trade.

This was the era of the East India Company, whose influence contributed to the Revolt of the Netherlands against King Philip II of Spain led by William the Silent. From this the Republic of the Seven Provinces emerged as an independent nation, and the 'Golden Age' began. During the second half of the seventeenth century the United Provinces were at war with England, culminating in the battle of the Medway in 1667. The war ended when the English deposed James II in 1688 and offered the crown to William of Orange and his wife Mary, James' daughter.

After further wars with England and France in the eighteenth and nineteenth centuries, the constitutional monarchy gradually developed into a parliamentary democracy, and the Dutch have emerged as a nation contributing much to both European and world civilisation. Their scholars, artists and scientists are well-known. Their Stock Exchange is the oldest in the world. Their traders to the Indies made great discoveries. In modern times they have proved their courage, having suffered terribly during World War II. Their courage also shows in their daring advances in engineering techniques, allowing the construction of huge storm barriers in areas which would have been unthinkable only a few years ago, and the reclamation of vast areas of land from the sea.

Art, Culture and Everyday Life

It is inevitable that Dutch culture is thought of in terms of the seventeenth century, because that is when Dutch influence spread world-wide. Much of the wealth — gold, silver, fine furniture and porcelain —brought back by merchants is preserved in more than 500 museums throughout the country. The many works by Dutch painters of the Golden Age are also to be found in these museums, as well as paintings and sculptures of the nineteenth and twentieth centuries.

There are many magnificent castles, country houses and estates, dating back many centuries, and modern architecture also has its place. Many old brick buildings from the Golden Age remain intact, although after restoration these can look deceptively new, as the mortar has to be renewed and the surface cleaned during the process.

Music plays an important part in Dutch culture today. Most large cities have concert halls and music societies, and many of the large churches have magnificent organs on which concerts are regularly given. Festivals of music of all kinds from pop to classical take place regularly, and on the streets music from colourful organs and student buskers can be heard.

The Dutch are a hard-working nation, who make the most of their spare time. They are particularly fond of the open air, and many families prefer to spend their weekends in the countryside rather than by the sea, although many enjoy watersports of all types. Cycling is a national pastime, both for commuting to work and for pleasure.

Food

The Dutch enjoy their food, which is plentiful, though there is not a great deal of variety. Breakfast normally consists of bread, rusks and *ontbijtkoek* (a spiced cake) served with sliced cheeses and cooked meats, jam, chocolate strands, and sometimes a boiled egg accompanied by tea or coffee. Much the same is served at midday, preceded by soup. The evening meal, served at about 6pm, consists of meat or fish, with plenty of fresh vegetables, followed by fruit, yogurt or *vla*, a kind of custard.

Some Dutch specialities are *uitsmijters*, which consist of two slices of bread and butter, topped with ham, roast beef or cheese, and two or three fried eggs, served with pickles, and a salad. *Pannekoeken* — pancakes — are delicious, large and served with a great variety of toppings, from bananas to bacon, together with a thick brown syrup or *stroop*. Soups are thick and filling; try *erwtensoep*, a thick pea soup with sausages or bacon. Fish specialities include smoked eels and fresh, raw herring, both of which are very tasty. Indo-Chinese food is available in abundance; try *Ba-mie* — noodles, vegetables and pork mixed together with spices — or *Rijsttafel*, different savoury or curry dishes, served with rice and chutneys, but some can be very hot, so beware. Pastries are mouthwatering (and fattening!); try *Appeltart* and *Limburgse Vlaai* — fruit flan served with thick cream.

Customs, Costumes and Folklore

These three traditions are inseparable from each other; they remain an everyday part of Dutch life. For example the women in the villages of

Bunschoten/Spakenburg, Marken, Volendam, and Staphorst wear their colourful costumes every day as a matter of course, not for the benefit of tourists. Many of these costumes are works of art, with fine needlework, knitting and crochet. Costumes may also be seen in other regions, particularly on market days and on Sundays. Look for the beautiful bonnets of Huizen, and the strange elongated cap or *poffer* of Scheveningen. Each costume is different and distinctive. Interested visitors should look for shops specialising in genuine costume dolls, dressed in accurate copies of the various costumes, which are not found in general souvenir shops. The shop in Edam, opposite the cheese market, sells dolls which are perfect replicas of the adult costumes, made in the villages from where the costumes come. Another source, at a more reasonable cost, are the shops of Arbeid Adelt, an association of women working in their own homes. The Amsterdam shop is in the Leidseplein.

Wooden shoes, or *klompen*, are often though to be part of traditional Dutch costumes. In reality, they are a working clog, used on farms, on fish quays, and by families when working in their gardens. They are never worn inside the house, but are left outside the door.

Many customs in Holland are linked with church festivals, or older pagan rites. Easter traditions include dancing through Ootmarsum's streets and bonfires in Twente. Children hunt for painted eggs and eat Easter men, made from bread dough, for breakfast. *Sinterklaas* (St Nicholas) arrives on 5 December, with his assistant, *Zwart Piet*, who tries to ensure that children have been good. Children may be given *speculaa*s — spiced biscuit in the shape of *Sinterklaus*— or their initial in chocolate.

In Brabant and Limburg, Carnaval is linked with pre-Lent festivities, and there are festivals with traditional ceremonies in other parts of the country. On Queen's day (30 April) many towns and cities are festooned with orange balloons, coloured lights and red, white and blue buntings.

Sporting customs include the Eleven Towns race on the frozen canals in Friesland in winter, and jumping the dyke, which takes place in several regions. Banner waving competitions and parades take place in Brabant and Limburg; 'tilting the ring' and other medieval sports are also popular. Windmills are also part of Dutch folklore; the miller can set his sails in such a manner to signal messages to other millers; during World War II many secret messages were passed in this way.

1

SOUTH-WEST HOLLAND: THE OLD AND THE NEW

Originally this area consisted of the islands of Zeeland and Zuid Holland, separated by a complex network of waterways forming the estuaries of the rivers Rhine, Maas and Schelde. Defence of expanding maritime and fishing interests, together with the need to protect the land from storms and flood, were the key factors in the development of this region. Now the separate islands have been linked by modern dams, dykes and bridges, leading to the growth of extensive recreation areas and nature reserves. The motorway system serving the rest of the country has been extended here so that easy access is possible.

However, much of the area's original character has been preserved and those wishing to see the islands can take minor roads at a more leisurely pace. These routes visit much of Zeeland which is often passed by.

Route 1: Around the Southern Delta. Approx 110km

This tour begins at **Vlissingen** (Flushing), where many visitors from Britain arrive on the ferry. The town itself is often by-passed, but it is worth taking time to walk along the Boulevard (2km long). Near the fish harbour entrance there is a statue of Admiral de Ruyter, who sailed up the River Medway in Kent (1667) and captured several British ships including the *Royal Charles* on which Charles II had returned to England in 1660. The carved stern of this vessel is preserved in the Rijksmuseum in Amsterdam. At the other end of the Boulevard is the Gevangentoren or prison tower (1490), now a restaurant. Old frontages can be seen along Nieuwendijk (near the fish harbour) and in Hendrikstraat, while the tall 'Oranjemolen' windmill and a monument to commandos and civilians who died during World War II are located on the Oranjedijk.

Along the coast, to the north-west of Vlissingen, are some excellent sandy beaches and a number of campsites and bungalow parks; most of these are situated behind the high dunes and are thus sheltered from the winds. The whole coast here is a busy holiday area and is particularly popular with the Germans. From Vlissingen, take the direct route north to **Middelburg** (6km). Cyclists may avoid the cycle path alongside the main

Middelburg Town Walk

It is worth spending a whole day here, beginning with a town walk (2¹/₂-3 hours). A good place to start is the Markt, with the beautiful town hall. This was extensively damaged in 1940 and has been rebuilt to the original plans. Look down Pottenmarkt to the magnificent Flemish Renaissance-style building, known as the Kloveniersdoelen, which once belonged to the East India Company and is now a music school. Not far from the Markt is the 280ft high tower of the abbey church known as 'Lange Jan'. By climbing the 207 steps to the top, a magnificent view over the town and surrounding countryside can be seen. The abbey itself is now the seat of the Zeeland Provincial Government, and houses the Zeeland Museum with its fine collection of local costumes and jewellery. Between the museum and the main provincial building is an arched gateway leading to the St Jorisdoelen, former home of the St George Company of Archers dating from 1582. Walk down Spanjaardstraat and immediately turn left into Haringsplaats Bleek. At the end cross over to Koepoortlaan and continue to the Koepoort (1735), the only remaining town gate. Opposite, entered from Molenwater, is Miniature Walcheren, with models of old buildings and landscapes from all over the island. From here there is a pleasant walk along the old ramparts which are now laid out as gardens.

road by taking a very attractive path which runs beside the Walcheren Canal and goes right into the centre of the town — follow 'Centrum' cycle signs. The capital of the province of Zeeland, Middelburg is one of the finest towns in Holland. Badly damaged in World War II, it has been beautifully restored using old building methods and often the original plans and materials. Parking in the centre is not easy, and parking fees are payable. It is better to park on the edge of the town and walk in. Thursday is market day, when traditional costumes can always be seen. During the summer a *son et lumier* spectacle is staged in the abbey.

A pleasant diversion from Middelburg is to take a boat from the Loskade (near the station) to Veere at the northern end of the Walcheren Canal. **Veere** is about 7km away, and is easily reached by road. Once one of Holland's busiest seaports, it has some lovely old buildings. From the fifteenth to eighteenth centuries it handled the bulk of the Scottish wool trade with Europe — a privilege granted in 1444 when a Lord of Veere married a daughter of King James of Scotland. The wool merchants had their headquarters here, and their homes are still known as the 'Scots Houses', now providing a home for a museum. The great Onze Lieve Vrouwekerk, dating from 1348, dominates the town, its huge tower once housing Napoleon's cavalry, including their horses. Other buildings not

Zierikzee Town Walk

Cross the bridge into Weststraat and walk towards the large square tower, St Lievens or Monstertoren, begun in 1454 but never completed. Originally planned to be 207m tall, it only reached 58m. Keep to the right of the tower along Kerkhof and, on the right, is the attractive Weeshuis (orphanage) of about 1740. Continue along Poststraat and turn left to see the ornate tower of the town hall which houses a museum — and turn right on reaching Meelstraat. The left-hand side of the town hall was built as the meat market hall in the fifteenth century. Later, it was enlarged in Flemish style and a tower added with a gilded statue of Neptune, reflecting the sea connections of the town. Continue to the Dam, along Appelmarkt and into Havenplein. Ahead are the Noord and Zuid Havenpoorts, but to the left, in the street called Mol, is the old Gravensteen prison, with an attractive stepped gable. It is now the maritime museum. Behind is a medieval garden, open during museum hours. A diversion at this point is to go down Lange Nobelstraat past the tall corn mill to Korte Nobelstraat and the Nobelpoort before returning to the town centre. On Havenplein is an interesting colonnaded building. Built in 1651 as a market hall, it has a church room above it for the Elisabethsgasthuis church, which had become too small.

Continue along Havenpark and the old harbour towards the Havenpoorts. These give the town its characteristic appearance of a seaport town from the Middle Ages. The gates date from the fifteenth century but have been restored more than once. In the open cupola of the Zuidhavenpoort hangs the old town hall carillon dating from 1550, the oldest in Holland. Walking along Nieuwe Havenleads to Bolwerk and the windmill 'De Haas', where a good view over the area can be obtained. A number of boat trips, including sailing trips, can be made from the town. Return along the ramparts.

to be missed include the fifteenth-century Campveerse Toren, once the fortress gate to the harbour and now a hotel/restaurant, and the town hall (1470). The original fortifications of Veere are preserved, and a walk around the ramparts is very pleasant. The view over the Veerse Meer created by the dams of the Delta Plan is impressive, this being one of the largest lakes in Holland. Formerly a busy fishing port, and commercial centre, Veere is now a very popular sailing centre with its own marina.

From Veere marina, travel north-west along the dyke road towards Vrouwenpolder, and the turn right onto the Veersegatdam towards Zierikzee. This was the first of the major Delta Plan dams to be completed. At the beginning of the dam is a monument marking its completion,

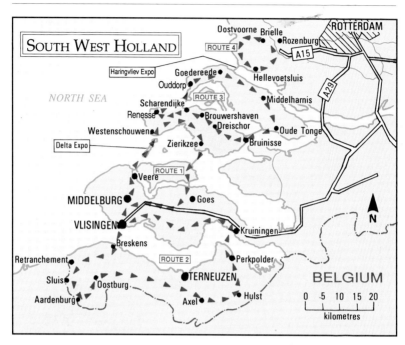

The Oosterschelde Storm Surge Barrier, part of the Delta Plan

Noord Havenpoort, Zierikzee

where it is possible to park and climb to the top. From this vantage point there are good views of the whole area, including a large area of dunes to the west, parts of which are accessible to the public. Cross the dam, still following signs to Zierikzee and Neeltje Jans. After crossing the first set of barrier sluices, follow Delta Expo signs and turn right towards a building where an excellent film about the barrier is shown during the holiday season. There is a 45-minute boat tour with commentary on the barrier and its ecology. The main control building, 'J. W. Tops Huis', a short walk or drive away, has an exhibition with models. A visit can be made inside of one of the sluices, which are only lowered in exceptional circumstances. One entrance ticket covers everything, but allow at least 3 hours. There are good refreshment facilities, and a good bus service from Middelburg to Zierikzee, which stops near the exhibition site. From the exhibition continue along the top of the remaining two sets of sluices towards Zierikzee, then follow the ANWB 'Schouwen Duiveland' route along the dyke roads The old church tower of the drowned village of Couderkerc is passed, where the last known dwelling existed in 1750.

The road leaves the dyke just beyond the tower and rejoins the main road. Turn right and continue straight ahead to **Zierikzee**. It is worth spending some time exploring this historic town and port, with fine buildings and three beautifully preserved town gates.

From Zierikzee, take the main road east out of the town and then turn south towards Goes. This road leads to the Zeelandbrug, the toll bridge over the Oosterschelde which, at over 3 miles long, is the longest bridge in the Netherlands. Cyclists and moped riders must use the cycle path alongside, which can be quite an experience in a strong wind, but the path is now toll-free. When the weather is clear it is possible to see the outline of the storm-barrier downstream. Once over the bridge, follow the signs to **Colijnsplaat**, an attractive fishing village where fresh fish can be purchased from the quayside each day. From the nearby dyke there is a fine view of the Zeelandbrug and across the Oosterschelde estuary to Zierikzee, whose massive Monstertoren is almost always visible.

Leaving Colijnsplaat, follow the road south again across the Zandkreekdam to **Goes**, with its fine eighteenth-century town hall with Gothic tower. Maria Magdalena church (1427) has an interesting lantern-style roof with an eighteenth-century carillon. Goes is the northern terminus of a tourist steam railway line to Oudelande in the south of the island.

From Goes, return to Vlissingen by way of the old main road via Wissenkerke, Eindeweg, and Lewedorp to Nieuw en Sint Joosland. From this point, motorists will find it more convenient to use the motorway into Vlissingen, but cyclists must follow the signed route along minor roads.

Route 2: Forgotten Zeeland. Approx 90km

This route begins at Sluis, the border town on the Belgian/Dutch frontier. Motorists disembarking at Zeebrugge in Belgium tend to drive straight on to the motorway and get away from the ferryport as quickly as possible. However, by following the Knokke-Heist road, and continuing towards Sluis, the Belgian/Dutch frontier is reached at St Anna-ter-Muiden. This part of Holland is often completely neglected by visitors, yet it offers a number of interesting places to see.

Just inside the frontier is **Sluis**, which has a long and eventful history, having received its charter in the thirteenth century. It was once the port for Bruges in Belgium before the estuary of the Zwin silted up. This, together with a succession of wars, led to the town's decline, until the emergence of the Belgian resorts on the nearby coast provided the impetus for Sluis to become a tourist centre. Eighty per cent of the town was destroyed during World War II, but it has been rebuilt, with much of the characteristic atmosphere being retained. The fourteenth-century town hall has a unique belfry tower, and the council chamber is one of the finest in Holland. Grass-covered ramparts almost completely surround the town and a pleasant walk can be taken along them, passing the fine corn mill which is in working condition and may be visited. Because of the town's position on the border, shops are allowed to open in the evenings and on Sundays, and many visitors take advantage of this.

From Sluis, the ANWB 'Westerschelde Route' signs may be followed to **Aardenburg**, known to be the site of a Roman station, preceded by a Stone Age settlement. It is considered to be one of the oldest towns in Holland. The church dates back to the thirteenth century, being a good example of 'Schelde Gothic', while parts of the ramparts, notably the Kaaipoort (1650), can still be seen.

Passing Oostburg to the north, the route comes to **IJzendijke**, a fortified town once an important centre for the wool trade. The market square was used as the exercise ground for the military garrison in former times, and the first Protestant church in Zeeland was built here in 1612.

About 5km further along is **Biervliet**, where a monument in the square testifies to the fact that one Willem Beukelszoon introduced a method of curing herrings. The town hall weathervane has a herring as a pointer. Leave the signposted route and continue along the main road N61, crossing the Gent to Terneuzen canal, then after the first set of traffic lights turn right to **Axel**. This is an agricultural area where local costumes can be seen at the Saturday market. The Axel farmhouse museum contains two fully furnished rooms from 1830 and 1880.

Leaving Axel, the signed route passes along tree-lined dykes via the hamlet of Luntershoek; a more direct main road also leads to the lovely medieval fortified city of **Hulst**, completely surrounded by moats and ramparts. The fine church, founded in 1200, was used during the last century by both Catholics and Protestants, each using a different part of

the building. After 1929 it reverted to the Catholics and was converted to a basilica in 1935. After war damage in 1944, the tower was rebuilt in modern style. Many other fine buildings exist, including fifteenth- and sixteenth-century abbey refuges, the town hall (1528-1547), and the ramparts and defence works which repay a walk for the extensive views over the town. One of the loveliest corn windmills in Holland, built in 1792, is here, while near the Gentse Poort stands the strange monument to 'Reynard the Fox'. Hulst and the surrounding countryside is the setting for this ancient fable.

Leave the town and continue in a northerly direction along the main road to the ferry at Perkpolder. The crossing takes about twenty minutes, and refreshments are available on board. Times of ferries may vary according to season, but there is normally one every hour. Check with the local VVV for times. Once off the ferry, continue to Kruiningen, then take the old main road (not the motorway) in the direction of Biezelinge and Kapelle. Do not turn off the road at Biezelinge but continue towards 's-Gravenpolder and Ovezande. From this point a short diversion to the south leads to **Oudelande**, terminus of the steam railway from Goes. From Ovezande, follow the signed ANWB route through Remmekens hoek and back to Vlissingen.

Ferries leave Vlissingen every half-hour for Breskens, and again the journey time is about twenty minutes. **Breskens** itself is a fishing and sailing centre, with a number of holiday parks and campsites along the coast to the west. It is possible to follow the coast road along the dyke by Nieuwesluis and Nieuwvliet-Bad to Cadzand-Bad. From here the road leads inland to **Retranchement**, with the well-preserved ramparts of a fortified border village, and a very fine open trestle windmill built in 1643. A small road to the west of the village offering good views of the ramparts leads south to Sluis. An alternative from Breskens is to take the road through Groede and Nieuwvliet and then turn north to Cadzand and Retranchement. This part of the route may easily be followed in the opposite direction by those wishing to go direct to Vlissingen from Zeebrugge. In this case, follow signs from Groede to Vlissingen, and not to Breskens. This leads directly to the ferry terminal.

Route 3: Around the Grevelingen. Approx 89km

The **Grevelingen** lake was formed by the building of the dam which links the former islands of Schouwen-Duiveland and Goeree. Like the smaller Veerse Meer, it is very popular with sailors and surfers, the latter using both the inland waters and the North Sea breakers. On the lake shores are the old fishing ports of Brouwershaven and Ouddorp, both with good marinas. The boundary between Zeeland and Zuid Holland runs through the centre of the lake.

← *Sluis, the fourteenth-century town hall and belfry*

Brouwershaven is an attractive little town with a rich history, having had town status since 1285. The busy harbour lies in the centre of the town, and the market square hass a number of interesting old façades, including the town hall with a Flemish Renaissance gable (1599). The thirteenth-century church is very large for the size of the town, and can be seen from afar. In the market square is the statue of Jacob Cats, the sixteenth-century poet who was born here.

Continue west along the dyke road, pausing at Scharendijke to see how well the Dutch have used the essential sea defence works to create an enormous recreation area. At the beginning of the nearby Brouwersdam ia a large sea aquarium, the 'Aquadrome', containing fish (including small sharks) from the North Sea, Grevelingenmeer and Ooster-schade.The road leads now to **Renesse**, a popular holiday resort, on the outskirts of which is the picturesque castle of Moermond (not open to the public) with its elegant towers. There are many popular North Sea beaches to the north of the village. Return to the Brouwersdam via Ellemeet, where there are two choices of route. On either side of the main road across the dyke are narrow roads which must be used by cyclists, but which may also be used by motorists to gain access to the beaches. One, on the seaward side, runs parallel to and below the main road above a sandy beach and leads to a carpark about halfway along the dam before continuing towards Ouddorp. This road is covered in sand after stormy weather and can be dangerous; also beware of windsurfers who tend to cross without looking. The other road is on the Grevelingenmeer side of the dam, and again lies below the main road. Here there are also car parks at intervals, and opportunities for launching small dinghies and sailboards. There are open-air swimming facilities at each end of the dam on the lake side. There is also a new holiday marina village halfway along the dam at **Kabbelaarsbank**.

Cross the dam to **Goeree**, where there are plenty of beaches, holiday houses and campsites; cycle paths through the dunes and adjoining lanes make for pleasant riding. Continue into **Ouddorp**, the main holiday centre, an attractive little town with good shopping and restaurant facilities and two campsites as well as a large marina. From here, follow the road to **Goedereede**, an attractive village whose huge church tower can be seen for miles. Originally built to serve as a beacon and lighthouse, it now houses a small museum; the view from the top is worth the climb.

From Goedereede, take the road towards Hellevoetsluis, but at the beginning of the Haringvlietdam keep to the minor road which leads to a new exhibition 'The Haringvliet Expo'. Although less technical than the Delta Expo, it is very interesting with films in English. The visit includes a tour inside one of the sluices, with a model showing how they work.

Return from the dam and continue via Stellendam and Dirksland to **Middelharnis**, the main town of the island of Overflakkee which has an attractive seventeenth-century town hall. The whole island is predominantly agricultural, and is noted for its gladioli bulbs. Take the road towards Oude Tonge, and turn south over the **Grevelingendam** towards Bruinisse. In the centre of this dam is a large recreation area with beaches and parking, picnic places and a good restaurant. From the centre of the dam, near the restaurant, a new road leads over the Philipsdam to the agricultural islands of Sint-Philipsland and Tholen.

Continue across the Grevelingendam to **Bruinisse**, a small fishing village renowned for its mussels. From Bruinisse, follow the ANWB-signed 'Schouwen-Duiveland Route' west towards **Dreischor**, a picturesque 'ring village' with its church on a mound in the centre. The church has an interesting staircase turret built on to the main tower. From here, continue following the signs back to Brouwershaven.

Route 4: The Old Island of Voorne. Approx 55km

Starting at the northern end of the Haringvlietdam, follow signs to **Hellevoetsluis**, the old fortified port from which William III set sail for England in 1688. To reach the old town centre, follow 'Vesting' signs; the road cuts through the old ramparts, and a leaflet outlining a walk is available from the VVV. The old fortifications, lighthouse and old naval buildings can be seen. The fire service museum is housed in two of the eighteenth-century naval buildings in the Industriehaven, and another museum in the town deals with the maritime history of the area. Boat trips to view the town from the Haringvliet are also available.

From Hellevoetsluis, follow the road alongside the Voorne Canal to Heenvliet, and continue in the direction of Brielle. Cyclists have the opportunity of using the road on the eastern side of the canal, then continuing into the little fishing village of Zwartewaal and along a pleasant cyclepath on the dyke to Brielle.

Brielle is first mentioned as early as 1257, and was created a town in 1330. It has many links with England. The ramparts of the fortified town can still be seen, and large cannons in the town centre stand as reminders of its strategic importance in the Middle Ages and later. It was the first town to be liberated from Spanish invaders in 1572 by the so-called 'sea-beggars', Protestant pirates based in Dover who had been expelled from England by Elizabeth I. From 1585 to 1616 the town was occupied by English troops, but in 1872 it lost its strategic importance when the river Maas was linked to the sea. Near the town hall (1793) is the Tromp Museum, housed in the former town prison and weigh-house. Nearby, in a small square, is a large pump dating from 1610. The Great or St Catharijnekerk is a showpiece of the town, dating from the fifteenth century. It is said that in 1688, Mary, the wife of William III, stood on the top of the tower and watched him sail for England from Hellevoetsluis. Certainly there is a fine view of the town its ramparts, and the surrounding countryside. There are many fine and interesting gables on houses, notably in Voorstraat and Maarland.

A small ferry taking foot passengers and cycles only runs from the north-east side of Brielle across the Brielse Meer to a long strip of land, known as the **Krabbeplaat** which is an oasis amid industry, for just the other side of this landscaped area is the Hartelkanaal and the huge oil storage tanks of Europoort. It is possible to cycle along the whole length of this recreation area, as far as the Botlekbrug, a total of about 10km, from where signs may be followed to Rotterdam. Motorists can reach the recreation island either from the Europoort road and the Suurhofbrug to the west, or over the Brielsebrug on the way towards Rozenburg. The island has plenty of parking places, picnic areas and places where one can walk and watch the shipping.

Return to Brielle and take the road to **Oostvoorne**, a popular holiday resort with the excavated ruins of a twelfth-century castle. There are fine sandy beaches, with surfing as an added attraction, and among the dunes are nature reserves with plenty of opportunities for walking and cycling. There are plenty of car parks and picnic areas. Continue via minor roads close to the dunes to **Rockanje**, another popular holiday village noted for its nature reserves in the dunes which support rare flora and fauna, including a large colony of cormorants. From here return along the coast road past the end of the the Haringvlietdam to Hellevoetsluis.

← *The Old Weeshuis, formerly a Protestant orphanage, in Voorstraat, Brielle. The plaque commemorates the liberation of the town by a 'sea-beggar' with a flag and axe in his hand*

Additional Information

Places of Interest

Axel
Streekmuseum 'Het Land van Axel'
Noordstraat 11
Open: Apr to Sept, Wed to Sat 1.30-5pm. Also July and Aug, Friday evening 7-9pm.

Brielle
* Trompmuseum
Venkelstraat 3
Open: Daily except Sun 9am-5pm.
Closed on Feast days.

Hellevoetsluis
Museum Gesigt van 't Dok (maritime museum)
Oostzanddijk 20
Open: all year Tues to Sun 1-4pm

Nationaal Brandweermuseum (fire service museum)
Industriehaven 8
Open: Apr to Oct, Mon to Sat 10am-4pm; Sun and Feast days, 11am-4pm.

Middelburg
Miniature Town of Walcheren
Molenwater
Open: Daily Easter to June and Oct 9.30am-5pm, July and Aug 9.30am-6pm.

* Zeeuwse Museum
Abdijplein 3
Open: Tues to Fri 10am-5pm, Sat to Mon 1.30-5pm.

Scharendijke
Zee Aquarium Aquadome
Randweg 13
Open: end Mar to end Sept daily 10am-6pm, mid-July to Aug 10am-8pm.

Retranchement
Windmill
Molenstraat 3
Working: July to Aug, Saturdays 1-3pm.

Stellendam
Haringvliet Expo
Haringvlietplein 3
Open: Apr-Oct 10-5pm.

Veere
* De Schotse Huizen Musem
Kaai 25-27
Open: Apr to Sept, Tues to Sat 10am-5pm, Mon 1-5pm.

Westerschouwen
Delta Expo, 'Neeltje Jans' Information
  Centre
Oosterschelde Flood Barriers
Open: Apr to Oct, daily 10am-5pm; Nov
to Mar, Wed to Sun 10am-5pm.

Zierikzee
Stadhuismuseum
Meelstraat 8
Open: May to Sept, Mon to Fri 10am-5pm. Closed on public holidays.

Maritiem Museum *Het Gravensteen*
Mol 25
Open: May to Sept, Mon to Sat 10am-5pm, Sun noon-5pm.

Transport

Ferry Services
(Services all year round)

Vlissingen-Breskens
Every half-hour during the day. Journey
time: 20 minutes. No reservations.

Kruiningen-Perkpolder
Every half-hour weekdays, every hour
Sat and Sun. Journey time: 20 minutes.
No reservations.

Steam Train Lines
Goes-Oudelande
July and Aug, daily except Saturdays.
May, June and Sept. Sun only.
Depot, NS Station, Goes
☎ 01100 20577 (VVV Goes)

2

ROTTERDAM, DELFT AND DEN HAAG

These three cities form part of the complex of towns and cities known as the Randstad or Ring Town. Forty-five miles long and 40 miles across at its widest point, this huge horseshoe-shaped conurbation contains the major cities and towns of Dordrecht, Rotterdam, Delft, Den Haag, Leiden, Haarlem, Amsterdam, Hilversum and Utrecht. Each town is a separate entity, the country in between remaining as open space with parks and pasture, while the western side is bounded by the seacoast.

Rotterdam, a city which has risen from the ashes of war, has in its Europoort the biggest harbour in the world; Delft, an ancient town, is famous for its porcelain, its artists and its University of Technology; Den Haag, seat of the Dutch Government, is a busy commercial centre with a flourishing seaside resort on its outskirts. All have much of interest for the tourist.

Rotterdam and Neighbourhood

Rotterdam is easy to reach by motorway and by public transport. Cyclists coming from the south should use the Maassluis ferry to the west of the city. There is a cycle lane through the Maastunnel, but it involves an escalator which makes it difficult with a loaded bicycle. The Benelux-tunnel is motorway only. Bicycles may be taken on the Metro (Underground), but only after 7pm on weekdays, and all day Saturdays and Sundays. Carriage is free, although no special facilities are available.

As in any city, parking can be a problem, and although there are plenty of car parks, charges can be high. It is better to use one of the multi-storey car parks near Centraal Station or near the Lijnbaan shopping centre.

Rotterdam is a fine city for visitors, offering plenty of hotels, excellent shopping facilities and a wide range of entertainment, in addition to museums and other tourist attractions. There is a casino, more than 200 restaurants and interesting modern architecture. One of the best ways to see the city is by tram. There is an old tourist tram which departs from Centraal Station every day, taking a slow ride (with a guide) all around the city. Or a free brochure (in English and several other languages) and map

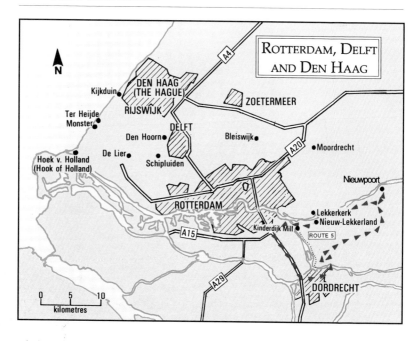

of the city public transport (bus, tram and Metro) and major tourist attractions is available from the ticket office on Stationsplein. Trams go to the waterside near Willemsplein, from where the 'Spido' boat tours start. A 1 hour tour of the harbour takes in the world's busiest waterway, and a commentary in various languages points out special features, making this an ideal way of getting the feel of the port. Longer boat trips can be taken, including one taking in the whole of the Europoort complex.

Another way of seeing Europoort is by car, following the well-signed ANWB 'Rotterdamse Havenroute'. This is designed to show the visitor as much of the area as possible, and an excellent map with full route description in English, with additional notes, is available from the local VVV office in Rotterdam. The tour is 90km in length, and ends with a drive along the Brielse Maas recreation area. The return may be made by crossing the Brielsebrug south to Groene Kruisweg then joining the motorway A15 just north of Rhoon. In this way, other interesting places may be seen including Heenvliet, once a port before Brielle became important, and the village of Rhoon which has a sixteenth-century castle.

Rotterdam's most famous landmark is the Euromast. Originally built to a height of 350ft (100m) in 1960, it towered over the city. From the 'Crow's Nest' at this height there is a wonderful view of Rotterdam. In the late 1960s, the Medical Faculty of the university opened their new building, which was even higher. Not to be outdone a 'Space Needle', ascended by an external rotating lift car, was added to the Euromast. Opened in 1970, the extra height brought the total to 600ft (185m) enabling one to see as far as Den Haag, Delft and beyond on a clear day.

The Euromast in Rotterdam gives a magnificent view on a clear day

An archetypal Dutch scene: cyclists passing the tower windmill at Groot Ammers

A short distance from Euromast there are two interesting museums which are both situated in Delfshaven, reached by walking along the Westzeedijk, or by taking a tram. One is De Dubbelde Palmboom, a restored warehouse in Voorhaven which is part of the Historical Museum complex, and the other, situated in nearby Voorstraat, is the restored Zakkendragershuisje with a pewter workshop which may be visited. This area is one of the oldest parts of Rotterdam and it was from here, in 1620, that the Pilgrim Fathers sailed to America in the *Speedwell*. The church where they held their last service before setting forth is in Albrechtskolk, a continuation of Voorhaven, where every year, on the fourth Sunday in November, a traditional American Thanksgiving service is held.

Other museums in Rotterdam which should not be missed include the Maritime Museum and museum ship *Buffel*, The 'Toy-Toy' museum of antique dolls and mechanical toys, and the Boymans Museum, containing paintings, sculpture, ceramics, glass, pewter, lace and furniture. This museum is particularly well-known for its modern art collection. The Schielandhuis Historical Museum is also worth seeing. Blijdorp Zoo, with its exotic animals, aquaria, reptiles and amphibians is only 1km from Centraal Station, and north-east of the city, beyond the motorway, are the recreation areas of Plaswijckpark, Lage Bergse Bos and Hoge Bergse Bos, offering many opportunities for cycling and walking. There is also an arboretum in the city with shrubs and flowers as well as trees.

West of Rotterdam is **Schiedam**, where the famous Geneva distillery mills can be visited as well as a museum of spirits and distilling. **Vlaardingen** is a historic fishing town with an excellent Fishery Museum, colonnaded fish market, and a town hall dating from 1650. Its position has made Vlaardingen an ideal place to develop a marina, where Crusaders once sailed for the Holy Land and fishermen landed their herring catch.

Route 5: Dordrecht and the Kinderdijk Mills. Approx 66km

To the south-east of Rotterdam lies **Dordrecht**, the first known town of Holland (as distinct from the Netherlands) whose charter dates back to 1220. Until the sixteenth-century it was the most important and powerful town in Holland.

Dordrecht makes an ideal starting point for a tour of the Kinderdijk windmills, either by car or cycle. Follow the main road out of the town to Papendrecht, then continue through the town to cross the motorway to join another main road which bears to the left. (Cyclists can take the small ferry to Papendrecht from the Riedijkshaven at the end of Rie Dijk, which is a continuation of Voorstraat, then continue straight ahead through the town to join the main road to cross the motorway.) In about 2km take the minor road to the left to the three windmills, then turn right and follow the river Albas to Vuilendam. Turn left here and follow the road to **Groot Ammers**, which has a protected stork colony. This is situated on a minor

Dordrecht Town Walk

Start at the carpark in the town centre near Arend Maartenshofje, an old almshouse which has remained virtually unchanged since 1625. Walk down Museumstraat to the Dordrechts Museum, which has a very good collection of Dutch paintings from the seventeenth century to the present day. Continue along the same street and turn left into Steegoversloot, then left again into Hofstraat, which leads to the *hof* or court. It was here in the States Hall that, in 1572, the foundations for the independence of the Netherlands were laid. Go through the archway into Voorstraat, turn right and continue as far as Boomstraat. Turn left and cross the Boombrug into Wijnstraat, then to the Groothhoft or Great Head. From the quayside there is a a fascinating view of the confluence of two major rivers, with a continual flow of traffic on the Oude Maas and the Merwede.

The magnificent Groothoofdspoort has a number of elaborate carvings, including pictures of the patron saint and the coat of arms of the town. Walking along Wolwevershaven, past some superb old warehouses, brings you to Nieuwe Haven and the Museum Mr Simon van Gijn at No 29. Housed in a beautiful nobleman's house, the interiors are reminiscent of paintings by Vermeer, while the top floor contains a fine collection of antique toys. Continue down the quay to Engelenburgerbrug, pausing on the way to glance down Korte Engelenburgerkade to the Catharijnepoort. Beyond the bridge is the Grote Kerk, dedicated to Our Lady, on the site of a chapel possibly dating from 1064. The tower, like many of the houses in the town, leans noticeably due to the marshy ground beneath its foundations. The church is one of the largest in Holland, with a lovely pulpit (1756) and a fine organ (1671) on which concerts are given in the summer.

Return via Grootekerksbuurt and Groen Markt to the Visbrug, then up Visstraat and Bagijnhof to Lenghen Straat, turn left and continue ahead to Lindenstraat and the car park.

road leading east towards **Nieuwpoort**, an old fortified town whose ramparts still exist, with a town hall built on a bridge over the canal. From Nieuwpoort, return to follow the dyke road beside the river through Groot Ammers, Streefkerk and Nieuwe-Lekkerland to **Kinderdijk**.

The Kinderdijk mills, nineteen in all, were built in 1740 to drain the surrounding polder. The mills are in operation on Saturday afternoons during the summer, and one mill is open to the public. Cars must be left in the car park and visitors walk along Molenkade past the mills, although cycling is permitted. After visiting the mills, motorists should take the road towards Krimpen a/d Lek and then, before crossing the river, turn left to Alblasserdam along minor roads to join the motorway and return to Dordrecht through Papendrecht. Cyclists can continue along the path beside the mills to Alblasserdam and Oud-Alblas, and then return to Papendrecht from there.

In and Around Delft

Just 11km north of Rotterdam centre and only 8km from the centre of the Hague, lies the medieval town of **Delft**. From the thirteenth to seventeenth centuries it became well known for its pottery, silverware, tapestries and woollen goods, but was also known as a centre for arts and sciences. William the Silent, who founded the United Netherlands, lived in Delft and the town was also the headquarters of the East- and West-India Companies. Today it is a centre for science and industry, with an internationally famous technological university, and is also important as a centre for the horticultural industries of Westland.

While in Delft take the opportunity to visit one of the factories making the world-renowned Delftware. At the Royal Delftware factory 'De Porceleyne Fles' in Rotterdamsweg, Atelier de Candelaer in Kerkstraat,

The busy Kuipers Haven at Dordrecht, seen from the Damiatebrug

and at 'De Delftse Pauw' in Delftweg, visitors can see how Delft Blue ware is made. The factories have shops, but if buying elsewhere make sure that you get the genuine article, not cheap imports from Germany and the Far East.

To the north-east of the town is an arboretum and the large recreation area 'de Delftse Hout' with facilities for swimming, miniature golf, ✳ cycling etc and a children's farm. To the east is the huge market-garden

The fourteenth-century Nieuwe Kerk rising above town houses in Delft

A Walk Around Delft

Delft is a town of narrow tree-lined canals, picturesque bridges, narrow alleyways and courts, dominated by the tower of the Nieuwe Kerk in the Markt where this walk starts. The building of the Nieuwe Kerk, dedicated to St Ursula, commenced in 1381, and contains the family vault of the House of Orange. At the opposite end of the Markt lies the town hall. This Renaissance building was erected after the original town hall was destroyed by fire in 1536, leaving only the tower standing. This was included in the new building, and included a carillon of forty-eight bells. Later they were transferred to the Nieuwe Kerk, and they are played regularly on Tuesday, Thursday and Saturday mornings. The market place is always busy and is the setting for the weekly markets and the Delft Tattoo, as well as other events. It is surrounded by attractive old buildings, souvenir shops and cafés. Face the church and walk to the right and down Oude Langendijk (once a canal) and round the back of the church to Kerkstraat. Turn left along Volders Gracht, where there are some fine sevententh-century façades, to Hippolytus-buurt, site of the Thursday Flower Market. Turn right to Oude Kerk or St Hippolytuskerk, founded in 1240; the present building dates from about 1500. In the tower, which leans visibly, hangs the great Bourdon bell cast in 1570; weighing 9 tons with a circumference of 7m, it is now only rung on special occasions.

Behind the church is the Prinsenhof, built as a convent in the fifteenth century and later to become the residence of the Prince of Orange. It was in this building that William the Silent was murdered in 1584, and it now houses the Historical Museum. The Museum Nusantara, an ethnological museum with an outstanding collection of masks, weapons and other articles from Indonesia, is nearby. A short distance along Oude Delft is the Huis Lambert van Meerten. This nineteenth-century mansion contains an outstanding collection of tiles and tile-pictures from many countries. Walk back along Oude Delft to cross the Boterbrug and turn right into Wijnhaven, then turn left into Oude Langendijk. To extend the walk to include the Oostpoort, the only remaining one of Delft's original eight fourteenth-century town gates, continue to the far end. Here turn right to follow the canal to Oostpoort, resting on its own little island among the canals.

A Walk Around Den Haag

Start at Centraal Station, by the Koningin Julianaplein and opposite the large open space known as Koekamp. Turn left along Herengracht and continue ahead along Korte Poten to the square at the end with its statue of William the Silent. Turn right into the square and cross diagonally to the famous Mauritshuis, once the residence of the Duke of Marlborough. It has a wonderful collection of paintings by Rembrandt, Rubens, Vermeer, Holbein and Frans Hals.

Go down Korte Vijverberg and turn left into Lange Vijverberg. On the left is the Hof Vijver, an attractive lake with fountains. Ahead is the Gevangenpoort or prison gate; originally an entrance to the castle (fourteenth century) and later used for political prisoners, it is now a museum.

Turn left at the end of the Hof Vijver past the large equestrian statue of William II to reach the entrance to the Binnenhof, for centuries the centre of political life in the Netherlands. Its history extends back to the thirteenth century, and the original building of the Ridderzaal (Hall of Knights) dates from this period. This has now been restored to much of its original form, and it is now used for state occasions, such as the opening of Parliament. Other buildings around the Binnenhof house the First and Second Chambers of the States General, the Parliament of the Netherlands.

Return past the statue of William II to the Buitenhof, the old outer court of the castle, and walk through to the main shopping area, which includes many pedestrian precincts. Beyond is the Oude Stadhuis or old town hall dating from 1565, and the Grote Kerk or St Jacobskerk, which dates mainly from the mid-fifteenth century.

Walk back towards the Buitenhof and turn left down the pedestrianised Hoogstraat. Continue along Noordeinde to cross Hogewal and Mauritskade, where the canal is part of the original city moat. Across the canal is Zeestraat, with its world-famous Panorama Mesdag — a very realistic 360° panoramic view of the old fishing village of Scheveningen and the surrounding dunes, sea and landscape. With a circumference of 394ft and a height of 46ft, the painting covers 18,000sq ft of canvas. Further along Zeestraat is the Netherlands Postmuseum, covering aspects of communications, including postage stamps, telegraphs and radio.

Still following Zeestraat, cross the junction of Laan van Meerdervoort and Javastraat into Scheveningseweg and Carnegieplein, site of the Vredespaleis or Peace Palace, home of the International Court of Justice. Most countries of the world contributed towards the building, initially financed by Andrew Carnegie as an international court of arbitration intended to reduce or prevent future wars.

From this point a tram can be taken can be taken either back to Centraal Station or on to Scheveningen.

area of Westland, with thousands of acreas of glasshouses producing cucumbers and tomatoes, cut flowers and houseplants.

Den Haag and Scheveningen

The city which is known to English-speaking visitors as The Hague has two names in Dutch — Den Haag or 's Gravenhage. Originally it was called Den Haag or 'The Hedge', and later it became 's Gravenhage or the 'Count's Hedge'. Today the more common name is Den Haag, which is used in this book.

✳   Den Haag is the seat of the Government of the Netherlands, and Queen Beatrix has made her official home there. Because of the proximity of the court, the diplomatic corps and the large foreign community there is a demand for luxury items. Consequently, shopping can be pleasurable, but expensive. Much of the city displays the dignity and elegance of the eighteenth and nineteenth centuries, with a number of broad streets and avenues lined by fine residences.

As in many cities, parking is difficult and expensive, so park outside the city — look for the P+R (park and ride) signs. The bus map from bus

Madurodam miniature town, near Den Haag ➡

The modern pier at the seaside resort of Scheveningen

information offices lists the major museums and attractions and has explanations in English. The best way to see Den Haag is on foot, although trams and buses may be used to get to the more outlying areas.

❄   **Scheveningen** is a thriving holiday centre on the coast to the north-west of Den Haag. Famous for its casino, luxury hotels and fresh fish landed in the harbour, the town presents a variety of faces to the visitor. There is multi-storey and metered parking (both expensive), but the P+R at Den Haag and public transport from there is recommended. From the tram terminus walk south along the Boulevard to the famous Kurhaus, with its typical nineteenth-century exterior. It has, however, been thoroughly modernised inside to make it into a major leisure complex, with casino, hotel, restaurants and up-to-date conference centre. The pier is modern, replacing one which was destroyed in World War II.

At the far end of the Boulevard lies Scheveningen Haven, site of the old fishing village and the harbour which served as the port for Den Haag from the sixteenth to the nineteenth century. It was from here that Charles II embarked in May 1660 for his return to England at the Restoration.

Scheveningen is still a very busy port with a thriving fishing industry and a modern roll on, roll off ferry terminal. In spite of modern developments there are still some traces of the old town to be seen, including the tower of the church in Keizerstraat which dates from the fifteenth century.

Those wanting good sandy beaches will find plenty on this stretch of coast. In addition to Scheveningen itself, with its pier, beaches and other attractions, there is **Kijkduin**, a small attractive resort to the south, with the largest campsite on the Dutch coast at **Ockenburg**; there is also a large youth hostel adjacent. To the north is **Wassenaar**, a select suburb where

♣   the beach is partly reserved for residents. There is also Recreatiepark Duinrell, a large country estate which has been developed into a country park and amusement park with attractions for the whole family, including a modern fully equipped campsite. It is possible to find resorts to suit every taste in the area, from the most sophisticated, with casino, through family holiday beaches for the children, to quiet restful places where the only sounds are from the waves and the birds in the dunes.

Those wishing to explore this beautiful coastline will find a network of cyclepaths and footpaths in the dunes both to the north and south of the town; cars are banned in these areas. Cycles may be hired from the local VVV office. It is possible to follow paths through the dunes to **Katwijk** and beyond to **Zandvoort** to the north, or go south to **Kijkduin** and along the coast as far as Hoek van Holland.

❄   From Scheveningen take the tram to **Madurodam**, the miniature town described as 'Holland in a nutshell'. This is a complete miniature Dutch town built to a scale of 1:25, with buildings modelled on actual examples from all over Holland. It is beautifully landscaped with miniature trees and flowers. If you cannot spare the time to visit all of the places in Holland that you would like to see, it is probable that many of the buildings are represented at Madurodam, in miniature. Quite apart from the interesting way in which the whole project has been carried out, and is still being added to, Madurodam is, in fact, a war memorial. The original financing was by the parents of George Maduro, a student who distinguished himself and subsequently lost his life during World War II. Together with many donations from firms and other interests, the scheme has grown, and all the profits are donated to charity, mostly for the benefit of young people. There are full facilities for disabled visitors. Return to Centraal Stationin Den Haag by tram.

Another place worth visiting if you are in Den Haag during May is the Japanese Garden at Clingendael, adjacent to the head office of the ANWB on Wassenaarseweg (follow signs ANWB Kantoor). This lovely garden is a haven of peace and quiet and is beautifully laid out in true Japanese style, with streams, small shrubs and statues. The parkland at Clingendael is also open throughout the year.

Additional Information

Places of Interest

Delft
Atelier de Candelaer (porcelain factory)
Kerkstraat 13
☎ 015 131848
Open: Apr to Sept Mon to Fri 9am-6pm, Sat 9am-5pm, Sun 10am-6pm. Oct to Mar Mon to Sat 10-5pm.

De Delftse Pauw (porcelain factory)
Delftweg 133
☎ 015 124743
Open: Daily 9am-4pm (weekends Oct to Mar 11am-1pm).

De Porceleyne Fles (porcelain factory)
Rotterdamseweg 196
☎ 015 560234
Open: Mon to Fri 9am-5pm; Sat, Sun and public holidays 10am-4pm.

* Museum Nusantara (ethnological museum)
St Agathaplein 4
Open: Tues to St 10am-5pm, Sun 1-5pm. Also Mon afternoon June-Aug.

* Stedelijk Museum Het Prinsenhof
St Agathaplein 1
Open: Tues to Sat 10am-5pm, Sun and 1-5pm. Also Mon afternoon June-Aug. Closed mid-Sept to mid-Oct, 1 Jan and 25 Dec.

* Museum Huis Lambert van Meerten
Oude Delft 199
Open: Tues to Sat 10am-5pm, Sun 1-5pm. Also Mon afternoon June-Aug.

Dordrecht
* Museum Mr Simon van Gijn
Nieuwe Haven 29
Open: Tues to Sat 10am-5pm; Sun and public holidays, 1-5pm. Free admission on Wed afternoon.

* Dordrechts Museum
Museumstraat 40
Open: Tues to Sat 10am-5pm; Sun and public holidays, 1-5pm.

Den Haag
Binnenhof Ridderzaal (Hall of Knights)
Binnenhof 8a
Open: All year, Mon to Sat 10am-4pm, also July and Aug Sun 10-4. Closed public holidays.

Clingendael Estate
Wassenaarseweg
Open: All year, daily, Japanese garden only open daily from May to mid-June.

* Mauritshuis
Korte Vijverberg 8
Open: Tues to Sat 10am-5pm; Sun and public holidays 11am-5pm. Closed 1 Jan and 30 Apr.

* Rijksmuseum Gevangenpoort
Buitenhof 33
Open: All year Mon to Fri 10am-4pm.
Also Apr to Sept Sat, Sun and public
holidays 1-4pm.

Panorama Mesdag
Zeestraat 65
Open: Mon to Sat 10am-5pm, Sundays
and public holidays noon-5pm.

Madurodam Miniature Town
Haringkade 175
Open: Daily Apr and May 9am-
10.30pm; June to Aug 9am-11pm; Sept
9am-9.30pm; Oct to Jan 9am-6pm.

Nederlands Postmuseum
Zeestraat 82
Open: Mon to Sat 10am-5pm; Sun and
public holidays 1-5pm.

Kinderdijk
Complex of eighteen windmills (1740)
along the Molenkade
Mill visits: Apr to Sept, Mon to Sat
9.30am- 5.30pm. Mill days: July and
Aug. All mills in operation Sat 2.30-
5.30pm.

Rotterdam
Arboretum Trompenburg
Honingerdijk 64
Open: All year, Mon to Sat 9am-5pm.
(Apply for free tickets to VVV,
Stadhuisplein 19.) Closed Easter,
Whitsun and Christmas holidays.

Blijdorp Zoo
Van Aerssenlaan 49
Open: May to Oct daily 9am-6pm, Nov
to Apr daily 9am-5pm.

* Boymans- van Beuningen Museum
Mathenesserlaan 18-20
Open: Tues to Sat 10am-5pm; Sun,
11am-5pm.

Euromast
Parkhaven 20
Open: Apr to Sept, daily 10am-9pm. Oct
to Mar daily 10am-6pm, Space Tower,
daily 11am-4pm. Jan and Feb Sat and
Sun only.

Historic Electric Tram
One run per day, from Centraal Station
through part of the old city to the
Willemsplein, on one of the old city
tramcars.
Booking from the VVV office at
Coolsingel 67 or in Centraal Station.
Tickets include 75 min boat trip around
the harbour.
Tram departs daily from Apr to Sept at
1.15pm.

*Maritime Museum *Prins Hendrik*
Leuvehaven 1
Open: Tues to Sat 10am-5pm; Sun and
public holidays, 11am-5pm.
Museum ship *Buffel* moored nearby is
part of museum.

Plaswijckpark Recreation Park
CNA Looslaan 23
Open: Daily, 9am-5pm.

* †De Dubbelde Palmboom (restored
warehouse)
Voorhaven 10-12
Delfshaven

†Historische Museum Schielandhuis,
Korte Hoogstraat 31

†Zakkendragershuisje (Sack-Carriers
Guildhall)
Voorstraat 12-15
Delfshaven

The museums marked † comprise the
Historic Museums of City of Rotterdam.
All are open: Tues to Sat 10am-5pm, Sun
and public holidays 11am-5pm. Closed
1 Jan and 30 Apr.

Toy-Toy Museum Flos and Pieter Mars
Groene Wetering 41
Open: Jan to June and Sept to Dec, Sun
to Thurs 11am-4pm.

Schiedam
De Noord Windmill
Noordvest 38
Distillery mill working every Sat, is also
a restaurant.

Stedelijk Museum (with National Spirits
Museum)
Hoogstraat 112
Open: Tues to Sat 10am-5pm; Sun and
public holidays, 12.30-5pm.

De Vrijheid Windmill
Noordvest 40
Distillery mill working Sat.
Open: Mon to Sat 10am-4pm.

Vlardingen
Visserijmuseum Vlaardingen
Westhavenkade 53-54
Open: Mon to Sat 10am-5pm. Sun and
most public holidays 2-5pm. 30 April, 5
May, Ascension Day, 31 December
10am-5pm.

Wassenaar
Duinrell Recreation and Fairytale Park
Duinrell 1
Open: Mid-Apr to mid-Oct, daily,
10am-5pm; July and Aug 9am-6pm.

Boat Trips

Rotterdam
Spido Havenrondvaarten
Willemsplein
☎ 010 4135400
Various trips departing from
Willemsplein. Rotterdam harbour tour,
and tour of Delta-works are two examples, the former going daily all year, the
latter during July and Aug.

3

Gouda, Utrecht
and the Central Lakes

Gouda, famous for its cheese, is only 33km by motorway from Utrecht, a former Roman fortress town at the eastern end of the Randstad. The area between these towns contains many pleasant surprises for the tourist who leaves the beaten track.

Gouda is a pleasant town which was granted its first charter in 1272. During the fourteenth and fifteenth centuries it was a centre for the cloth trade, later turning to a variety of industries including the making of smokers' pipes, pottery, bricks, candles and, of course, cheese. The market square is the largest in Holland, and in its centre stands what is possibly the oldest Gothic town hall, dating from 1450.

Much of the town centre is pedestrianised, and parking is easier in the free parks on the outer edge of the town.

Route 6: A Circular Tour of the Lopikerwaard. Approx 70km

Lopikerwaard is the name given to the country lying between the rivers Lek to the south, the Vlist to the west and the Hollandse IJssel to the north. The name Lopik is derived from a natural stream in the peaty soil called the Lobeke. The embankments, or dykes, built of earth to enclose and retain the water became natural routes for roads. The landscape is pleasantly broken up by clumps of trees, small picturesque houses built behind the dykes, and reed-thatched farmhouses.

A very pleasant tour of the area can be made from Gouda. Leave the town via the bridge to the south, across the river, and take the road leading to Haastrecht. This road follows along the south bank of the river, but cyclists will find that a more pleasant way is to take the dyke road along the north side. At Haastrecht, take the minor road leading south to Vlist and Schoonhoven and, ignoring turnings to Stolwijk, continue alongside the river to the centre of Vlist. Just past here, cross the bridge over the river on the left, signed to Bonrepas. Cyclists can cross at another bridge before reaching the village; by crossing the river, a much prettier road is followed, and in springtime the whole route is extremely attractive. A short distance before reaching the outskirts of Schoonhoven the road passes

A Walk in Gouda

Begin the walk in the market square. If you can time it to begin on the hour, you can watch the little figures on the east wall of the Stadhuis move when the carillon plays; they depict Count Floris V bestowing civic rights on the town in 1272. Also look out for the beautiful Renaissance staircase on the south side of the building. Behind the Stadhuis, on the northern side of the Markt, is the Waag or weigh-house. Built in 1668, and formerly used for weighing the cheeses at the weekly market, it is now only open on Thursday mornings during July and August, when an old crafts market is held. There are demonstrations of clog-making, pottery, pipe-making, candle-dipping and *stroopwafel* baking. *Stroopwafels*, or syrup waffles, are a speciality of the district.

From the south end of the Markt, through Kerkstraat, the great St Janskerk is reached; its 123m long nave is the longest in Holland. Dating from the fourteenth century, the church is renowned for its seventy stained glass windows, mostly sixteenth century, and these illustrate scenes from the Bible and Dutch history. They are fully described in a detailed guide which is available in English.

On the south side of the church, the Lazarus Gate (1609) leads from Achter de Kerk into the Catharina Gasthuis, a building from 1665 which served as a hospital from 1306 to 1910. It is now the municipal museum with period rooms, collections of old and modern art, an old dispensary and surgeons' instruments.

Leave the building by the exit into Oosthaven, cross the bridge and turn left along Westhaven. On the right is a seventeenth-century merchant's house named 'De Moriaan' (The Blackamoor) which houses a museum of tiles, earthenware and clay and other pipes. Gouda's pipe-making history goes back to the early seventeenth century, when Puritan refugees included several pipe-makers fromEngland. Until 1637 the English had a monopoly of the industry in Gouda, after which their Dutch competitors took over.

Continue along Westhaven to the next bridge and turn left into Lange Noordooststraat, then left again into Spieringstraat. Here is the old Weeshuis (orphanage) which has a fine collection of rare books and documents. On the other side of the street is the Willem Vroesenhuis (1614), a former almshouse. At the west end of the St Janskerk is Torenstraat, leading to Lage Gouwe, with the canal on your left. Across the water are picturesque colonnaded buildings: the cornmarket and the fish market, the latter now used for pottery and art demonstrations. From the fish market, turn right up the narrow Visstraat and right again into Achter de Vismarkt, following this street until Lange Groenendaal opens on the left. Here are two shops selling the Gouda specialities of cheese and *stroopwafels*. Return along Korte Groenendaal to the Markt and the Stadhuis.

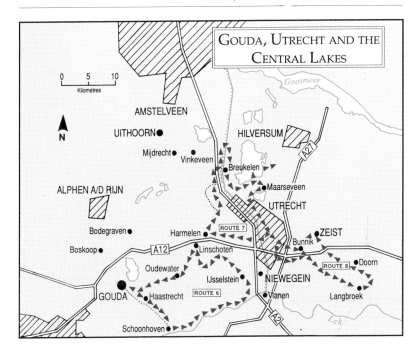

GOUDA, UTRECHT AND THE
CENTRAL LAKES

quite close to a fine example of a *wipmolen* pumping windmill.

Schoonhoven, an old fortress town on the banks of the River Lek, is ❄
noted chiefly for silver manufacture, especially the ornaments worn with
traditional costume. In the centre of the town is the former weigh-house,
now a recommended pancake restaurant. The building dates from 1617,
but the Stadhuis is even older, built in 1452. The Gothic St Barth-
olomaeuskerk has an interesting sixteenth-century official pew. Beside
the harbour are many restored old buildings housing silver and other
craft workshops. The Edelambachtshuis at 13 Haven has the largest
collection of antique Schoonhoven silver in Holland and an old fashioned
workshop. 't Silverhuys, 1-5 Haven, also has a very fine collection of
silver. The Nederlands Goud- Zilver- en Klokkenmuseum is in Kazerneplein.

Leave the town via the harbour which leads to the Veerpoort (1601), the
only remaining town gate of the original five, where a ferry operates
across the River Lek to Nieuwpoort. Do not take the ferry, but turn left
and follow the north bank of the river with views of the shipping on the
waterway. The huge observation mast of the Meteorological Institute is
passed about 10km from Schoonhoven, while just before the Lekbrug
motorway bridge high television masts can be seen to the left. Here, at
signpost 7409, turn away from the river to **Lopikerkapel**, a typical village

◄The 'fairytale' town hall at Gouda, probably the oldest in Holland

of the area with a fifteenth-century Dutch Reformed church with a beautiful interior.

✳   Continue into **IJsselstein**, a town with a long history. Inhabited since Roman times, the medieval street plan can still be traced. The remains of the thirteenth-century castle tower with a beautiful arched staircase houses a permanent photographic exhibition dealing with its history. The municipal museum is located in the restored town hall, originally built in 1560. Holland's first Renaissance tower, dating from 1535, forms part of the Dutch Reformed Church; the original building was constructed in 1310. There was only one road leading to Utrecht, and access to it was by the IJsselpoort. Near this gate is a little building, the Brandspuithuisje, originally built in 1622 to house a small fire pump, but now containing historic fire-fighting equipment, which may only be seen through the windows.

Leave the town by a minor road running north, parallel to the river Hollandse IJssel, towards Achtersloot then left to **Montfoort**, meaning 'castle on a ford'. The gatehouse of the castle still stands and the seventeeth-century IJsselpoort (town gate) stands adjacent to the eighteenth-century town hall. The layout of the town centre still recalls the Middle Ages.

From Montfoort, take the road out of town to the south-west, then turn ✳ right along road N212 to **Linschoten**, a beautiful rural village in a loop of the river Linschoten. Many houses are in their original seventeeth and eighteenth-century condition. Settlements existed in the polders of the area in AD900, and between 1290 and 1490 there were four castles, although only traces remain. The fine Grote or St Janskerk has a fifteenth-century tower, and the village is situated in the centre of a large nature reserve along the Hollandse IJssel and the Lange Linschoten.

The road south along the Lange Linschoten is particularly beautiful, lined by pollarded willows on the bank of the winding river, and particularly pleasant for cycling. The road finally leads to **Oudewater**, which was granted a city charter in 1295, and was beseiged during the Eighty Years' War. Here is the famous weighhouse, known as the Heksenwaag, with stepped gable dating from 1595, which, because of its reputation for honesty and accuracy, was used for weighing people accused of witchcraft. A person was deemed to be a witch if their weight was not compatible with their size and height. Today, visitors can still be weighed, and receive a certificate stating that their weight is 'in accordance with the natural proportion of the body'. The town has many attractive seventeeth-century façades and backwaters, including a town hall with a Renaissance façade of 1588. The Gothic St Michael's Church has a thirteenth-century tower and vestry. You may even see storks nesting on the roof tops. The market square is built over the river and parking, even for cycles, is forbidden.

Leave Oudewater by the road to Hekendorp, which runs along the northern side of the Hollandse IJssel, with old farm houses below the dyke on the right and fields leading to the river on the left. There are many fruit farms in the area. Beyond the junction for Haastrecht, on the left, the road continues back towards Gouda. In about $1^1/_2$km, at *paddestoel* 21509, a steep road leaves the dyke on the right, leading to the Reeuwijkse Plassen. This is an area of water which is the result of peat cutting over hundreds of years. Popular with sailors and fishermen, it is an ideal place for viewing water birds. It is possible to drive along the narrow lanes across the lake, although there is restricted access at weekends and holidays. The roads are very narrow, so care is needed. A bicycle is the best form of transport for exploring the area. Return to Gouda via Reeuwijk-Brug.

To the north of Gouda, **Boskoop** is the centre of Holland's shrub-growing industry. This area was once so remote that no peat cutting took place , so the sandy soil and underlying peat provide ideal growing conditions for trees and shrubs. An arboretum and tree research station may be visited and there are boat trips around the nurseries (enquire locally).

Beyond Boskoop is **Alphen a/d Rijn**, noted for the Avifauna bird park, where visitors wander through a sub-tropical house with free-flying birds, tropical plants, and even fruit-producing banana trees.

Utrecht is the fourth largest city in Holland, and the capital of Utrecht Province, often called the heart of Holland. It is easily reached by motorway, but it is pleasant to take the old road from Gouda via Bodegraven, Woerden and Harmelen, following the Oude Rijn river.

There is plenty of parking space (fee payable) in the Hoog-Catharijne, the largest covered shopping centre in Europe. Because of its size, it can be extremely confusing, although well signed. Since there are seven car parks within the complex, it is essential to take careful note of where you are parked, and it is recommended that the illustrated guide (*wegwijzer*) is obtained from the centre's information office.

Utrecht was built on the site of a Roman fort where Dom Square is now located. During the prosperous years of the twelfth to fourteenth centuries a network of canals was dug within the city walls, with merchants' houses, cellars and quays. The huge cathedral tower, separate from the adjacent church building, dates back to the fourteenth century, and is topped by a weathervane depicting St Martin (to whom the cathedral is dedicated) cutting off part of his coat to give to a beggar. The 112m tall tower is the tallest in Holland and is open to visitors.

Ther are many museums in the city, but those of special interest include the Catharijne-Convent, depicting the history of Christianity in the Netherlands, housed in the sixteenth-century hospital of the Knights of St John, in Nieuwegracht; the Netherlands Railway Museum at the Maliebaanstation; the Centraal Museum in Agnietenstraat; and the National Museum van Speelklok tot Pierement in the Buurkerkhof. The latter has early musical boxes, fairground and street organs, pianolas, etc.

A boat trip can also be made to **Loenen**, one of the prettiest villages on

A Walk Around Utrecht

Starting at the Hoog-Catharijne centre, where the bus and railway stations and central car parks are situated, make your way to the Vredenburgkwartier and along Lange Viestraat. Cross the Viebrug and turn right along Oudegracht. On the left, at the corner of Drakenburgstraat, is the medieval house Drakenborch, while across the canal may be seen Huis Oudaen. Built in the fourteenth century, it was the residence of the French Ambassador at the time of the Treaty of Utrecht (1713). Cross over to the Jansbrug and look below, where the old cellars (now housing small cafés) are visible along the quayside. Walk along the quay past the next two bridges, Bakkerbrug and Bezembrug. At the Stadhuisbrug, almost a square built over the water, cross to the Stadhuis, parts of which date from the thirteenth century. Continue along Vismarkt to the Maartens-brug and turn left to the great tower of the Dom. The large arch in the base of the tower is big enough for a city bus to pass through. Here also are the Dom church, the university buildings and a copy of a Danish Rune Stone from Jutland, commemorating the fact that St Willibrord, the English founder of the cathedral, introduced Christianity to Denmark.

Just by this memorial is an archway leading to a peaceful fourteenth-century cloister. Go through and turn right into Achter de Dom and Pausdam. Here you will find the Paushuize (Pope's House) built for Pope Adrian VI, the only Dutch Pope, who in fact never lived here. Turn into Achter St Pieter and St Pieterskerk will be seen on the right. Continue to Korte Janstraat where, at the end of the street, the Janskerk can be seen. These two churches were built as collegiate churches linked to the cathedral, forming part of a cross around the Dom. The other two churches are St Catharijnekerk and the Buurkerk or parish church. Walk down Oudkerkhof, cross the bridge and turn left into Choorstraat, then right into Zadelstraat. The Buurkerk is on the right, but continue to Mariaplaats where, behind the university's Arts and Sciences building, are the twelfth-century cloisters of the Mariakloostergang. From here, return to the start in Hoog-Catherijne.

Another method of viewing the city is by a boat trip on the canals, starting from the Oude Gracht near the Viebrug. This trip lasts about 1 hour and many of the most interesting sights of the city can be seen.

◀ A quiet corner near the main square in Oudewater

the river Vecht, noted for country estates and castles. A drive or trip by cycle through this area is also well worthwhile.

Route 7: The Castles and Lakes of the Vecht Area. Approx 67km

Leave Utrecht by the road to **De Meern** and **Harmelen**, which follows the Leidse Rijn. At Harmelen, turn right at signpost 3112 towards the Vijverbos nature reserve, continue across the railway, and at signpost 937 turn right and look for Kasteel de Haar. This beautiful castle was rebuilt last century on the ruins of a fifteenth-century castle, in the Romantic style — a real fairy tale castle. Inside is a fine collection of sixteenth and seventeenth century Gobelin tapestries, furniture, carpets, Chinese vases and many paintings, and the castle is surrounded by a park and gardens.

Continue along the road fronting the castle moat and grounds, turning left at signpost 6639, passing the large wrought-iron gateway to the park. Continue through the beautiful village of **Haarzuilens** to Laagnieuwkoop and on to Portengensebrug, turning right towards Breukelen.

Motorists can join the motorway A2 north for 6km to Loenersloot, then take the N201, turning right (signpost 2125) into **Loenen**, one of the prettiest Vecht villages. Cyclists follow the road alongside the railway and canal to Loenersloot. Cross the river and follow the road south beside the river towards **Breukelen**. This is an area noted for its castles and manor houses. Although many of the buildings have disappeared over the centuries, its name was taken by Dutch emigrants and became the present-day Brooklyn, New York. The town of Breukelen is now the centre for an outstanding water sport area based on the Loosdrecht lakes.

About 1km further south, on the right, is the rather impressive Nijenrode Castle, based on an original thirteenth-century foundation and considerably altered and enlarged from 1632 on. It is not open to the public as it is now a college for business management studies.

In about 500m the route turns left (signpost 240) and follows alongside the lake before turning right through Tienhoven and Oud Maarsseveen. Just before reaching Tienhoven, at signpost 2620, a diversion can be made along the road to Nieuw-Loosdrecht across the lakes. This road passes another castle, Kasteel Sypestein. The original castle was built in 1288, but the present building was completed at the beginning of this century, carefully reconstructed using the original foundations and old materials from other castles of the same period. The result is quite impressive, and the castle houses a fine museum of old masters, furniture, porcelain, silver and glassware. The gardens and park have been laid out in the style of the late sixteenth and early seventeeth centuries, and are open to visitors to the museum.

Return to signpost 2620 and continue through Tienhoven to Maarsseveen and **Oud-Zuilen**, where there is the castle known as Slot Zuylen. The first references to a castle here date from AD838, and the present building was commenced in 1300. The park around the castle is open to visitors to the museum within the building, and has a unique garden sheltered by a so-called 'snake-wall' which traps the sun's warmth, making it possible to grow sub-tropical fruit.

From Slot Zuylen return to Utrecht by the main road.

Route 8: Zeist, Doorn and the Langbroek Castles. Approx 50km

To the south-east of Utrecht, between the Utrecht hills and the rivers Rijn and Lek, lies an area particularly rich in castles. There are three good reasons for this: good hunting was available, sufficient land for tenant farmers could be found, and much of the area was protected against attack from the east and south by natural barriers.

Along the Kromme Rijn and the Langbroeker-wetering, a small canal running parallel with the river, lies a string of castles. Although most of them are not open to the public, a tour of the area or a walk around those which are open will give a good insight into the countryside and the sixteenth- and seventeenth-century castles and mansions, many of which have been built on the sites of older structures.

Leave Utrecht along the A12 motorway, in the direction of Arnhem. After about 5km, leave at the turn-off for Bunnik, and go south following signs for Odijk and Wijk-bij-Duurstede, past the village of Odijk, then take a minor road at signpost 9329. This leads to Beverweerd castle, dating from the thirteenth century but rebuilt in neo-Gothic style in 1751. It is not open to view, but the grounds, apart from the immediate vicinity of the castle, are open for walking.

Continue past the castle for about 1km, turning left, then right alongside the Langbroeker-wetering, to castle Sterkenburg on the right. Other castles can be seen on both sides of the road, including Kasteel Hinderstein, originally built in 1320, and completely rebuilt in 1847, but retaining the original tower. As before, free access to the grounds is possible, but not to the castle.

Cross the main road in the village of **Langbroek**, and in 1km the two castles of Sandenburg (left) and Walenburg (right) will be seen. Sandenburg is an ornate turreted nineteenth-century edifice, white-plastered in neo-Gothic style, but built on the site of a medieval castle. It stands in an estate which is the largest in the district, including about twenty-one farms. The estate includes Kasteel Walenburg, purchased by the owners of Sandenburg in 1865, and restored in 1967. Neither castle is open to the public, but walking is permitted on the estates.

In approximately 1km, turn left at the crossroads, right at the next T-junction, then second left (following local signs) to Kasteel Broekhuizen on the right. This is a massive building with a portico supported by Ionic pillars. In the fourteenth century, a castle stood here surrounded by moats, but it was demolished in 1794 and a larger structure built, being further enlarged in 1810. After a fire in 1906 it was rebuilt once again. Now the buildings are occupied by the national institute for landscape management, so are not open to view. Part of the surrounding park is used for zoological and botanical research, but the remainder, which is open to the public, is landscaped in the English style, with hedges and copses and a fine nineteenth-century beech avenue.

Although the main N225 road is very pleasant, it is better to take the country lane from Broekhuizen to **Doorn**. In the centre of the small town is St Maartenskerk, with a stone-built twelfth-century nave and a brick tower in Gothic style. There is a Norman doorway and leper-squints in the church wall. The main interest in Doorn is the Huis Doorn, since the fourteenth century the summer residence of the Diocese of Utrecht. From 1920 it was the residence of the exiled Kaiser Wilhelm II of Germany, who died here in 1941. During extensive reconstruction and enlargement in 1780, the house incorporated parts of the original medieval castle. It now belongs to the Dutch Government who maintain it as a museum with fine collections of paintings, tapestry and silverware; there are also many items belonging to the ex-Kaiser. The interior is preserved as it was when he lived there. The surrounding park is most attractive, with centuries old trees, a pinetum and deer park. The orangery is now a tea room.

From Doorn, follow the main road to **Zeist**, a small town surrounded by beautiful wooded countryside. Its early origins are recalled by the mound upon which the church stands, and the town has some stately houses and delightful villas built in the last century by wealthy merchants.

On the edge of the town lies Slot Zeist, a very large seventeenth-century

Kasteel de Haar near Utrecht

mansion built on the site of a medieval castle. Inspired by the French baroque style there are painted walls and ceilings, and gardens in the fashion of Le Notre, similar to those at Versailles. The mansion changed hands many times, until in 1924 the local authority bought it and restored it to its original state. It is now used as a conference and exhibition centre, with a music school and restaurant. Little of the original gardens remain; in the eighteenth century the grounds were landscaped in English style, and only a small part is still as planned on the Versailles model. The main area contains lawns, paths and canals, with trees, and an open-air theatre which is used on summer afternoons.

From Slot Zeist, take the road south-west at signpost 6697 towards Bunnik, then follow the Utrecht road through Bunnik, keeping north of the railway. Watch for a signpost for **Rhijnauwen**, on the right after about 1km (signpost 7300). From this point there is a one-way system which must be followed to the car parks within this large estate, which was purchased by the city of Utrecht in 1919. The eighteenth-century mansion is now a youth hostel, while the grounds, together with two adjoining estates, are open to the public. Within the park, the 'Theehuis Rhijnauwen' is famous for its wide selection of pancakes.

From Rhijnauwen, it is a short journey back to Utrecht. It is possible to visit this estate by boat from the city, the journey taking about 90 minutes.

Additional Information

Places of Interest

Alphen aan de Rijn
Avifauna Bird Park
Hoorn 56
Open: Apr to Sept daily 9am-9pm, Oct to Mar 9am-6pm.

Doorn
* Huis Doorn
Langbroekerweg 10
Open: Mid-Mar to Oct, Mon to Sat 9.30am-5pm; Sun 1-5pm.

Gouda
* Het Catharina Gasthuis Museum
Oosthaven 9-10
Open: Mon to Sat 10am-5pm; Sun and public holidays noon-5pm. Closed 1 Jan, 25 Dec.

* De Moriaan (pipe museum)
Westhaven 29
Open: Mon to Sat 10am-5pm; Sun and public holidays noon-5pm. Closed 1 Jan and 25 Dec.

Haarzuilens
Kasteel De Haar
Kasteellaan 1
Open: Mid-Oct to mid-Nov and Mar to mid-Aug, Mon to Fri 11am-4pm. Sun and public holidays guided tours on the hour 1-4pm.

Loosdrecht
Kasteel Sypesteyn
Nieuw Loosdrechtsedijk 150
Open: May to mid-Sept, Tues to Sat, 10am-4pm; Sun , Easter, Ascension Day and Whitsun 2-4pm. Guided tours on the hour.

Maarssen
Slot Zuylen
Tournooiveld 1
Open: Guided tours mid-Mar to mid-May, mid-Sept. to mid-Nov, Sat 2pm, 3pm, and 4pm. Mid-May to mid-Sept, Tues to Thurs 10am and 4pm, Fri 10am and 11am, Sat 2pm, and 4pm, Sun 1pm and 4pm.

Schoonhoven
Edelambachthuis (silver collecion)
Haven 13
Open: Apr to Sept Mon 1-5.30pm, Tues
to Fri 10am-5.30pm, Sat 10am-5pm. Oct
to Mar Mon 1-5pm, Tues to Sat
10.30pm-5pm. 30 Apr and Ascension
Day 1-5pm. Closed 25 Dec and 1 Jan.

* Nederlands Goud-, Zilver- en
  Klokkenmuseum
Kazerneplein 4
Open: Tues to Sun noon-5pm.

't Silverhuys (silver collection)
Haven 1-5
Open: Mon 1-5pm, Tues to Sta 9.30am-
5.30pm.

Utrecht
* Rijksmuseum Het Catharijne-Convent
Nieuwe Gracht 63
Open: Tues to Fri 10am-5pm; Sat, Sun
and public holidays 11am-5pm.

Centraal Museum
Agnietenstraat 1
Open: Tues to Sat 10am-5pm; Sun and
public holidays 1-5pm.

* Nederlands Spoorweg Museum
  (railway museum)
Johan van Oldenbarneveltlaan 6
(Maliebaanstation)
Open: Tues to Sat 10am-5pm; Sun and
public holidays 1-5pm. Closed 1 Jan,
Easter, Whitsun and Christmas.

* Nationaal Museum van Speelklok tot
  Pierement (mechanical music)
Buurkerkhof 10
Open: Tues to Sat 10am-4pm, Sun and
public holidays 1-4pm. Guided tours
every hour on the hour, last tour 4pm.
Closed 1 Jan, 30 Apr, Easter, Whitsun
and Christmas.

Zeist
Slot Zeist
Zinzendorflaan 1
Open: All year Sat and Sun 2.30-4pm;
July and Aug Tues to Fri 2.30pm.

IJesselstein
Stadsmuseum IJsselstein
Utrechtsestraat79
Open: Wed, Fri and Sat 2-5pm.

4

LEIDEN, HAARLEM AND AMSTERDAM

These three cities form the north-west and northern edges of the Randstad. All three have long and varied histories, and are full of interesting places to see. Between Leiden and Haarlem lies the centre of the bulb-growing industry, and along the coast the resorts of Katwijk, Noordwijk and Zandvoort attract many holidaymakers. Extensive dune areas open to the public include the Amsterdam water purification scheme and the Kennemer Dune Reserve, while further inland is the Haarlemmermeer polder, once a huge inland lake and now containing Schipol International Airport. Amsterdam itself is continually expanding, both south and north of the busy North Sea Canal, but within its boundaries some of the old villages still retain some of their former charm.

Leiden

A sixteenth-century poet described Leiden as a labyrinth of canals, streets, bridges and ramparts. The castle was built in the twelfth century on a mound of either Saxon or Roman origin. Leiden has always offered asylum to refugees from religious persecution; these include the Pilgrim Fathers, and the Flemish weavers, which explains the growth of the cloth industry. The wars with Spain during the sixteenth and seventeenth centuries had their effect on Leiden, which was beseiged during 1573-4. After the seige, the courage and loyalty of the citizens was recognised by Prince William the Silent who endowed a university in 1575, which has enjoyed international renown ever since. October 3, the day the seige was lifted, is still a public holiday in Leiden.

1606 saw the birth of the painter Rembrandt, just one of many great Dutch painters who lived and worked here during the Golden Age. The spirit of liberty shown by the resistance to Spanish invaders was further demonstrated in 1609 when the Pilgrim Fathers found refuge here, and their pastor, John Robinson, attended the university. He remained behind after the Pilgrims sailed for America, and died in the city in 1625. The Pilgrim Collection in the city holds copies of their records.

Around 1670, Leiden was the second largest city in Holland, so it is not

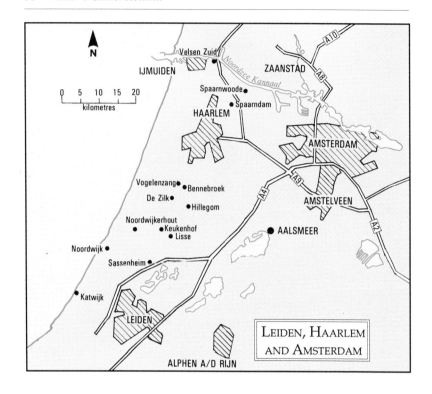

LEIDEN, HAARLEM
AND AMSTERDAM

surprising that there is much of interest to see. Four waymarked walks are marked by coloured arrows set into the pavements, and leaflets detail the routes and interesting places. The routes are: 'A true Dutch Heritage' (red arrows), 'A town full of monuments' (blue), 'The road of freedom' (green) and 'Following in Rembrandt's footsteps' (yellow). The walk here takes in some of the more interesting places from all four routes.

To the north-west of Leiden is a stretch of the North Sea coast with fine sandy beaches backed by large areas of dunes. Because of the risk of erosion, access for cars and cycles is restricted.

The fishing village of **Katwijk** lies about 9km north-west of Leiden, and is now the centre of a popular beach resort, ideal for families with children. Permits to visit the dunes to the north of the village are obtainable from the local VVV. Among these dunes is the European Space Centre ESTEC. The dunes to the south are freely accessible but visitors must keep to the waymarked paths. Parking is available at both ends of the esplanade. A trip worth making from Katwijk is by boat to the Kager Plassen or lakes, and the windmills, or to the Avifauna bird garden at Alphen a/d Rijn.

Just 3km north of Katwijk is **Noordwijk**, another very popular resort with an extensive beach. Both horses and cycles can be hired here, and the dunes form a natural setting for an 18-hole golf course.

To the north of the village these dunes stretch for miles, and have been planted with trees by the Staatsbosbeheer (State Forestry Service); many trails and cycle paths have been established. At the northern end of the woods is Langevelderslag, a popular holiday area with campsites, holi-

The Keukenhof gardens, Lisse, open in the spring when the bulbs are at their best

Holland's famous bulb fields are a popular attraction in the spring

A Walk Around Leiden

Starting at the railway station (plenty of parking nearby), walk down Stationsweg and cross the outer moat into Steenstraat. At the Blawpoortsbrug, turn right into Morsstraat, at the end of which is the seventeeth-century Morspoort, one of the two remaining town gates. Turn left and cross the Rembrandtbrug. Look back to see the old City Carpenters Yard, an attractive seventeeth-century building. Rembrandt was born in the Weddelsteeg, through which you pass before turning left into Noordeinde. Turn right into Oude Varkenmarkt and pass the Loridanshofje, a 1657 almshouse now used by the university. Cross the bridge, turn left along Groenhazengracht then right into Rapenburg, and continue to the university building at the end of the street, where, on 20 May 1620, Rembrandt registered as a student. Here also is the entrance to the oldest botanical gardens in Europe, belonging to the university. These may be visitied on payment of a small fee, and they make a pleasant diversion. Crossing the Nonnenbrug into the Kloksteeg brings you to the Jean Pesijnshofje, built on the site of the Groene Poort house. This is where John Robinson, spiritual leader of the Pilgrim Fathers, lived from 1611 to his death in 1625. A plaque on the wall of the fifteenth-century Pieterskerk commemorates the voyage of the *Mayflower* to America in 1620.

Turning left at the church brings you to Het Gravensteen, once the county jail and now used by the university. Rembrandt's studio was in the nearby Muskadelsteeg. Almost opposite Het Gravensteen, on the corner of Lokhorststraat and Schoolsteg, is the fine gabled building of the Latin School, in use as a grammar school until 1864.

Continue the walk up Lokhorststraat and Diefsteeg into Breestraat, where, on the left, a short way along the street is the restored sixteenth-century Rijnlandshuis. Returning along Breestraat, at the crossing with Maarsmansteeg and Pieterskerkchoorsteeg near the Stadhuis, is the 'Blue Stone', marking the former place of executions and the spot where faulty cloth was burned before it could be marketed.

The sixteenth-century Renaissance façade of the Stadhuis was the only part of the building which could be restored following a disas-

day houses and a youth hostel. Not far from here is a small gliding field, and at De Zilk is the entrance to the dune area known as the Amsterdamse Waterleiding Duinen. Tickets, permitting entry for walkers only, are obtainable at the nearby café. Once inside the gates, visitors are free to walk anywhere on the vast network of paths within this area of natural dune-land, which is the site of the water purification system for Amsterdam, and a nature reserve. The water is allowed to flow through concrete channels or leats, during which it is aerated and also allowed to filter trous fire in 1929. Notice the rings where visitors tethered their horses, the town crier's stand and, behind this, the *Rijnlandse Roede*, the standard measure of twelve Rijnlandse feet or 3.7674m.

Beyond the Stadhuis, turn left towards the beautiful Koornbeurs-brug or corn exchange bridge which was built in 1440, with twin colonnaded buildings added in 1825. Cross over and walk up Burg-steeg. On the left is the gated entrance to De Burcht, Leiden's twelfth-century citadel built on an artificial mound. Climb the steps to the top for a magnificent view over the town. From the battlements the view is even better. To the south-east is the St Pancras or Hooglandsekerk (sixteenth century), behind which, in the Hooglandse Kerkgracht, is the entrance to the former Holy Ghost orphanage, now the National Museum of Geology and Mineralogy. Continue across the drawbridge and into Hooglandse Kerksteeg, left into Haarlemmerstraat, then in a short distance left again through Donker–steeg into Hoogstraat. To the left, across the water, is the seventeeth-century Waag or weigh-house.

Return to Haarlemmerstraat again and turn left, then right into Vrouwenkerkkoorstraat. Ahead is the dome of the seventeenth-century Marekerk, and to the left are the remains of the fourteenth-century Vrouwenkerk, the original outline of which may still be seen. Not far from here, in Oude Vest, is the Museum of Clay Pipes.

Turn left into Vrouwenkerkhof and continue into Lange Sint Agnietenstraat, where, on the right, is the sixteenth-century Boerhaave Zalen, considered to be the world's first teaching hospital.

Continue across Klooster, then turn right into Lange Lijsbethsteeg, passing on the left the beautifully restored Sint Elisabethgasthuis (1428), still used as a hospice. Across the bridge is the Municipal Museum De Lakenhal, originally the guildhall of the clothmakers, with fine paintings. Past here is the Lammermarkt, at the end of which is the huge corn-mill 'De Valk', now a museum of milling. A beautiful park, Het Plantsoen, with an aviary, is on the moats of the old town.

Return to the station by crossing the bridge beyond the mill into Schuttersveld, then left into Stationsplein.

through the sand of the dunes. The footpaths are well signed, and maps are available.

The area inland from the dunes, running north from Leiden, includes the villages of **Sassenheim**, **Lisse**, **Hillegom** and **Bennebroek**, which are the heart of the Dutch bulb-growing industry. From Lisse, signs direct visitors to the **Keukenhof**, site of perhaps the most famous flower show in the world. In its 70 acres of parkland are magnificent displays of flowering bulbs, shrubs and old trees, all landscaped among lakes and fountains, forming a show-case for the Dutch bulb growers and nurseries. There are also 5,000sq m of greenhouses full of all kinds of flowers, and exhibitions are mounted in the pavilions. The gardens are only open in the spring, when the bulbs are at their best, but it is a superb way to spend a day, wandering along the paths between the lawns, lakes and flower beds. Climb to the stage on the windmill for a breathtaking view of the surrounding bulb fields, the scent of which is almost overpowering at times.

About 4km north-east of Bennebroek, alongside the N201 main road at **Vijfhuizen**, is the distinctive round castle-like building of 'De Cruquius'. This is one of three steam pumping stations used to drain the Haarlemmermeer during 1849-52, thus creating what was then the largest polder in Holland. They continued to keep the polder drained up to 1933, when the other two were modernised. Cruquius became redundant but the building, with its unique Cornish steam beam engine and pumps, has been preserved. The 144in diameter engine is the largest steam engine ever built. It operated many different pumps at once, all situated around the building. Together with scale models of the country, of wind and steam pumps, old machines, maps and drawings, and superb examples of cast iron work the building has been turned into a museum to show the story of the struggle against the water, and to demonstrate the use of steam for this work.

Between De Cruquius and the village of **Bennebroek** is the Linnaeushof

De Cruquius steam pumping station at Vijfhuizen

Recreation Park, with many attractions for children, while a short distance to the west is the village of **Vogelenzang**, site of the well-known Frans Roozen nurseries.

Haarlem

Lying a few kilometres to the north of the bulb-growing area, the city of Haarlem is an attractive place with many old and interesting buildings. The city lies on the river Spaarne, and like so many old Dutch towns, it was built on a ring of canals, with ramparts on the north side of the town. These were landscaped as a park during the nineteenth century. Haarlem is noted for its beautiful *hofjes* or almshouses, many of which are still in use for their original purposes. The best way to see the city is by following the recommended walking route.

To the west of the city are the 'garden suburbs' of Bloemendaal and Aerdenhout, with fine country houses, parks and gardens. Beyond them, towards the sea coast, is the National Park 'De Kennemer Duinen', an area of surprisingly hilly dunes in which a whole day can easily be spent walking and cycling. Within the park is a campsite, and a number of car parks are provided at the entrances along the road from Haarlem to the coast. Where this road reaches the beach approaches, it turns south past the famous Zandvoort motor racing circuit to the popular holiday resort of **Zandvoort**. The main beach area along the promenade is constantly patrolled, and quieter beaches can be found further away.

To the north of the dune reserve are the great sea locks at **IJmuiden**, at the entrance to the North Sea Canal which links the sea with the port of Amsterdam. Originally opened on 1 November 1876, it was soon realised that the locks were too small, so the size of the canal and of the locks was increased in 1896 and again in 1930, when the great lock, more than 1,300ft long, 160ft wide and 50ft deep, was opened. It is an experience to see the lock complex at night, with all the lights of the waterway installations, backed by the lurid flames from the steel works at Hoogovens, across the water.

The fishing harbour at IJmuiden serves as a base for trawlers from many other ports, and from the nearby beaches visitors can watch the constant flow of shipping negotiating the lock entrance.

Nearby **Velsen**, with numerous pleasant walks and estates open to the public, is the location of the Velsen road tunnel under the North Sea Canal.

To the east of the motorway leading to the tunnel is the recreation area of Spaarnwoude, with a number of car parks, a cycle track, canoe courses and a 27-hole golf course. There is also a campsite.

It is possible to drive alongside the River Spaarne from Haarlem to the village of **Spaarndam**, a typical North Holland village of green and white painted houses with old wooden gables, built along the dyke. Here too is the little statue of Hans Brinker, the boy whom legend says put his thumb

A Walk Around Haarlem

The walk starts at the railway station, where there is a well-signed multistorey car park, also the local VVV office.

From the main entrance of the station, turn right then left along Kruis Weg, crossing Parklaan to the bridge over Nieuwe Gracht. From the bridge, looking east, may be seen some attractive old houses alongside the canal. Continuing along Kruis Weg, there is a particularly fine carved façade of an old apothecary's house on the right, followed a little later by the lovely 'Hofje van Oorschot' dating from1770 with a wrought iron gate and garden in front of the elegant buildings. Turn right along Krocht into Ursulastraat, passing the Remonstrants Hofje (1744), and cross the wide Nassau Laan into Magdalena Straat. Halfway along, turn left into Witte Heren Straat, with the Lutheran church and *hofje*, whose courtyard has an open-air pulpit. Nearby is the seventeenth-century Frans Loenen Hofje with an attractive little gate. At the end of the street, turn left into Zijl Straat, then back to the Grote Markt in the centre of the town. Across the square is the great church of St Bavo built between the fourteenth and sixteenth centuries, with its tower standing high above the surroundings. Frans Hals, the artist who lived and worked in Haarlem, is buried here, and the interior has a magnificent organ built in 1738, played by Mozart and still used for recitals. In the centre of the Markt is a statue commemorating Lourens Janszoon Coster who, in the fifteenth century, founded the printing industry in Haarlem which still exists.

Other fine buildings surrounding the Markt include the old Hoofdwacht or guard house dating from about1650, the Vleeshal, a lovely gabled building in Dutch Renaissance style (1603), and the Vishal. Once used as markets, these are now museum and exhibition centres. On the opposite side of the Markt from the church is the Stadhuis. Once a thirteenth-century hunting lodge belonging to the Count of Holland, it has been in use as a town hall since the fourteenth century. Behind the building, leading off Zijl Straat, is a small alley called 't Pand leading to the Prinsenhof, once a monastic garden, and later a herb garden (1721-1865). Walk through Prinsenhof to Jacobijne Straat, then turn right to Gedempte Oude Gracht, a wide street that was once an old canal, now filled in. A left and right turn leads to Zuider Straat, followed by a left turn into Gasthuis Straat; half way along is the former Kloveniersdoelen, on the right at No 32. This sixteenth-century building was the headquarters of the local militia. The inner courtyard through the arched gateway may be visited during weekdays. In Barrevoete Straat, a short distance along on the right, is the fifteenth-century 'Hofje van

Loo'. The typical courtyard appearance has been lost because one row of houses was demolished when the street was widened during the nineteenth century.

Return to Gasthuis Straat, turn right into what now becomes Tuchthuisstraat. Continue past the Brouwershofje, along Lange Anna Straat to the Hofje van Guurtje de Waal then turn left along Doel Straat to the junction with Gier Straat and Grote Hout Straat. On the right is the Proveniershuis, built in 1591. The almshouses around the courtyard date from 1700, are the largest of the *hofjes* in Haarlem.

Walk down Grote Hout Straat to the bank of the canal called Raamsingel, turn left along Gasthuis Vest then left into Groot Heiligland. Along the right are some fifteenth-century cottages. Opposite them, in an old almshouse dated 1608, is the world-renowned Frans Hals Museum, containing works by the Haarlem masters including Frans Hals himself, all displayed in period settings.

By cutting through into the parallel street known as Klein Heiligland, and turning right, across into Franke Straat, right along Anegang then left again into Warmoesstraat, the walk passes another *hofje*, 'In Den Groenen Tuijn' (in the green garden), originally built in 1614. At the end of the street, turn right into Oude Groenmarkt and continue along Dam Straat to the river, where stands De Waag or weigh-house. Built in 1598, goods were weighed here after being brought by boat along the river Spaarne. Nearby, on the river bank, is Teylers Museum, the oldest museum in Holland, built by the bequest of a cloth and silk merchant and manufacturer who died in 1778. Devoted to both arts and sciences, it has exceptionally fine paintings and old scientific instruments.

Spanning the river nearby is the picturesque Gravenstenenbrug, a lifting bridge which leads across to Wijdesteeg, and then to Spaarnwouderstraat. Turn left, and in about 500m is the only surviving city gate, the Amsterdamse Poort, standing on an island between busy roads. Returning to the museum, continue past the river bridge to Bakenesser Gracht, then turn left along the canal bank past the fourteenth-century Hofje van Bakenes, continuing along to Groene Buurt on the left and into the Begijnhof. The Walloon church, originally a fourteenth-century nunnery, is here and nearby, in the Goudsmidspleintje, is the seventeenth-century guildhall of the Haarlem gold and silversmiths.

The walk continues back along Jansstraat and Jansweg, passing the elegant Hofje van Staats (1730) to the station, itself a listed building of 1908.

in a hole in the dyke to prevent a flood. The river opens into a lovely lake, the 'Mooie Nel', with an excellent marina and water sports facilities.

Amsterdam

Amsterdam is the capital of the Netherlands, with the greatest number of listed buildings in Europe. With a recorded history going back over 800 years it is, nevertheless, one of the most modern and progressive cities in the world, as evidenced by the large number of ultra-modern office and other business developments and the continually expanding residential areas surrounding the city. One of the less-pleasing aspects of this international city is its reputation as a meeting place for drug addicts, and its notorious red-light districts, and visitors should be warned, especially if walking in the streets at night.

Haarlem makes a good base for visiting Amsterdam. It is not recommended to take a cycle into Amsterdam; lock it securely in a guarded *Rijwielstalling* somewhere outside the city, and go in by train. Never leave a cycle unattended, even if locked. Any vehicle with other than Dutch numberplates should be parked off the road or where it is not visible, as many foreign cars are broken into.

The origins of Amsterdam lie in the medieval 'Dam on the Amstel', the river from which it takes its name, and the network of canals dug in the

The Gravenstenenbrug over the River Spaarne at Haarlem

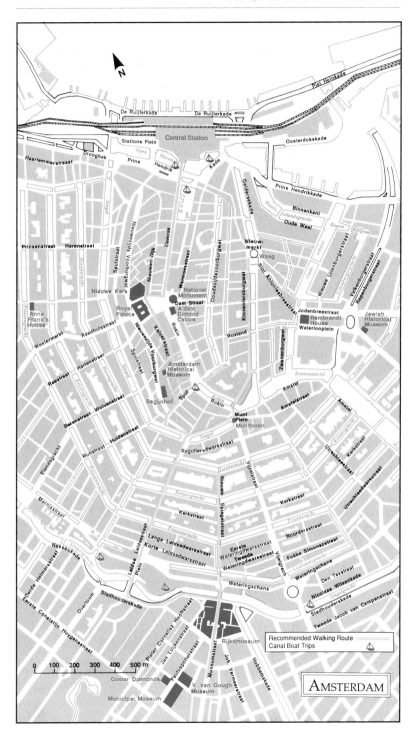

AMSTERDAM

Recommended Walking Route
Canal Boat Trips

A Walk in Amsterdam

Starting from Centraal Station, cross Stationsplein from the tram and bus station and walk down the wide street across the harbour basin towards the city. This leads down Damrak to Dam square. Any of the narrow streets to the right off Damrak lead into Nieuwendijk, one of the busy pedestrian shopping streets. Facing onto the Dam is the Royal Palace, built in the seventeenth century as the town hall. Traditionally it is from here that the new monarch is proclaimed. In the centre of the square is the National Monument to victims of World War II, and the surrounding open space is a favourite meeting place for groups of people, not all of whom may be welcome. The nearby Nieuwe Kerk (1500-1650) has been used for royal coronations since 1815, and beyond it can be seen the pear-drop shaped towers of the Old Post Office.

Continue beyond the Dam along Kalverstraat, another busy pedestrianised shopping street, and about two thirds of the way along, look on the right for a narrow alley ending in a magnificent sixteenth-century arched gateway surmounted by the city coat of arms. This is the entrance to 92 Kalverstraat, which in complete contrast to the bustling modern shops on the street leads to a former orphanage. Through the arch is the Amsterdam Historical Museum where there is also a good restaurant. The collection of paintings, prints and other historical objects makes a fitting introduction to further tours of the city. Almost opposite the restaurant is a passage roofed over with glass, the Schuttersgalerij, the walls of which are lined with enormous paintings of seventeenth-century marksmen. Passing through the gallery, a narrow alley leads to what must be one of the surprises of the

city — a peaceful and secluded close with trees and flower beds, surrounded by beautiful and elegant houses dating originally from the fourteenth and fifteenth centuries, restored and still occupied. This was the Begijnhof, for centuries a home for Lay Sisters. At the far end

of the garden is the 'English Church', a Presbyterian church granted to the English community in the seventeenth century and still very much in use. Opposite this building is a very small Roman Catholic church dating back to 1671 and used as a clandestine place of worship until 1795. Tucked into a corner is Amsterdam's oldest surviving house, built of wood in 1475.

From the Begijnhof an exit leads directly into the street called Spui, opposite the Maagdenhuis, the main building of the University of Amsterdam. Walk past here to Singel, once the outer defence line of the

early seventeenth century which encircle the old town.

With over 7,000 houses and other buildings under the care of the Dutch equivalent to the National Trust in Britain, the city has a unique atmosphere. The Dam square is the focal point, with the Royal Palace on one side city. Turn left alongside the canal then right via Koningsplein to cross Herengracht, a lovely canal lined with exceptionally fine houses. Follow alongside the canal to the left as far as Nieuwe Spiegelstraat, the 'antiques street' of Amsterdam. To the right at the far end of this street is the large building of the world famous Rijksmuseum, justly noted for its display of works by Rembrandt, especially the great painting *The Night Watch*. There is, however, much more to be seen in the museum, and to do justice to the many and varied collections an English guide book should be obtained and ample time allowed for a visit.

A wide central archway through the centre of the museum building leads to Museumplein, along the right side of which will be found the Vincent van Gogh Museum with an impressive collection of paintings and drawings by this artist, together with his personal collection of works by contemporary artists. Beyond here is the Municipal (Stedelijk) Museum containing mainly collections of modern art. At the far end of Museumplein is the Concertgebouw, known to music lovers world-wide. From near the concert hall a return to Centraal Station may be made by bus or tram, or one of the boat trips along the canals can be joined.

Alternatively, the walk may be continued by returning to Singel Gracht and turning left along Stathouderskade as far as the bridge across the water to Leidseplein, a cosmopolitan area with numerous hotels, restaurants of many nationalities, and some good shops nearby. In the summer tables are set out along the pavements, there are street entertainers and the whole area is bustling and vibrant. Continue along Leidsestraat, crossing three major canals, and back to Koningsplein. Turn right beside Singel, passing the flower market, to Muntplein with the old Munttoren (1490-1620). Walk along Nieuwe Doelenstraat on the other side of the water then along Kloveniersburgwal to the Nieuwmarkt, where the weigh-house was originally built in 1448 as a city gate, being converted in 1617 to weigh cannons which were made nearby. The upper room was used by various guilds and Rembrandt painted his famous *Anatomy Lesson* here.

The area to the west and north of Nieuwmarkt towards Warmoesstraat is the red light district and is not to be recommended to those who may be offended. In any case this area and the surroundings of Centraal Station should be avoided at night, so the best way to terminate the walk may be to take the Metro from Nieuwmarkt back to Centraal Station.

and the city spreading out over a spider's web pattern of canals, roads and bridges. From the Dam radiate some of the famous shopping streets, many now pedestrianised, selling goods ranging from cheap souvenirs to top quality works of art and antiques. At several points it is possible to join

A trip on a sightseeing boat is a good introduction to Amsterdam

The decorative façade of the Rijksmuseum, Amsterdam

The Rijksmuseum has one of the world's finest collections of art

a boat for a tour of the canals and it is even possible to rent a 'canal bike' and pedal around the city's waterways.

Undoubtedly the best way to see many of the old buildings and sights of the city is to take one of the guided tours by canal boat. Details of these round trips by boat (*rondvaart*) may be obtained from the VVV office in Stationsplein in front of Centraal Station. Other sight-seeing possibilities include a walk through the city to the Rijksmuseum, then either a further walk or a return to Stationsplein by tram, bus or Metro. Details of the public transport system including maps are available from the information office opposite Centraal Station. Although the walk in Amsterdam passes a number of museums and other places of interest, use public transport to visit them if more time is to be spent there.

There are many other interesting aspects of the city and places worth visiting in addition to those passed during the recommended walk, and the public transport system will be found useful here. To the west of the centre, in Prinsengracht, is the Anne Frank House, a canal house whose preserved rear part has become famous as the hiding place of Anne and her family during World War II, before their betrayal and deportation. The Anne Frank Foundation maintains the building and an exhibition to serve as a warning against future persecution. To the east of the centre, in Jodenbreestraat near Waterlooplein, is the Rembrandthuis, a former residence of the artist which houses a collection of his original etchings. Beyond Waterlooplein and Visserplein lies J. D. Meyerplein where the Jewish Historical Museum is now located in a restored seventeenth-century synagogue. By way of contrast, along Prins Hendrik Kade near the entrance to the IJ Tunnel is the Netherlands Maritime Museum. Located in a former naval arsenal dating from 1656, this is based on a private collection but has rapidly become a major museum of its kind with ambitious plans for the future. A full size replica of the former East Indiaman *Amsterdam* has been built using information from the actual wreck and other records and is now moored alongside the museum building.

Almost hidden from the city centre by the Centraal Station building is the busy harbour complex based on the River IJ which separates the south of the city from its northern suburbs. Two vehicle tunnels traverse the river, the Coentunnel to the west and the IJ Tunnel to the east of the station, in addition to which there are free ferries for foot passengers and cyclists running from behind the station building. Not far from the IJ Tunnel is the Artis Zoo. To the east of the IJ Tunnel the Amsterdam Ring Road (opened in 1990) crosses the approach to the IJsselmeer by the Zeeburgerbrug and Zeeburgertunnel, so taking through traffic away from the older Schellingwoude Brug. The Ring Road completes the circuit of the city by using the Coentunnel on the west side.

Any account of Amsterdam would not be complete without mentioning the diamond trade and industry, first established here in 1586 and now renowned worldwide. A number of establishments in the city allow visitors to view the cutting and polishing of these, the most valuable precious stones in the world. Details of visits can be obtained from the VVV, who also publish leaflets describing walks relating to various aspects of the city.

To the south-west of the city lies the Amsterdamse Bos, claimed to be the largest landscaped park in the Netherlands. Laid out in the 1930s to give work to the unemployed, the area includes attractive walks and cycle rides through the woods, a childrens' farm, varied sporting facilities, and a municipal campsite. An old 'museum tram-line', operated by a voluntary society, runs along the eastern side of the Amsterdamse Bos.

The great international airport of **Schipol** is separated from the Bos by a road and a drainage canal. Schipol is situated in the Haarlemmermeer polder, and the name recalls the days when this was an inland sea, and westerly gales blew ships on to the northern shore to be wrecked in the 'ship hole'. Near the main entrance to the airport, is a hemispherical aluminium building, the 'Aviodome', where exhibits portraying the history of aviation, together with many models and actual historical aircraft and spacecraft, can be seen.

Not far to the south of Schipol airport is the town of **Aalsmeer**, in the ❋ centre of the Dutch flower-growing industry. With about 70 acres of greenhouses, more than 3,000 growers send their flowers and plants to be auctioned daily, before being sent all over the world. Between 7.30-11am, visitors can sit in on the unique flower auctions (they are best visited as early as possible), and also visit the historical garden in the nearby town.

Additional Information

Places of Interest

Aalsmeer
Flower Auction
Legmeerdijk 313
Open: Mon to Fri 7.30-11.30am.

* Historical Garden
Uiterweg 32
Open: May to Sept Mon to Fri 10.30am-1.30pm, Wed also 1.30-4.30pm. Sat and Sun 1.30-4.30pm.

Amsterdam
Amsterdam Diamond Centre
Rokin 1
Guided tours daily except Thurs 10am-5.30pm;Thurs 10am-6pm, 7-8.30pm.

* Amsterdams Historisch Museum
Kalverstraat 92
Open: Daily 11am-5pm. Closed 1 Jan.

Artis Zoo
Plantagekerklaan 40
Open: Daily 9am-5pm.

Coster Diamonds
Paulus Potterstraat 2-4
Open: Daily 9am-5pm.

A. van Moppes and Zoon (Diamond Centre)
Albert Cuypstraat 2-6
Open: Daily 9am-5pm.

*Nederlands Scheepvaart Museum (Maritime Museum)
Kattenburgerplein 1
Open: Tues to Sat 10am-5pm, Sun and holidays 1-5pm.

* Rijksmuseum
Stadhouderskade 42
Open: Tues to Sat 10am-5pm; Sun and public holidays 1-5pm. Closed 1 Jan.

The Stadsschouwburg or municipal theatre on Leidesplein, Amsterdam

The Singel, like many of Amsterdam's streets and waterways is illuminated at night

Pleasure boats line the riverbank at Aalsmeer

*Rembrandthuis
Jodenbreestraat 4-6
Open: Mon to Sat 10am-5pm; Sun and
public holidays 1-5pm. Closed 1 Jan.

*Joods Historisch Museum
J. D. Meyerplein 2-4
Open: Daily11am-5pm, closed 9 Oct.

*Rijksmuseum Vincent van Gogh
Paulus Potterstraat 7
Open: Tues to Sat 10am-5pm; Sun and
public holidays 1-5pm. Closed 1 Jan.

Anne Frankhuis
Prinsengracht 263
Open: Mon to Sat 9am-5pm; Sun and
public holidays 10am-5pm. Closed 1
Jan, 25 Dec and Day of Atonement.

Royal Palace
Dam
Open: Easter, summer and autumn
school holidays only. Mon to Sat 12.30-
4pm.

* Stedelijkmuseum
Paulus Potterstraat 13
Open: Daily 11am-5pm, closed 1 Jan.

Bennebroek
Linnaeushof (recreation park)
Rijksstraatweg 4
Open Apr to Sept Mon to Sun 10am-6pm

Haarlem
* Frans Hals Museum
Groot Heiligland 62
Open: Mon to Sat 11am-5pm; Sun and
public holidays 1-5pm. Closed 1 Jan
and 25 Dec.

* Teylers Museum
Spaarne 16
Open: Tues to Sat 10am-5pm, Sun 1-
5pm. Ascension Day 1-5pm. Closed on
public holidays.

Leiden
* Stedelijk Museum De Lakenhal
Oude Singel 28-32
Open: Tues to Sat 10am-5pm; Sun and
public holidays 1-5pm. Closed 1 Jan
and 25 Dec.

* Molenmuseum De Valk
2e Binnenvestgracht 1
Open: Tues to Sat 10am-5pm; Sun and
public holidays 1-5pm. Closed 1 Jan, 3
Oct and 25 Dec.

Pilgrim Collectie
Vliet 45
Open: Mon to Fri 9.30am-4.30pm.
Closed 3 Oct and public holidays.

Rijksmuseum van Geologie en
  Mineralogie
Hooglandse Kerkgracht 17
Open: Mon to Fri 10am-5pm, Sun 2-
5pm. Closed 3 Oct and public holidays.
Admission free.

Pijpenkabinet (museum of clay pipes)
Oude Vest 159a
Open: Sun 1-5pm. Occasional demon-
strations of pipemaking when open.

* University Botanical Garden
Rapenburg 73
Open: Apr to Sept, Mon to Sat 9am-
5pm, Sun, Good Fri, Easter Mon,
Ascension Day and Whit Sun 10am-
5pm; Oct to Mar, Mon to Fri , Sun and
holidays 10am-5pm. Closed 8 Feb, 3 Oct
and 25 Dec to first weekend in Jan.

Lisse
Flower Exhibition Park
Keukenhof
Open: End Mar to mid-May, daily, 8am-
6.30pm.

Schipol
Nationaal Luchtvaart Museum
Aviodome
Westelijke Randweg 1
Open: Apr to Sept, Mon to Fri 10am-
5pm, Sat and Sun noon-5pm.

Vijfhuizen (near Haarlem)
* Museum Cruquius
Cruquiusdijk 32
Open: Apr to Sept, Mon to Sat 10am-
5pm; Sun and public holidays noon-
5pm. Oct and Nov, Mon to Fri 10am-
4pm, Sun noon-4pm.

Boat Trips

Amsterdam
A number of firms cruise along the
canals and the harbour area. Some start
from opposite Centraal Station. Details
from VVV or from signs on quayside.

5

NORTH OF THE
NORTH SEA CANAL

The North Sea Canal, stretching from IJmuiden to Amsterdam, cuts the Province of North Holland in two, and can be crossed by tunnel (for cars and trains) or by ferry. The only road bridge is that at Schellingwoude, across the eastern end of Amsterdam harbour.

North of the canal, the city of Amsterdam extends its boundaries virtually without a break until it meets the boundaries of Zaanstad, an industrial complex along the river Zaan which includes the towns and villages of Zaandam, Koog a/d Zaan and Zaandijk. To the east is the polder area of Waterland, and the picturesque villages of Monnikendam, Edam, Volendam and Marken, together with the expanding old town of Purmerend. The western part contains the extensive North Holland Dune Reserve and the well-known old town of Alkmaar, east of which lie the polders of Schermer and Beemster, first drained in the early seventeenth century. Further north are more bulbfields, dunes and holiday resorts extending to the naval base at Den Helder. The eastern boundary of the area is the former Zuiderzee coast, along which are to be found the old West Friesian towns of Medemblik, Enkhuizen and Hoorn. From the former island of Wieringen, in the north east corner of the province, at Den Oever, the great Afsluitdijk or 'enclosing dyke' runs 32km across the water to the other side of the IJsselmeer.

Alkmaar

The importance of this busy town increased with the reclamation of the surrounding polders in the late seventeenth century. The cheese market for which Alkmaar is famous is more than 350 years old. The exceptionally fine weigh-house, originally built as a chapel in the fourteenth century, was converted to its present use in the sixteenth century, and is still used during the traditional Friday market in the summer; it also houses the VVV and a cheese museum. The tower of the building dates from 1595 and contains an interesting clock with jousting horsemen and a trumpeter.

The polder landscape to the south and east of Alkmaar provides a very pleasant area for exploring, either by car or by bicycle.

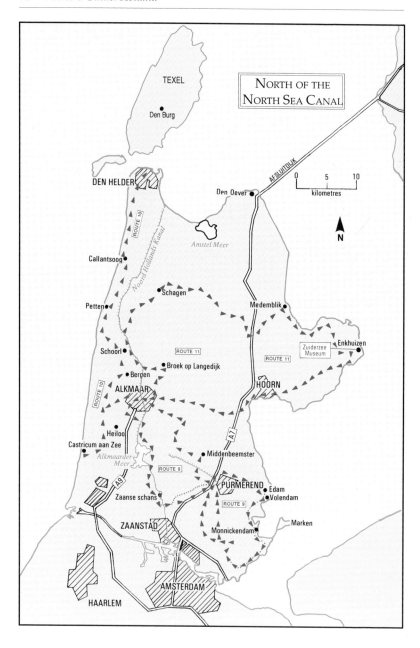

Route 9: The Seventeenth-Century Polders and Waterland. Approx 110km

The Beemster, Purmer, Wormer and Schermer lakes were drained by the use of windmills during 1612-35, and the flat polder landscape thus created is typically what visitors imagine to be representative of Holland. However, despite the flat landscape, the distant views and the quality of light above the large areas of water present a great attraction.

The route leaves Alkmaar by the road to the south towards Heiloo and Castricum. In about 3km (signpost 299) turn left towards the hamlet of Boekel which lies on the far side of the motorway A9. On reaching the Noord Hollands Kanaal, turn right and in about 2km cross the canal by ferry, continuing alongside the Alkmaardermeer for 3km before turning

The Friday Cheese Market at Alkmaar is a popular attraction for visitors

A Walk Around Alkmaar

From the Waag, cross over the Bathbrug, named after the English city of Bath with which Alkmaar is twinned, and walk down the narrow street ahead called Fnidsen. Turn left into Appelsteeg and walk to the bridge, then turn and look at the wooden house on the right. High up on the front of the house is a cannonball dating from the Spanish seige of 1573, embedded in the wall. Return towards the Bathbrug but before the bridge turn left along the Mient past some houses with fine gables. At No 23 the gable displays the arms of Alkmaar, but as the owner was in dispute with the city council, he deliberately reversed the lions! The walk is continued past the Fish Market (1591) to the square by St Janskerk. Look down the Verdronkenoord canal to the Excise Tower at the far end. Built in 1622, and moved to its present position in 1924, it now houses the harbourmaster's office, and serves as a reminder that although Alkmaar, like so many Dutch towns, is situated away from the sea, it still handles much waterborne trade on the canals and other waterways.

Turn back to the church; originally built by the Knights of Malta but rebuilt after a fire in 1760, it contains a fine organ. Pass the church, cross over the street named Laat and walk to the Oude Gracht, cross the bridge and turn left to the attractive Wildemanshofje, built in 1714 for elderly Catholic and Protestant women.

Return across the bridge and turn left. Walk along Oude Gracht, admiring the old buildings with their gables. The style of the gable indicates the age of the building: triangular in the sixteenth century, stepped in the seventeenth century and bell-shaped in the eighteenth century. At the end of Oude Gracht is the junction with Koorstraat to the right and Ritsevoort to the left. Along Ritsevoort, immediately on the right, is another almshouse, the Hofje van Splinter, while at the end of the road is Molen van Piet, a windmill built on the ramparts in 1769 and used as a flour mill.

Back along Koorstraat, on the left, is the Grote Kerk or Church of St Lawrence, a most beautiful building from between 1470 and 1516. It contains two organs, a large one from the seventeenth century, and a small one from the early sixteenth century, one of the oldest still in regular use. From the east front of the church, turn down Langestraat, a busy shopping street, to the town hall or Stadhuis, parts of which date back to the late fifteenth and early sixteenth centuries, and whose entrance has a fine double stairway. Just past the town hall, turn left and walk through to Nieuwesloot, where opposite, on the corner, is the Huis van Achten, a home since 1656 for eight old men, both Catholic and Protestant. Next to this is the Hof van Sonoy, which now houses several good craft shops, boutiques and a restaurant. Straight ahead are the Waag and Cheese Market, the starting and finishing point of the walk.

right on the road to Markenbinnen and Zaanstad. At this junction (sign-post 560) is a car park and a very pleasant picnic area by the lake. Continue past Markenbinnen, following signs to Zaandijk and Zaanse Schans. Cyclists can turn left 1km after leaving Markenbinnen, cross on the ferry to Oost Knollendam, then follow the river Zaan through Wormer to Zaanse Schans.

Zaanse Schans is a village museum of buildings from the Zaan area 🏠 dating from around 1700, re-erected together on an attractive site by the river. Many of the old houses are lived in, and some are open to the public. In addition, there are old shops and several different types of windmill typical of the area, including a sawmill, a paint-mill, a mustard mill, and 🎏 an oil-seed mill. Other places of interest in the neighbourhood which may be visited include the windmill museum at **Koog aan de Zaan** and the Czar Peterhuisje in **Zaandam**, where Peter the Great lived when he came to study ship design.

On leaving Zaanse Schans, take the road leading east to the A7 main road to Purmerend. Cyclists may take the parallel road to the north, turning left at signpost 10726. The town of **Purmerend** is a busy and ex-panding community with an old centre. The Koepelkerk is now used as a cultural centre, and the Renaissance town hall houses the Historical Museum. This is open when the cheese market is being held, on Thurs- 🏛 days; it is no longer held in nearby Edam. There is plenty of parking in the town.

From Purmerend, take the road eastwards to **Edam**. Parking discs are ❄ required in the town, so park just outside. Edam was formerly a settlement of farmers and fishermen which became an important shipbuilding centre. When the polders began to be created in the sixteenth century, the foundations for a flourishing cheese trade were laid. From 1573 to 1922 a cheese market was held weekly, and much of the cheese produced in the area today is stored and matured in the warehouses in the town. There are some lovely old houses, some having surprisingly large gardens with elegant 'summer-houses' by the water's edge. The town hall dates from the eighteenth century, and the square in front of the building is actually a stone-covered bridge built across the locks.

In Edam's oldest house (1530) is a 'floating cellar', and the story goes 🏚 that the retired sea-captain who built the house wanted to spend the rest of his life at sea. Walk along Spui and look at the Speeltoren, all that is left of the fifteenth-century Onze Lieve Vrouwe church. It houses one of the 🛕 oldest carillons in North Holland, dating back to 1561. Return to Spui and walk past the eighteenth-century Waag and cheese market. Opposite here is a shop specialising in beautiful costume dolls, as well as pottery and silverware. Continue alongside the water along Matthijs Tinxgracht to the Grote Kerk or St Nicholas Church, with its early seventeenth-century 🛕 stained glass windows. On the other side of the water, on J. C. Brouwers-gracht, is the Provenniershuis, built for a nursing order founded in 1555, and now used as an almshouse for both young and old.

From Edam, a diversion may be made to the old fishing port of **Volendam**, home of the well-known and (incorrectly-named) 'Dutch National Costume'. It is now very commercialised and always over-crowded, and many other places merit more time.

Continue south along the road N247 from Edam to the small 600-year-old town of **Monnickendam**; parking is possible near the edge of the town. The original method of smoking eels is still carried out, this being one of the most important industries, now supplemented by watersports. Many old buildings exist, some with new uses. The Speeltoren houses an archaeological museum, and the seventeenth-century Waag is now a restaurant. Also worth a visit is the Grote or St Nicolaaskerk, built in the fifteenth century. A number of traditional ships are moored in the inner harbour, which is surrounded by eel smoke-houses. Middendam is the spot where Frisian monks founded the town in the twelfth century, and the nearby locks were restored in 1968.

To the south is the area known as Waterland, a typical polder landscape stretching to the outskirts of Amsterdam. From Monnickendam, the coast road may be taken south along the dyke towards Uitdam, diverting to visit **Marken**. Once an island, it was only connected to the mainland in 1957 by a dyke and road, and for this reason, it still retains much of its old character. The islanders are strictly Protestant and tend to intermarry. Many of them wear traditional dress, which is much more attractive than that of Volendam, but visitors with cameras are not always welcome, particularly on Sundays. It is possible to see inside a traditional Marken house where the old way of life can be seen. A museum in some old smoke houses shows how fishermen used to live, plus exhibits showing the history of the former island.

On returning from Marken to the mainland, turn south again passing through typical landscape of the Waterland district. The road is narrow and winding, with a few parking places alongside, from which the dyke may be climbed to look out over the former Zuiderzee, now Lake IJssel. As the road continues towards Durgerdam, a number of little lakes on the right show where the sea broke through in former times. Many of these lakes are now nature reserves, and the whole of the Waterland is a conservation area. After about 2km beyond the parking place on the Kinselmeer, turn right towards the village of **Ransdorp** with Waterland houses, often made of wood and painted green and white. Continue along narrow roads to **Zunderdorp**, another very small protected village, then right to **Broek in Waterland**. Here is a cheese dairy which may be visited by appointment, a clog-maker, and again many picturesque old houses.

From Broek, follow the main road N247 in the direction of Amsterdam, until the junction with the road alongside the Noord Hollands Kanaal is reached. From here a diversion may be made to visit 'Het Twiske', a country park with footpaths, cycle paths and plenty of opportunities for watersports of all kinds. From the road junction, cross the canal by ferry and follow signs for Het Twiske via Landsmeer and Den Ilp.

The return to Alkmaar may be made by taking either the main road alongside the canal, or the road through Den Ilp and Purmerland to the outskirts of Purmerend, then along the northern side of the Noord Hollands Kanaal for about 3km, and turn right towards Middenbeemster. In the village turn left towards De Rijp. Here, follow signs 'Doorgaand Verkeer' and Graft, until signs for the car park are seen. Walk into the pleasant little polder village of **de Rijp** with its interesting town hall, and weigh-house. The old house, 't Wapen van Munster, is now a pancake restaurant and coffee house, and the whole place is most attractive.

Continue to Graft, and turn right, following the winding road to **Grootschermer**. Here, unexpectedly for such a small place, you will see a fine old town hall dated 1652. The road carries on to Schermerhorn, but just before the main road, turn immediately left along the minor road on the south side of the water. Park by the three windmills, the middle one is a museum showing how the polder was drained and kept dry. The mills were built in 1634 and have been beautifully restored and maintained.

The road is followed back to Alkmaar, and offers good views across the polders with windmills in the distance.

Route 10: The Coastal Road to Den Helder and Texel.
Approx 52km

The town of Alkmaar makes an excellent starting point for exploring the whole of this area. Leave the town by the road to Egmond, joining the coast road at Egmond a/d Hoef. Turn south, and at Bakkum take the road towards **Castricum aan Zee**. About 1km along this road is a parking area and visitor centre, where maps and admission tickets to the dune reserve (which is open during daylight hours) may be obtained. From this point many paths may be followed through the high dunes and woodland which stretch for 19km from Wijk aan Zee in the south to Bergen aan Zee in the north. Cycles may be hired in Castricum, and all paths are way-marked.

The dunes are Holland's natural defence against the sea, and at only one point in the whole of this coastline is there a man-made dyke. Beyond the dunes are family holiday resorts with miles of sandy beaches, mostly developed from farming and fishing villages.

After visiting the dune reserve, return via the coast road north to the village of Bergen, inland from Bergen aan Zee where there is an aquarium. **Bergen** is particularly popular with artists, who regularly hold open-air exhibitions. Here also is an old seventeenth-century step-gabled house converted into a museum with period rooms and old costumes, and the remains of a medieval church. Follow the winding road north from Bergen towards Schoorl, passing country houses with attractive gardens. On the outskirts of **Schoorl** is a visitor centre explaining the work of the Forestry Commission who control the dunes in this area. These contain particularly fine walks, giving spectacular views inland from the highest points, especially in the bulb season.

The road bears towards the coast, and at the north end of the dunes, at **Camperduin**, a long sea dyke known as the 'Hondsbosse Zeewering' begins. In 1421 the villages of Camperduin and Petten were washed away, and the local population began building a dyke. In 1780 the sea broke through again, so a new dyke was made. **Petten**, at the north end of the Hondsbosse Zeewering, now a holiday resort, has been rebuilt four times, the latest being in 1947, having been completely destroyed by the Germans during World War II. The dyke has also been raised several times, and although it held during the flood disaster of 1953, in 1977 it was decided to increase the height to 11.5m above sea level, to reduce the risk of disaster ever happening again. The history of the dyke and the neighbourhood can be seen during the summer in a free exhibition entitled *De Dijk te Kijk* ('The dyke on show').

To the north of Petten, in the dunes, is the Dutch Alternative Energy Centre, where research on nuclear, wind and sun energy is carried out. The nearby Zwanenwater nature reserve has one of the largest breeding colonies of spoonbills in Europe, together with rich flora and fauna.

The road from Petten runs through Callantsoog, then close under the dunes past access roads to a number of beaches, eventually coming to **Den Helder**. On the straight main road away to the right are many new wind turbines which make a spectacular sight when working. Den Helder is the main Dutch naval base, called by Napoleon the 'Gibraltar of the North'. It is also the departure point for the ferries to Texel, largest of the Wadden Islands. There are several holiday parks and campsites in the area, with numerous hotels. Foot and cycle paths wind through the Donkere Duinen nature reserve on the edge of the town, which itself has two interesting museums, namely the marine museum on the Hoofdgracht near the Texel ferry landing stage and a lifeboat museum.

Texel is completely different from the other Wadden islands, but has much to offer in the way of beaches, dunes and nature reserves. At the end of the last Ice Age, the melting ice-cap left a gently-sloping hill covered with scattered boulders from Scandinavia, and it was here that the first people settled. With 25km of sea beaches, wide dunes and forested areas, there are plenty of opportunities for recreation. At one point there is a gap in the dunes, and the water entering through a network of channels has formed a marshy area known as 'De Slufter', which provides a unique breeding place for masses of birds, and is now a nature reserve. Bulb-growing is an important industry of the islanders, the south being particularly colourful when the flower fields are at their best. There is a considerable contrast between the north and south due to the fact that originally there were two islands, Texel and Eierland. In 1630, dykes were constructed and the two islands joined, with the creation of polders. These are typical of North Holland polderland, whereas the southern, older part of the island, has narrow winding lanes, old farms and sheep-folds.

The main town of Texel is **Den Burg**, built in rings around the church. **De Koog**, on the North Sea coast, is the principal resort, while the villages of **Den Hoorn**, **Oosterend** and **De Waal** are conservation areas. The harbour at **Oudeschild** has a long history and was originally the ferry port before the service was transferred to 't Horntje at the southern end of the island. It is still used as a yacht harbour and fishing port. There are three museums: a historical museum at Den Burg, an agricultural museum in De Waal and a maritime museum in Oudeschild. In the Nature Recreation Centre 'Ecomare' there is a natural history collection, seal nursery and a bird hospital. At the extreme north of the island is the newest village, **De Cocksdorp**, developed for the tourist industry. By far the best way to explore is on foot or by bicycle, and a folder in English describing four cycle rides on the island is available from the VVV in Den Burg. Although cars can be taken, the ferry is very expensive and a car passage cannot be booked from Den Helder. The modern roll on, roll off ferries leave every hour, and tickets (return only) may be bought only at the departure place in Den Helder. Nature lovers might prefer to take a cycle in the off-season and make arrangements through the local VVV to visit the nature reserves. There are a number of campsites on the island.

Route 11: The Old North — Around the Westfriesdijk. Approx 125km

Before the long dyke at Petten, on the coast, was built in the fifteenth century, West Friesland was separated from the dunes by the waters of the Zijpe, and bordered on the south by the Schermer and Beemster lakes. To the east was the Zuiderzee, so West Friesland was quite isolated. To protect the area from the sea, a dyke had to be built, and almost the whole length of it may be followed. Some roads follow the line of other, older secondary dykes. Some are very narrow single-track roads, so care is needed. The route takes in the old towns of Schagen, Medemblik, Enkhuizen and Hoorn.

Leave Alkmaar in the direction of Heerhugowaard and **Broek op Langedijk**, where there is a unique museum combined with the world's oldest vegetable auction, established in 1887. Called the Broeker Veiling, it includes waymarked walks around the museum area, and an English guidebook is available.

From Broekerveiling, travel west to Koedijk, then turn north alongside the Noord Hollands Kanaal to Schoorldam. Here, take the dyke road north to Krabbendam, then onto a narrow winding road to **Sint Maarten**. Away to the left are the mills used to drain the Zijpe and Haze polders, while to the right are small ponds made when the sea broke through hundreds of years ago. Leave the dyke road at Sint Maarten and drive east to **Schagen**, famous for its summer folklore market and festivals.

From here, the road along the Kanaal Schagen-Kolhorn runs parallel to

Lighthouse near De Cocksdorp, at the northern tip of Texel island

Walking in the sand-dunes on the north-west coast, Texel

the old sea dyke. **Kolhorn** is an attractive old whaling port, now completely surrounded by polder. Follow the main road to where it crosses the Groet Kanaal, then turn right to the main road at signpost 511. Here, cross over the main road and turn right towards Aartswoud, then left at the next junction (signpost 3489). Continue for about 5km, then turn right again to **Abbekerk**, through the village, and continue to cross the motorway by a bridge on the left, then left and right following signs to **Twisk**, a picturesque village with a fourteenth-century church and some lovely old houses in the long village street.

Continue through Opperdoes to **Medemblik**, the smallest and oldest town in West Friesland. Although small, the town is most attractive and is the terminus of the Hoorn-Medemblik Steam Train. Note the little cottages along Heere-steeg, the orphanage gateway in Torenstraat, and old buildings in Nieuwstraat, including the weigh-house at one end and the town hall at the other. Look at the east harbour, beyond which is Kasteel Radboud, first recorded in the thirteenth century, and now open to visitors. The dyke enclosing the Wieringermeer Polder, first of the IJsselmeer Polders, stretches away in the distance to the north of the town.

From Medemblik, take the coast road south towards Wervershoof. After 1km the old steam pumping station, 'De Vier Noorder Koggen'is on the right; it is now a museum of steam engines and machinery.

From Wervershoof, keep to the dyke road along the coast towards the hamlets of Geuzenbuurt and Broekoord. After passing the old Grootslag pumping station (now a museum) on the left, the site of the experimental Andijk Polder, constructed to test the feasibility of the schemes for closing the Zuiderzee is reached. The dyke road may be followed all the way to Enkhuizen, but the main road through Andijk is more convenient.

Enkhuizen was once a very prosperous sea port, and this is shown by houses built by East India Company merchants. Here, too, is the award-winning Zuiderzeemuseum. More than one day is needed to see Enkhuizen properly, as the museum alone can take a whole day. The open air museum should, perhaps, be visited first. On approaching the town, follow signs for Zuiderzeemuseum and Lelystad. These lead to a free car park where tickets can be bought for the museum. A ferry then takes visitors direct to the Buiten Museum, giving an excellent view of the town en route. The tickets cover the return ferry journey and admission to the Binnen Museum, or indoor part, located in the town. After touring the outdoor section, walk through the old town to the station, where the ferry can be picked up, (note the time of the last ferry). If a longer time is to be spent in the town, it may be better to park by the railway station, and take the ferry from there to the museum.

The Zuiderzeemuseum really is a must for visitors, and if there is only time either for the museum or the town, then the museum takes precedence. It was established in 1950 to show the everyday life and work of the inhabitants of the Zuiderzee region as it was before the Afsluitdijk was built. Fishing, shipping and many associated trades were badly affected

A Walk in Enkhuizen

Starting at the railway station in the town, the quay immediately to the south is the point of departure for ferries to Stavoren, Urk and Medemblik in the summer. Walk around the Old Harbour, on the town side past the Visafslag (fish auction), from where the old locks may be seen. The grassed area was originally used for drying nets. Nearby is the large Drommedaris tower, or fortified watergate.

Cross the bridge by the tower, and follow the canal towards the Zuiderkerk, whose tall and elegant tower forms a distinctive landmark. With the church on the left, cross the end of the canal towards the Stadhuis, and the old prison from 1686. Beyond these buildings, across the bridge, is the little Staverse Poortje, and to the right along Wierdijk, which dates from 1567, is the entrance to the Zuiderzee

Binnenmuseum. The building, known as the Peperhuis (1625), was formerly the head office in Enkhuizen of the East India Company. The Binnen Museum has been completely re-organised, having been closed for some time.

Walk back to the Zuiderkerk, turn right and you reach the Waag, now the municipal museum. A left turn leads to the pedestrian precinct, where, on the right, is the Westerkerk or Gomarus Church,

commenced in 1472, which has a wooden belfry. Continue along Westerstraat to the Koepoort, once a land-gate. Turn right and walk along the ramparts to the other gates, the Boerenboom and the Oudegouwsboom, then return along the canals through the town to Westerstraat, after which a left and right turn leads back to the old harbour and the railway station. The yacht harbours are very busy, and old traditional sailing vessels can be hired for sailing holidays.

On the edge of the town is Sprookjeswonderland, a fary-tale park for children.

when the dyke was closed, so as much as possible as been preserved. A complete Zuiderzee town has been recreated in great detail, using actual buildings and materials brought here from their original locations and re-erected. Interiors have been furnished or equipped as workshops and other such premises, showing life as it was from 1880 to 1932. In 1983, just fifty years after the closing of the Afsluitdijk, the outdoor museum opened to the public. The site gained of the European Museum of the Year Award in 1984.

On leaving Enkhuizen, take the road west to Bovenkarspel, then left through Broekerhaven to the main Enkhuizen-Hoorn road. If time allows, take the narrow dyke road through Oosterleek and Schellinkhout to Hoorn, passing old dyke houses built below the embankment. Otherwise, follow the main road into Hoorn. There are plenty of car parks around the edge of the town, in which there is much to see.

Hoorn is another town which in former times was of world-wide importance through its connections with the East India Company, yet has lost much of its influence through the enclosing of the Zuiderzee. However, the town is enhanced by magnificent buildings which have been beautifully restored, particularly those dwellings and warehouses along Veermanskade, near the inner harbour. Here is also the Hoofdtoren or gunpowder tower, probably the most familiar landmark for visitors. Until the end of the seventeenth century, Hoorn was noted as a port for herring fishery, and records exist of net-making here in the fifteenth century. Cape Horn was so-named by the navigator Willem Schouten, a native of Hoorn. In the town centre is the fine Staten-College or council house, built in 1632 as the meeting place of delegates from the seven member towns of North Holland north of the river IJ, namely Alkmaar, Hoorn, Enkhuizen, Medemblik, Edam, Monnikendam and Purmerend. The building now houses the Westfries Museum. Opposite is the Waag, a typical North Holland building with veranda, built in 1609 and now used as a restaurant. Nearby, in Kerkplein, is the Boterhal, formerly St Jans Gasthuis (1563) and now part of the Westfries Museum complex.

There are many other attractive old buildings in the town and on the ramparts. The terminus of the Hoorn-Medemblik Steam Train, and the museum workshops of the railway are located here.

From Hoorn, the old Westfriesdijk is followed south to Scharwoude, turning right across the main road and under the motorway to Avenhorn and on to Ursem and **Rustenburg** where there are three windmills, then via Oterleek to Alkmaar.

Additional Information

Places of Interest

Alkmaar
* Kaasmuseum (cheese museum)
Waagplein 2
Open: Apr to Oct, Mon to Thurs and Sat 10am- 4pm; Fri 9am-4pm.

Andijk
* Poldermuseum 'Het Grootslag'
Dijkweg 319
Open: May to Sept Wed to Sun 2-5pm. Oct to April Sun and holidays only 2-5pm.

Bergen
* Gemeentemuseum 't Sterkenhuis
Oude Prinsweg 21
Open: May to mid-Sept Tues to Sat 10am-12noon, 3-5pm. Also mid-July to mid-Aug 7-9pm.

Bergen-aan-Zee
Aquarium
Van der Wijckplein 16
Open: Apr to Oct daily 10am-6pm, Nov to Mar Sat and Sun 11am-5pm.

Broek op Langedijk
*Broeker Veiling (vegetable auction, museum, boat trips)
Voorburggracht 1
Open: June to Sept, Mon to Fri 10am-5pm.

Enkhuizen
* Rijksmuseum Zuiderzeemuseum
Entrance at parking place behind station on dyke to Lelystad
Open: Outdoor museum, Apr to mid-Oct, daily 10am-5pm. Reorganisation of indoor museum in progress, enquire at outdoor museum.

Sprookjeswonderland Recreation Park
Wilhelminaplantsoen 2
Open: End Apr to early Sept, Mon to Sat
10am-5.30pm, Sun 1-5.30pm.

Stedelijk Waagmuseum
Kaasmarkt 8
Open: Easter to mid-Sept and Christmas
holidays Tues to Sat 10am-noon and 2-
5pm; Sun and public holidays 2-5pm.

Den Helder
* Helders Marinemuseum Het Torentje
Hoofdgracht 3
Open: Tues to Fri, 10am-5pm; Sat and
Sun 1.30- 4.30pm. Also June to Aug Mon
1-5pm.

* Reddingsmuseum Dorus Rijkers
(lifeboat museum)
Bernhardplein 10
Open: Mon to Sat 10am-5pm. Sun 1-5pm.

Hoorn
* Westfriesmuseum
Rode Steen 1
Open: Mon to Fri 11am-5pm; Sat and
Sun and public holidays 2-5pm.

Koog aan de Zaan
* Molen Museum (windmill museum)
Museumlaan 18
Open: Apr to Sept Tues to Fri 10am-
5pm, Sat and Sun 2-5pm. Oct to Mar
Tues to Fri 10am-noon and 1-5pm, Sat 2-
5pm, Sun 1-5pm. Closed 1 Jan, Easter
Sun, Whit Sun, and 25 Dec.

Marken
Marken Museum
Kerkbuurt 44
Open: Easter to October Mon to Sat,
Good Friday, 30 April, 5 May and
Ascension Day 10am-4.30pm. Other
holidays (not Sun) 12noon-4.30pm.

Medemblik
* Kasteel Radboud
Oudevaartsgat 8
Open: mid-May to mid-Sept, Mon to Sat
10.00am-5pm; Sundays all year 2-5pm.

Nederlands Stoommachinemuseum
Oosterdijk 4
Open: July and Aug Tues to Sat 10am-
5pm; Sun noon-5pm. Machines working
during opening hours. May and June,
Sept and Oct, Wed to Sat 10am-5pm,

Sun noon-5pm. Machines working on
Sat and Sun only.

Monnikendam
* Monnikendam de Speeltoren
Noordeinde 4
Open: mid-June to mid-Sept Mon to
Thurs and Sat 10am-4pm, Fri 10am-4pm
and 7-7pm, Sun 1-4pm. Mid May to
mid-June and mid-Sept to end Sept Sat
10am-4pm, Sun 1-4pm.

Petten
De Dijk te Kijk
Zuiderhazedwarsdijk
Open: July to Aug Mon to Fri 10am-
5pm, Sat and Sun 2-5pm. May to June
and Sept Sun public holidays 2-5pm.

Schermerhorn
Windmill (1635)
Noordervaart Zuidzijde 2
Open: May to Sept, Tues to Sun 10am-
5pm; Oct to Apr, Sun 10am-4.30pm

Texel
Ecomare Nature Recreation Centre (Sea
aquarium and seal nursery)
Ruyslaan 92
De Koog
Open: All year, Mon to Sat 9am-5pm.
Closed 25 Dec and 1 Jan.

* Maritiem en Jutters Museum
Barentzstraat 21
Oudeschild
Open: Mon to Sat 9am-5pm.

* Oudheidkamer (antiquities museum)
Kogerstraat 1
Den Burg
Open: Apr to Oct, Mon to Fri 10am-
12.30pm and 1.15-3pm. Closed public
holidays.

*Wagenmuseum
Hogereind 4-6
De Waal
Open: Mid-May to mid-Sept, Tues to Fri
10am-noon, 2-5pm, Mon 2-5pm. Sat
10am-noon and 2-4pm.

Zaandam
Czar Peterhuisje
Krimp 23
Open: Tues to Sat also second and
fourth sun in month 10am-1pm and 2-
5pm. Closed 1 Jan, 25-6 Dec.

De Zaanse Schans
Kalveringdijk
Open: Mon to Sun 10am-5pm. Nov to
Apr houses and museums open week-
ends and public holidays only.

Ferry Service

Den Helder-Texel
All year round, every hour. Journey
time: 20 minutes. No reservations.
☎ 02226 441

Boat Trips

Alkmaar
Rederij Woltheus
Kanaalkade
☎ 072.114840
Cruises to Zaanse Schans, Amsterdam
and Broeker Veiling. Summer only.

Steam Railway

Hoorn-Medemblik
May to Sept, also special trips and
events
Tramstation Hoorn
Van Dedemstraat 8
☎ 02290 14862

6

FLEVOLAND

In Roman times there was a great lake, with a narrow outlet into the North Sea — the Flevomeer. Owing to floods in the Middle Ages, this lake, now known as Lake Almere, grew in size to become the Zuiderzee. To protect the towns on its shore a bold plan for closing and partially reclaiming the land was proposed in the seventeenth century. Due to the lack of technology at that time, the plan was dropped. However in 1891 plans were accepted to reduce the size of the Zuiderzee to that of the original Flevomeer, although it was not until 1918 that the Zuiderzee Act was passed. Work began in 1920, with the dyke linking North Holland to the island of Wieringen, closing off the Amstelmeer. Many engineering problems had to be overcome, including the changing tidal heights in the Waddenzee. An experimental polder was reclaimed near Andijk to investigate these problems and the possible solutions. Unlike the huge inland lakes already drained, the water in the Zuiderzee was salt, so the problems of producing land fertile enough to grow crops had to be solved.

In 1932, the last gap in the Afsluitdijk (enclosing dyke) was closed and the Zuiderzee became the IJsselmeer. The spot, 8km from Den Oever, is marked by an observation tower which gives a view over the Waddenzee to the north, and the IJsselmeer to the south. A footbridge across the motorway at this point enables the visitor to climb to the top of the sea-dyke, and to a small exhibition about the project. The 30km long dyke was built wide enough to take a road (enlarged to a motorway in 1976), a railway (which was never built, the motorway taking its place) and a cycle path. At each end of the dyke large locks permit the passage of shipping and regulate the water level in the IJsselmeer.

The Wieringermeer Polder

Although not part of Flevoland (it is in North Holland), this was the first of the major polders to be drained from the old Zuiderzee, so it is inextricably linked with the new province of Flevoland. The Afsluitdijk, vital to the whole scheme, crosses to Friesland from the former island of Wieringen, from which this polder takes its name.

The first of the Zuiderzee polders to be drained, in 1927-30, it stretches 21km south from the former island of Wieringen to Medemblik. The old island itself has four main settlements, including Westerland, with a fifteenth-century church tower, and Hippolytushoef, which is even older, with many attractive houses and farms. In Oosterland the Norman church has been extensively altered, while Den Oever, the island's fishing port, is noted for shrimping.

Just 8km south of the island, is the spot where, 15 years after the draining, the ring dyke was blown up by the retreating German forces in 1945, flooding the polder and destroying 80 per cent of the land and property. A small lake has been designated a nature reserve, and the nearby woods are part of the recreation area created by the Dutch Forestry Service. This is the most sparsely populated area in the Netherlands, with only sixty people per sq km, compared with 2,400 in the Randstad. Most of the land is agricultural, with more than 10 per cent devoted to bulb-growing.

The North-East Polder

Work began in 1937 on the draining of the North-East Polder, which incorporated the former islands of Urk and Schokland. Drainage was completed during World War II, and became known as the 'Nederlands Onderduikers Paradijs'. The letters 'NOP' stand also for 'Noord-Oost Polder'. This was a 'safe' retreat for resistance fighters (Onderduikers) and other refugees. Work began on the task of bringing it into cultivation. The focal point of this area is the town of Emmeloord, which is continually expanding. The whole polder is primarily agricultural, although Urk retains its character and charm as a fishing village. In summer, a ferry service for pedestrians and cyclists operates from here to Enkhuizen on the opposite side of the IJsselmeer. The former island of Schokland, which was very small, has been used as the basis for a country park, and the old island church is now an interesting archaeological and geological museum, with artefacts dating from Roman times. There are exhibits showing the history of Schokland, which in former times was joined to Urk. However, in the face of continued threats from the sea, it was decided in 1859 to evacuate the whole population, and the church is the only building which survived the onslaught of the waves. The old coastline of the island can still be followed on foot or by cycle, and the old harbour with its huge wooden mooring posts, stands in the middle of fields.

The Flevo Polders

In 1950 work began on the huge 'Flevo-polders', starting with the south-east polder, now named Eastern Flevoland. It was soon recognised that new towns would be required to house the population which would settle

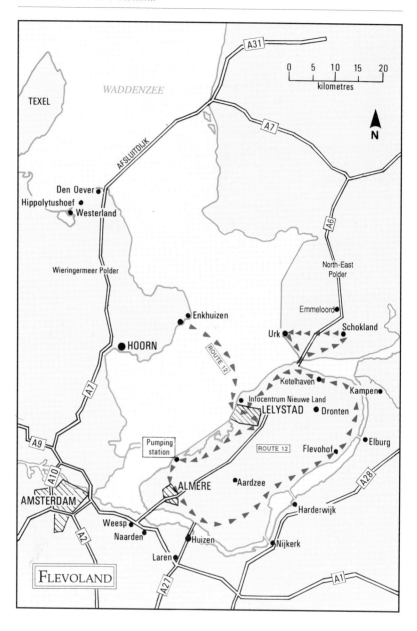

here, both to relieve congestion in the Randstad and to man the new industries which would be attracted to the area. In addition, large recreation areas were created for the new residents. In 1965, in the middle of a swampy area of reclaimed land, the foundations were laid for the new city of Lelystad. Today there are more than 60,000 residents, with ex-

The Afsluitdijk, now carrying a motorway across the IJsselmeer, with its observation tower

Fishermen by the Knardijk sluice, Flevoland

tensive shopping and other facilities, and a direct rail link from Amsterdam.

The last major new town, Almere, named after the former lake, is now well established. Because of excellent transport links, many of its residents commute to Amsterdam, although new local industry is developing. Almere is situated at the western end of the south-west polder, now named Southern Flevoland, work on which began in 1968. Most of this south-west polder has been devoted to agriculture, particularly growing rape seed. This in itself has provided a tourist attraction as there is a special Rape-Seed Route to follow when the bright yellow flowers are in bloom.

The final stage of the IJsselmeer Polders Plan is the creation of the Markerwaard, on the western side. Currently there is much debate as to whether this last stage should be carried out. There are many reasons for and against the plan, but it seems likely that the Markerwaard polder will eventually be created. The Houtribdijk, between Lelystad and Enkhuizen, forms one of the enclosing dykes for the projected polder, and, provides a major route from North to Central Holland, avoiding Amsterdam.

With the development of these polders there is now room for the growing population, and for recreation and leisure. The large waterways and lakes surrounding Flevoland are used for leisure, and new beaches, marinas and holiday resorts attract visitors from all over Europe. There are numerous nature reserves, the most important being the Oostvaardersplassen in the north, between Lelystad and Almere. Unique in Europe, it is an important wintering ground for many rare birds.

The woods in Eastern Flevoland are primarily commercial, but recreational facilities such as signed cycle and walking routes, campsites and picnic places are now included. Woodland being developed in other parts of Flevoland will follow the same pattern and, with landscaping, it is difficult to believe that these lovely afforested areas were, within living memory, at the bottom of the sea.

Route 12: A Tour of Flevoland. Approx 160km

There are two ANWB signposted tourist routes in Flevoland: one, the Zeebodem (sea bottom) route, covers part of the North East Polder and part of Eastern Flevoland to the east of Leystad. The other, the Nieuwland route, covers most of the Southern Flevoland and Lelystad.

Perhaps the ideal way to start this tour, which includes some of the places covered by the ANWB routes, is by crossing the Houtribdijk from Enkhuizen to Lelystad, a distance of 28km. There are parking places alongside the road, so it is possible to stop and look at the waterbirds, fishing boats and sailing craft. On reaching the far end across the Houtrib locks, follow signs for Informatiecentrum Nieuw Land, situated close by. Here photographs, maps and diagrams (with English captions) explain how the land has been reclaimed. A film (also in English) explains the history of Flevoland. Unfortunately the artefacts recovered from the seabed were destroyed in a disastrous fire in 1987. Outside are the special machines used to reclaim the land.

The nearby city of **Lelystad** is continually expanding. There is a good shopping centre (follow 'Centrum' and Parking signs), but it can be a little confusing as pedestrians and cyclists are totally separated from motor traffic. There are plenty of open spaces around the city, as well as a small zoo, the Natuurpark Lelystad, just south of the motorway, with collections of rare species.

Follow the dyke road to **Lelystad Haven**, cross the locks by the pumping station and continue in the direction of Almere past new housing and factory developments on the left. In about 2km turn off to the left along the Knardijk. From this high embankment, which was the first enclosing dyke of the Flevopolders, there are good views to the right over the Oost- vaardersplassen nature reserve, and access to the Hollandse Hout (woods) on the left. A small carpark a short way along the dyke allows access to one of the observation hides. Return to the sea dyke (Oostvaardersdijk) and turn left, continuing ahead to the huge 'Bloq van Kuffeler' pumping station, the largest in Holland. Nearby is the 'De Trekvogel' nature information centre, giving information about the migratory and other birds in the nearby reserves, with excursions to see the colonies of cormorants in the Oostvaadersplassen.

If you wish to visit **Almere** the best way is to follow the Nieuwland route signs into the city centre. Development is still taking place, but there are good shops and an attractive modern station building. But be warned, it is always windy.

Follow the route out of the city, returning towards Almere Buiten, then go south again towards Almere-Haven. The route follows mostly minor roads to **Almeerder Hout**, where the garden centre 'De Kemphaan' may be visited. This organic gardening centre has attractive display gardens showing how butterflies and bees can be attracted to the plants and which plants help keep down pests.

From De Kemphaan continue following the Nieuwland route along the Gooimeerdijk, past the end of the Stichtsebrug leading to Huizen, then by winding roads through the Horsterwold (a newly planted forest) to **Zeewolde**, another new town being deveoped mainly as a holiday centre. Follow the route out of the town as far as the main road, then turn right in the direction of Dronten. At the next junction turn right again towards Harderwijk, then follow local signs to Veluwemeer and Flevohof. The roads runs along the dyke, offering beautiful views.

Flevohof, described as a 'look, play and do' park, is a recreation centre, with some holiday bungalows, which is particularly suited to families. Numerous attractions include a miniature train to carry visitors around the park and a children's farm. Visitors can see cows being milked, and there are attractive floral gardens and agricultural displays.

Continue along the coast road in the direction of Elburgerbrug and Kampen. Just past the cross-roads by Elburgerbrug are the remains, on the left, of the old harbour entrance to **Elburg**. Still following the coast road continue past the locks at Roggebotsluis and cross the main Kampen-Lelystad road to continue along the Vossemeerdijk to Ketelhaven.

At **Ketelhaven** the Museum of Marine Archeology contains the remains of the many historic vessels which were wrecked centuries ago in the Zuiderzee, and have been recovered since the polders were drained. Their cargoes and other salvaged items are also on dislay, including some eggs from 1620.

In the nearby town of **Dronten** is the twisted propellor from an RAF bomber, displayed as a memorial to those who died in regaining Dutch freedom. Many aircraft remains were found when the polder was drained.

Continue along the Ketelmeerdijk and turn right at the minor cross-roads just before the Ketelbrug. This leads to a minor road running beside the motorway across the bridge. Follow this road and at the other end of the bridge, in the North-East Polder, follow the Zeebodem route signs to **Schokland**. Spend some time here visiting the museum (where cycles may be hired) and walking or cycling round the old coastline of the island.

From Schokland follow the main road west to **Urk**, another former is-

Fishing boats in the harbour at Urk

land, but still a busy fishing port. The old village centre has some attractive houses, and washing may often be seen strung across the street to dry. The old town hall houses an interesting local museum about the island's history, including some old furnished rooms. Many of the older people here still wear traditional dress, but they value their privacy and do not like being photographed without permission. North of the village the Dutch tradition of harnessing the wind is continued with a 3km long line of twenty-five wind turbines.

Emmeloord is the main town of the North-East Polder, and has a modern 65m high water tower which also contains a carillon. The tower may be climbed for a fine view across the town and polder landscape. Northeast of Emmeloord is **Luttelgeest**, which has a superb orchid farm with more than 7 acres of orchids. This may be more conveniently visited from the Old Coastline Route (see Chapter 12).

To complete the tour return to Lelystad via the motorway over the Ketelbrug.

Note that on the long straight polder roads with few trees in a flat landscape, there is a danger of drivers falling asleep. In some places it is mandatory to drive with headlights on in daylight, and this is a wise precaution anyway. The strong winds also cause problems for cyclists, who should always use cyclepaths where provided, and choose sheltered routes where possible. This is difficult in the Flevopolder, but there are a number of wooded areas with recreational cyclepaths, especially in Eastern Flevoland along the coast of the Drontermeer and Veluwemeer. The cyclepath from Dronten to Lelystad is also reasonably well protected by trees. The ANWB 'Touristenkart' shows the cyclepaths and its use is recommended.

Additional Information

Places of Interest

Almere
De Kemphaan Outdoor Centre
Kemphaanweg
Open: May to Oct, Tues to Sun, 10am-4.30pm; Nov to Apr, Tues to Fri 10am-4pm.

Natuur Informatiecentrum de
  Trekvogel
Oostvaardersdijk
Open: All year Mon-Fri 12noon-5pm.
April to Oct also Sat, Sun and public
holidays 12noon- 5pm.

Biddinghuizen
Flevohof Recreation Park
Spijkweg 30
Open: Apr to Sept, daily, 10am-6pm.

Ketelhaven
* Museum voor Scheepsarchaeologie
Vossemeerdijk 21
Open: Apr to Sept, daily 10am-5pm. Oct
to Mar, Mon to Fri 10am-5pm; Sat, Sun
and public holidays 11am-5pm.

Lelystad
Information Centre Nieuw Land
Oostvaardersdijk 1-13
Exhibition on land reclamation and

development of IJsselmeer Polders.
Open: Apr to Oct, daily 10am-5pm. Nov
to Mar, Mon to Fri 10am-5pm; Sun 1-
5pm.

Natuurpark Lelystad
Meerkoetenweg
Open: All year from sunrise to sunset.

Schokland
* Meseum Schokland
Middelbuurt 3
Open: Daily all year 10am-5pm. Closed
1 Jan and 25 Dec.

Urk
* Museum Urk
Wijk 2
Open: Apr to Sept Mon to Fri 10am-
5pm. Feb, Mar and Oct Mon to Fri
10am-1pm.

Ferry Services

Enkhuizen-Urk
(North Holland-Friesland)
May to Sept only. Twice daily (three in
July/Aug). Journey time: 1 hours.
Reservation compulsory. No cars, but
cycles and mopeds allowed.
☎ 05277 3407

7

FRIESLAND
AND THE WADDEN ISLANDS

When you enter Friesland you enter a different country. Here sign-posts and name boards are in both Dutch and Fries, for the people here, like the Welsh, are fiercely proud of their language and customs which they understandably wish to preserve as living entities. It may be a little disconcerting to find shop assistants who insist on speaking Fries, but once they know you are a visitor your welcome is assured. Recently some local authorities have insisted on only the use of Fries names on road signs. As these are not the names given on most maps (except one obtainable from local tourist offices in Friesland) this causes confusion, so in this book we use the Dutch name with any Fries variant in brackets.

The province offers a wide choice for the holidaymaker, and it is surprising to find few tourists here. Despite being in the north of the country distances are not exceptionally great and road and rail communications are continually improving. Friesland contains a unique lakeland paradise for watersport and sailing enthusiasts. There are large farms, for this is the dairy centre of the Netherlands, and centuries-old churches built on mounds (*terps*) for protection against floods. There are many miles of dykes, both along the edge of the sea and inland. Old wooden belfries (*klokkenstoels*) in village churchyards date from the days when the villagers could not afford to build church towers. Variety is provided by wooded areas in the south-east, interspersed with dunes, heathland and fen areas, while in the south-west is Gaasterland where sand martins nest in the sand cliffs along the edge of the IJsselmeer.

The towns and terp villages of the north form an interesting tour, as does the lake area in the south-west, while the south-east is less well-known than it deserves to be. The Wadden Islands form a separate but nonetheless interesting area to visit.

Route 13: Harlingen, Franeker and Leeuwarden. Approx 27km

Coming to Friesland from the west, across the Afsluitdijk, keep on the E10 main road which bears north to **Harlingen**, the historic port from which ferries leave for the Wadden Islands of Terschelling and Vlieland. The

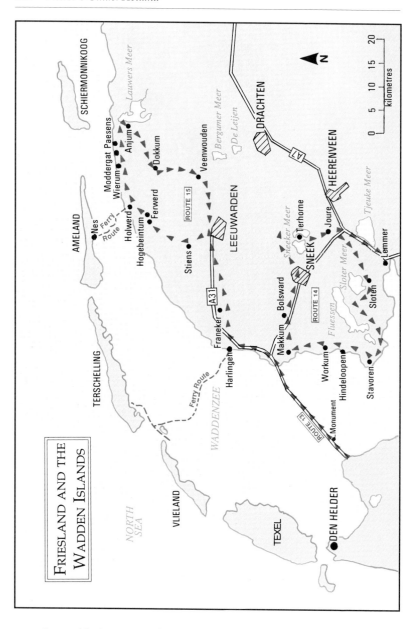

Friesland and the Wadden Islands

town is notable for its very fine old dwellings and warehouses — relics of the East India Company — the town centre being a conservation area.

Leave Harlingen via the dyke road, along Havenweg and Havenplein, Oude Ringmuur and Harlingerstraatweg on the north of the town, cross the motorway and follow the old road via Herbayum to Franeker.

Smaller than Harlingen, **Franeker** is another old town, once famed for

Old wine warehouse in Grote Bredeplaats, Harlingen, now used as a restaurant

The richly decorated facade of the town hall at Sneek

A Walk in Harlingen

Start from the Zuider Plein, close to the southern end of Zuiderhaven. Cross the square to the north side of Rozengracht where a little brick building originally used to house a fire engine. Across the canal are many old East India Company warehouses. Continue across Zuider Plein and along Brouwersstraat, which has some lovely bell-shaped gables on the fronts of houses. Turn left into Schritsen, and shortly after passing Raamstraat a typically Dutch alley or steeg, Woudemansteeg, leads between two old houses with stepped gables on the right. Walk through to Lanen, turn left, and after a short distance, right again into Kleine Bredeplaats, a street full of beautiful old buildings. No 12 in particular is richly decorated in Renaissance style with the Harlingen arms on the façade. At the end of the road turn left into Grote Brede-plaats. On the right is an old fruit and wine warehouse, beautifully restored and, like so many other of the town's buildings, put to another use. Continue to the end of the road, turn right into Prinsenstraat, then right again along Noorderhaven with more lovely buildings on both sides of the water. Part way along stands the town hall (1730), very similar to the British Georgian style. Behind it, in Raadhuisstraat, stands the octagonal Raadhuistoren. At the end of the street is Voor-straat, with the municipal museum in the Hannemahuis (No 56), a lovely eighteenth-century building containing a fine collection of silver, china, tiles, old maps and model ships.

Then return to the Nooderhaven and follow the waterside to the end. Cross the Leeuwenbrug and walk down Rommelhaven, along Scheerstraat and into Lombardstraat, to the English Gardens, laid out and planted in nineteenth-century style on the remains of the city walls. Walk through this peaceful part of the town, cross the bridge to the south side of Franekereind, and return to Zuider Plein along Heiligeweg and Brouwersstraat.

A Walk in Franeker

In the main street, Voorstraat, is the old Waag which houses the VVV offices, next door to two professors' houses dating from the seventeenth and eighteenth centuries. They now accommodate the town museum. Further on the right, is a beautifully-restored building, the Martenahuis, dating from 1498, with a beautiful garden. This building is now the office of the Rural District Council. At the end of Voorstraat turn left into Raadhuisplein, to the town hall, one of the earliest in Friesland, built in 1591 in Renaissance style. At the end of Raadhuis-plein, is Eise Eisingastraat, where in 1774-81 a wool merchant and amateur astronomer built a planetarium with the operating mecha-nism in the attic of his house. At the end of this street is the attractive

Korendragershuisj (grain-porters house) now used by local crafts-men, which visitors are welcome to view. Grain was brought in along the canals by boat, and was weighed here for tax purposes before being allowed into the town. Return along Groenmarkt, on the opposite side of the canal to the planetarium, to the Camminghastins, a fortified dwelling recently restored and now the Friese Munt and Penning-kabinet, an annexe of the Frisian Museum. Just beyond is the Martini-kerk, built in 1421. A stroll around the rest of the town shows that it was originally built within an encircling canal or moat with ramparts, the latter having been mostly levelled to provide a promenade.

A Walk Around Leeuwarden

Starting at the railway station, by the VVV office, cross Stationspleinan and walk up Sophialaan to Willemskade. Cross the Prins Hendriks-brug and continue up Prins Henrikstraat and Doelsteeg to Nieuwe-stad. Turn left and continue to the landscaped ramparts. Turn right, and walk through the gardens, past the Resistance Monument on the second bastion, then cross over to the huge sixteenth-century leaning tower of the Oldehove. This is part of a Gothic tower, built in 1529-32, intended as part of a cathedral, but because of ground subsidence, never completed. The outline plan of the building is laid out behind the tower in the Olde Hoofsterkerkhof, on one of the original mounds.

In nearby Grote Kerkstraat is the Princessehof which, with the ad-joining house, is one of the finest museums in the world specialising in ceramics. Walk along Grote Kerkstraat as far as Pijlsteeg, turn left, then right into Perkstraat where some lovely old almshouses, known as the Boshuizen-Gasthuis, can be found. Return to Grote Kerkstraat and cross into Beijerstraat, on the corner of which is Mata Hari's house, now the Frisian Literary Museum. At the bottom of the road, turn right into Hofplein, and continue into Raadhuisplein, down Weerd and on to Waagplein with the old weigh-house (1598). Continue along Peper-straat into Groentemarkt, bear left then right along the street 'Over de Kelders'. This runs along one of the town's canals, with an upper quay over a lower quay from which cellars open, similar to those in Utrecht. Along Over de Kelders, on the right, is Koningsstraat, down which is Turfmarkt. A left turn reaches the Frisian Museum, with very good regional collections of art, history, costume, archaeological finds, etc. On the opposite side of Turfmarkt is one of the loveliest buildings in the town, the 'Kanselarij'(1566) which was once the Frisian Court.

Walk back to Groentemarkt, along Peperstraat and turn left along Widumerdijk, a long street leading to Zuiderplein, with a huge sculpture of a Frisian cow, known as '*Us Mem*' (Our Mother). From here it is a short step along Stationsweg to the starting point.

its university, until Napoleon closed it down.

From Franeker it is just 15km to **Leeuwarden**, the provincial capital. It is another fortified town, originating from settlements on three mounds at the confluence of the rivers Ee and Vlie. Its centre is surrounded by a ring canal, with further intersecting waterways. The town makes a good base and has excellent shops. A detailed walk map is available from the VVV, but a tour of the most interesting places is described here.

To the south-west of Leeuwarden are two very small but interesting places. In the tiny hamlet of **Beers** (Bears) is a seventeenth-century fortified gateway, which stands in the middle of fields. In the little restored church nearby is a small district musem with a permanent exhibition about the estates, fortified towers and gateways in Friesland. About 8km to the southwest of Beers is the village of **Wieuwerd** where, under the chancel of the medieval church, is a vault containing four naturally mummified bodies believed to date from the early sevententh century. Apparently, there is something in the atmosphere that acts as a preservative. These places can be visited en route for Sneek, which is where the next route begins.

Route 14: The Frisian Lakes and IJsselmeer Towns. Approx 116km

Sneek, some 20km south west of Leeuwarden, is a beautiful old town, second largest in the province and a well-known yachting centre. The lovely old watergate dating from 1613 is the only remnant of the town's defence works, with a guardroom built over the water. It is possible to park near here, in Veemarkt on the Geeuwkade. After looking at the Waterpoort, walk down Waterpoortgracht to Martiniplein, where the sixteenth-century Martinikerk stands on foundations from the twelfth century. The unusual wooden belfry standing beside the church dates back to 1489, and has recently been restored. Beyond the church, in Marktstraat, is the beautiful fifteenth-century town hall with later additions including a fine double staircase to the entrance. Although the town is about 20km away from the sea, the network of waterways means that one is never far from sight of yachts and other craft. The importance of the town as a maritime centre is shown in the Fries Scheepvaartmuseum.

From Sneek it is possible to follow the signposted ANWB 'Friese Meren' route, but the shorter tour described takes in some additional places.

Leave Sneek by the road signed for Grouw (Grou), following the blue hexagonal signs for the 'Friese Meren' route. After passing through Offingawier, keep straight on instead of turning left, following the road running north-east towards Irnsum (Jirnsum), where at the crossroads beyond the village (signpost 3098) turn right, and cross the Prinses Margriet Kanaal. Cyclists can turn off along the north side of the Sneekermeer, cross the Terzoolstersluis and follow the road alongside the canal.

Windmill on the town ramparts at Sloten

The old sea lock and harbourmaster's house, Hindelopen

After crossing the canal, in about 1km turn right at signpost 357 towards Terhorne (Terherne), back on the signed route. Through the village are two good viewpoints with parking, for watching the sailing and wildlife on the Sneekermeer and Terkaplesterpoelen. At the next village, **Goingarijp**, is a *klokkenstoel* (wooden belfry). Continue south to **Broek-Noord**, where the road turns right at a T-junction (signpost 4896) passing another *klokkenstoel* at Snikzwaag before reaching **Joure** which has two important industries: the manufacture of Fries clocks, and the main factory of Douwe Egberts, the well-known Dutch suppliers of tea and coffee. The latter is well represented in the local museum. A diversion along the motorway A50 is to **Lemmer**, another town devoted to sailing and boating, where locks give access from the IJsselmeer to the Frisian lakes.

Otherwise, leave Joure along the signed route through Sint Nicolaasga to **Sloten**, the smallest of the eleven Frisian towns. Park outside the town near the Slotermeer, and walk along the street beside the central canal. Old locks stand at either end of the central waterway, and a fine windmill overlooks the whole town from the ramparts.

On leaving Sloten, continue to Wijckel, then turn right to **Balk**, which has an attractive seventeenth-century town hall with belfry and small central steeple. A short diversion may be made at this point to look at the Slotermeer; there is a car park at the edge of the lake. Back in the village, follow the signed route to the main road, at signpost 1728, cross over to **Harich**, turn right in the village and follow the minor road, which runs near the main road for about 1km. Where it bends sharply to the left, take the right turn, bearing right in about 2km to a T-junction (signpost 2410), turn left and continue to where the road turns left again alongside the Fluessen lake to **Elahuizen** and **Aldegea**. Here it is possible to turn left along the signed route which passes through Gaasterland, the most heavily wooded part of Friesland. There are plenty of walks and cycle paths, and a number of bird sanctuaries including Sybrandy's Bird Park and Recreation Centre at **Rijs**. This route is shorter, and at Aldegea you continue straight ahead to **Nieuw Buren**. After crossing the main road at signpost 594, take the next turning on the left, then after 1km turn right, back on the signed route. The road is now followed to the shore of the IJsselmeer, turning right along the sea cliffs. Although very low by British standards, these are real cliffs, not dykes or sand dunes. After following the shoreline for about 5km, to the monument at Rode Klif, a huge boulder bearing an inscription which translates as 'On 26 September 1345, the Frisians, in defence of their independence, stood as one man against an overseas attack by the Dutch, and repelled the enemy'. There is car parking nearby, and from this point a fine view is obtainable out across the water of the IJsselmeer. Along this stretch of coast there are many opportunities for observing waterbirds.

The road along the coast continues to **Stavoren**, a prosperous port in the Middle Ages, now mainly noted for the locks which give access to the yachting areas of the Frisian lakes, and for the summer ferry service across the IJsselmeer to Enkhuizen, available to pedestrians and cyclists only.

On leaving Stavoren, instead of following the signed route, turn left at the T-junction 2km out of the town (signpost 2405) and follow the road to Molkwar, then on to the dyke road to **Hindelopen**, where parking is only permitted outside the town. This little place was raised to the status of a town in 1255, and became a member of the Hanseatic League in the fourteenth century. Once a very busy seaport, it is now an equally busy centre for yachting. Behind the sealocks are many houses with old façades, linked by characteristic wooden bridges across the drainage canals. Many of the houses were the homes of sea captains, and the place is known for its beautiful painted furniture and unusual costumes, which may be seen in the Hidde Nijland Museum in the former town hall and weigh-house.

Behind the sealocks is the old lock-keeper's house with a wooden belfry, dating from 1619 and now used as the harbourmaster's office. Near the sea dyke is the church (1658) with a leaning tower dating from 1593, the weather vane on top being a model of a sailing ship. The old lifeboathouse on the quay is often open. During World War II, the local lifeboat was 'stolen', to take over forty refugees to safety in England. Today there are about eight large modern motor lifeboats stationed around the IJsselmeer, which seems excessive until one realises just how quickly the sea can get up and how rough it can become in a strong wind, with the shallow waters of the inland sea.

From Hindelopen, take the road inland towards the main road, where the signed route is rejoined along the parallel minor road to **Workum**, noted for its local pottery. The Waag (1650) stands in the market square, and houses the VVV office. The main part of the town hall is medieval, and was enlarged in about 1725. In the town are many fine gabled houses. The Grote or St Gertrudiskerk was commenced in the sixteenth century and its tower stands separately. Like the one in Leeuwarden, it was never completed. The organ, built in 1697, is one of the oldest in the province. Near the lock is the old shipbuilding yard 'De Hoop', where boats are being built and restored using traditional tools and methods.

The signed route is followed from Workum north to Makkum, passing two villages, Ferwoude and Piaam, which lie on what is called the 'Aldfaers Erf Route'. The name is best translated from the Fries as 'Forefathers' Heritage', and is a historical trail where various shops, old farms, workshops and dwelling houses have been carefully restored and furnished to show visitors how people lived and worked during the period at the end of the last century. The villages belonging to this project are located within a triangle bounded by the towns of Workum, Makkum and Bolsward, and the whole route is signed, literature being available locally.

Makkum is well-known for its pottery. The Waag (1698) is the site of the VVV, together with a museum devoted to Frisian pottery and earthenware. The church dates from 1660. The most interesting feature of the town is undoubtedly Tichelaar's Royal Makkum Pottery and Tile Factory. ※

The industry has existed here since the seventeeth century, and the present factory has been owned by one family for over 300 years. It is the only surviving factory in the world still using the original white tin glazing process introduced into the Netherlands in the sixteenth century. It is claimed that the products of Makkum rival those of Delft; certainly each piece, which bears the Royal Makkum mark together with the signature of the individual painter, is a real collector's item. Tours around the factory provide a fascinating insight into this old but thriving craft.

Turning again along the signed route from Makkum, turn right at signpost 7661, then left at 7665 to **Allingawier**, another 'Aldfaers Erf' hamlet with just twelve houses and two churches, and including an old restored farmhouse which may be visited. Before reaching the hamlet, the road passes the lovely Frisian mansion house called Allingastate. About 1km beyond Allingawier is **Exmorra**, where there is an antique grocer's shop and school, furnished and stocked with genuine old items.

Beyond Exmorra the road continues, passing under the A7 motorway to enter the town of **Bolsward**. Built on a *terp*, this old Hanseatic port first received its charter in 1455, and was at the height of its prosperity in the sixteenth century. The red brick town hall with Renaissance carved façade, and elegant tower with a carillon, dates from 1617. A former Franciscan church, the Broerekerk, has a moulded brick front from 1281, while the fifteenth-century Grote or Martinikerk has an older tower and some fine choir stalls and organ. From Bolsward, the route returns direct via Nijland and Ysbrechtum to Sneek.

Route 15: Frisian Terps and Towns. Approx 50km or 75km

An interesting tour can be made of the area north of Leeuwarden, particularly noted for the *terps* or mounds on which small villages were built.

Leave Leeuwarden by the road which turns off the ring road at signpost 4819, leading north to Stiens. A short distance away on the right may be seen the *terp* villages of Jelsum, Cornjum and Britsum, all on low mounds rising above the surrounding countryside. Continue past Stiens towards Hallum and Marrum, passing more *terp* villages on the left beyond which the sea dyke can be seen. At Ferwerd, turn right at signpost 7510, and keeping right, take the road to **Hogebeintum**, the highest of the existing *terp* villages. Park on the road and walk back into the village. A board can be found near the approach to the church, explaining the purpose of the *terp* which translates as: '*Terps* were lived on in 600BC. People first lived on the (normal) highest ground, then, because of the sea, the level of the high ground was raised by degrees. Houses and farms, and later the church itself, were built on the mound. There are about 1,000 known *terps* in Friesland, of varying ages and heights. Hogebeintum is the highest, 8.8m above sea level. By the year AD1000 building of sea dykes had commenced, which did away with the function of the *terps*. Around the

A Walk in Dokkum

From the car park walk across the bridge and along the side of the Grootdiep, the former inner harbour. This is called Diepswal, and on the right is the seventeenth-century Admiralty House, now the municipal museum. Further along Diepswal is De Zijl, a bridge where the sea locks were located. The town hall is situated by this bridge, from which a number of seventeenth-century houses may be seen. Nearby are two fine tower windmills standing on the ramparts, and many attractive small canals. From De Zijl, walk up Hoogstraat to the Markt and the Grote or St Martinus Kerk, dating from the fifteenth century. On leaving the Markt, along Boterstraat will be seen, on the left, the Fetzefontein, a fine eighteenth-century town pump. Continue to Grote Breedstraat and turn right. Look down the wide street to the Waag (1752), now the VVV, with ornate carving on the gable. From here, walk along Kleine Oosterstraat and De Dam to the Oosterbolwerk, and to the start.

The seventeenth-century town hall at Dokkum

year 1800 excavations had begun on several terps, and valuable information was discovered about the *terp* dwellers. Much of this is now in the Fries Museum in Leeuwarden.' The central part of many of the *terps* has been left intact, as old churches stand on them.

The road from Hogebeintum running north to Blija is very narrow as it runs across the fields, so motorists may prefer to return to the main road at Ferwerd, then turn right. On the left may be seen farmhouses built on terps. The road continues through Holwerd and Ternaard to signpost 10206, where a minor road leads off to the left to **Wierum**. On the sea dyke is a memorial made of anchors, commemorating an occasion when local fishermen were lost in a great storm. The twelfth-century church, opposite the memorial, has a typical saddle-roof tower, and is one of the most photographed churches in Friesland. At Wierum is the 'Wadloopcentrum Friesland', from where it is possible to go on a guided but strenuous walk across the mud flats at certain times of the year. Such walks vary in length, and must only be undertaken in company with local guides who know the tides, weather and the varying pattern of the mudflats. (The word *wad* means mudflat.)

Leave Wierum by the road below the sea-dyke leading to **Nes**, another *terp* village, then head back towards the dyke and the villages of **Moddergat** and **Paesens**, where there is a small fishermens' museum. From Paesens take the minor road past the windmill, across at signpost 2265 and so to **Anjum**, where the tall windmill houses the VVV office and a small shell museum. The church, built on a *terp*, dates back to the eleventh century. At nearby **Oostmahorn**, from where the ferry once left for the island of Schiermonnikoog, there is evidence of Napoleonic forts built into the sea-dyke. The stretch of water beyond is now the Lauwersmeer, having been closed off from the Waddenzee by a long dyke with sluices, so the ferries now leave from Lauwersoog.

From Anjum, follow the main road south-west to **Dokkum**, an interesting old town built on a series of mounds. Once a sea port, and headquarters of the Frisian Admiralty, its importance diminished when the sea inlet silted up, and the Admiralty moved to Harlingen. The best car park is in the Harddraversdijk near the campsite and sports centre.

If returning to Leeuwarden, take the road south through Damwoude to **Veenwouden**. Visit this little town to see the fourteenth-century square fortified tower known as Schierstins, the only surviving example of its type in Friesland. From Veenwouden it is about 2km to the main E10 motorway which leads back to Leeuwarden.

South-East Friesland

South and east of Drachten is a countryside totally different from that of the Frisian lakes or northern *terp* areas. It has extensive woods alternating with sand dunes, heath and fens. Attractive scenery surrounds **Beet-**

sterzwaag and **Bakkeveen**, near the border with Drenthe province.

Further south are the woods and heathlands of Appelscha, well provided with very pleasant cycle paths, and to the west is **Heerenveen**, a
town which is described as being on the border between wood and water,
referring to its position at the point where the lakes to the west meet the
wooded country to the east, with its farms and fens. The name of the town
shows that it is also in a land where peat was cut. To the east of the town
are the woods of the Oranjewoud estate, with many waymarked footpaths and cycle paths through fine old beech woods. Formerly the
property of the widow of Prince William IV of Nassau, in the seventeenth
century, it is now freely open to the public. In the town itself are a number
of fine old buildings, including the Willem van Horen Museum with
ehibits from the region and the elegant municipal offices in the seventeenth-century 'Crackstate' mansion. A restored cornmill dating from
1849 can often be seen working.

Finally, to the south of Heerenveen, is the small town of **Wolvega**,
where there is a statue of Pieter Stuyvesant, founder of New York, who
was born in the area. Wherever one goes in this part of Friesland, the
wooden bell towers and typical Frisian farmhouses will be seen, with
black and white Frisian cows in the fields. The farm barns have decorated
gable ends which protect the entrances left for owls to enter and leave the
loft space and so keep mice and other robbers of the grain under control.
All in all, Friesland deserves to be better known by visitors who can
appreciate what it has to offer.

The Wadden Islands

Stretching like a necklace across the northern coast of Holland, the
Wadden Islands, with the exception of Texel, lie in the Province of Fries-
land. Texel is different from the others as it lies in the Province of North
Holland, and can only be reached from Den Helder, so is included in
Chapter 5.

Vlieland is the most westerly of the Friesian Wadden Islands, and its
peace and quiet is ensured because visitors are banned from taking
motorised transport to the island. The only village is **Oost-Vlieland**, the
old village of West Vlieland having been washed away by the sea in the
eighteenth century. Some 20km long and about $2\frac{1}{2}$km wide, the island,
though small, has large unspoilt areas freely accessible to walkers. As well
as cycles, horses and ponies may be hired. A natural history museum
deals with the local scene, while the Tromphuys in Dorpstraat has a good
collection of Norwegian folk art and many items from Lapland. There is
a large marina on the island, frequently used by sailors sheltering from
sudden North Sea storms. The island is reached by ferry from Harlingen,
where there are special car parks for ferry-users. There are three sailings
daily, but these may be reduced in winter months.

Terschelling is, next to Texel, the largest of the Wadden Islands, with a length of 30km but still only between 2 and 5km wide. Beaches, dunes, extensive woodlands, heath and polders make up this outpost of Friesland, and a road links all the villages. Although cars may be taken on the ferry, it is expensive and bicycles are the best form of transport. The ferries dock at **West-Terschelling**, which together with the main village of **Midsland** and the other villages on the island, cater for tourists as their main occupation. The ferry service from Harlingen sails twice or three times daily, and it is essential to book in advance for cars. Ideally suited to those wanting a quiet holiday, there are also several places of interest, such as the fifteenth-century Brandaris lighthouse, and a small local museum showing craftwork, costumes and items relating to the whaling and shipping industries which were once the main source of the islanders' income.

Ameland is particularly noted for its flora and fauna, and is the only Frisian island where deer can still be found. The island is about 24km long and between 2 to 4km wide. The whole of the eastern end consists of a natural area of dunes and grassland, known as 'het Oerd', where rare birds and plants abound. The main village is Nes, near the centre of the island, and this is connected by road to Ballum and Hollum to the west and Buren to the east. Each village has its own characteristic charm. Once totally dependent on the whaling industry, now 95 per cent of the island's income is derived from tourism. However, this is kept under control so that the essential character of the island has not been destroyed. Nes is near the ferry landing, and a bus service connects with the other villages.

The VVV office is in **Nes**, near the fine saddle-roof tower, which bears two dates. The first is 1664, and originally a fire basket stood on top to serve as a beacon for ships. Later, in 1732, the tower was made higher and a light was displayed from an opening under the clock. In the neighbourhood there are a number of so-called captains' houses, identified by an extra row of bricks in the gables, forming a small step. Near the tower is a little square in which the old town pump can still be seen, together with the old school room and post office. To the north of the village is an attractive octagonal thatched windmill, the only one remaining of four which once stood on the island.

East of Nes is **Buren**, the only village with neither church nor cemetery. To the north of Nes and Buren, in the dunes, many beautifully secluded and sheltered holiday houses, have been built so they do not intrude on the landscape, and a cycle path runs right through to 'het Oerd' nature reserve. Recently, oil has been discovered here, but very strict conditions have been imposed on its extraction; work is only permitted between October and March, and all equipment has to be removed during the summer. All buildings and permanent installations such as tanks must be painted to blend with the landscape. The first year this was done, the

Terschelling

camouflage was so good that sea birds flew into the tanks and injured themselves, so the colours have had to be slightly modified. Certainly it is difficult to realise that modern industry has come to this place.

The villages of Ballum and Hollum stand in the western part of the island, with polders to the south. New farms were built here in 1950, with Government assistance, in the old Frisian style of '*kop, hals en romp*' ('head, neck and body'), so-called from the layout of a living house connected to a large barn by a short connecting passage, all under one roof. The inhabitants of these two villages are Protestant, and at one time they never went to the other end of the island which was predominently Catholic. Nowadays, however, the islanders mix more freely. **Ballum** is the quieter of the villages, and the family vault of the rulers of Ameland from 1424 to 1681 is in the churchyard. The 3m high figure of a knight standing between the columns gives an idea of the family's great power. The church itself contains a beautiful seventeenth-century pulpit.

Hollum has an old church tower from the Middle Ages, and many captains' houses, one of which has a small historical museum, the Amelander Oudheidkamer, dealing with the island and the whaling trade. In the dunes just to the west of the village stands the 58m high cast-iron tower of the lighthouse, one of the most powerful in Europe, whose light may be seen over 100km away. Hollum also has what must be the only modern lifeboat still to be launched with the aid of horses, who drag it from its boathouse in the village to the beach.

The ferry service to Ameland starts from Holwerd, with five or six sailings per day, and more in the summer and on Saturdays. Advance booking is essential for cars, but these may be safely left in the car park at Holwerd. It is quite an interesting experience to make the passage at low tide, as the boat follows a winding course through the mudflats.

Schiermonnikoog is the most easterly of the five Dutch Wadden Islands, and is about 11km long and 2km broad. It also is closed to visitors' cars. As the name implies, it was once owned by the monks from Klaarkamp, a Cistercian monastery in North Friesland, of which no trace remains. Apart from one village, which used to be called Oosterburen, the landscape consists of pine woods and sand dunes. The village is now usually known as Schiermonnikoog. The north-eastern corner of the island is very attractive, and the surrounding high dunes create a large bird sanctuary. The houses in the little village date mostly from the eighteenth century. The chief attractions for visitors are the beaches, pony riding, walking and cycling and the nature reserves. The ferry service departs from the new port of Lauwersoog, in north Groningen, with three or four sailings per day. Cars are left in the car park at the ferry terminal, and since there are only about 10km of road on the island, the ban on cars is understandable.

Additional Information

Places of Interest

* Aldfaers Erf Village Museums
Consists of five museums, listed below.
Open: Apr to Oct Mon to Sat 9am-
5.30pm; Sun and holidays 10am-5pm.

Farm Museum *De Izeren Kou*
Kerkbuurt 11 and 19
Allingawier

Woord en Beeld Kerkje
Meerweg 4
Allingawier

Grocery shop and school
Dorpstraat 52
Exmorra

Carpenter's workshop
Buren 5
Ferwoude

't Fugelhus (Bird house)
Buren 8
Piaam

Ameland
Amelander Oudheidkamer
Oosterlaan 31
Hollum
Open: Apr to Oct 9.30am-12.30pm and
2-4pm, also June to Sept Sat and Sun 2-
5pm.

Anjum
De Eendracht windmill
Mounebuorren 18
Flour mill still in use, with exhibits.
Open: Apr to Sept Mon 1pm-5pm, Tues
to Sat 10am-5pm.

Beers
* Tsjerke en Poarte fan Bears (district
museum)
Beers 1
Open: may to Aug Mon to Sat 10am-
4pm.

Dokkum
*Streekmuseum Het Admiraliteitshuis
Diepswal 27
Open: Apr to Sept, Mon to Sat 10am-
5pm; Oct to Mar, Mon to Sat 2-5pm.

Franeker
Gemeentenmuseum 't Coopmanshus
Voorstrat 49-51
Open: All year Tues to Sat 10am-5pm.
Also May to Sept Sun 1-5pm. Closed
1Jan, 25-6 and 31 Dec.

* Fries Munt en Penningkabinet
Voorstraat 2a
Open: may to Sept Mon to Fri 1-5pm.

Planetarium Eise Eisinga
Eise Eisingastraat 3
Open: Oct to Apr Tues to Sat 10am-
12.30pm and 1.30-5pm. May to Sept
Mon to Sat 10am-12.30pm and 1.30-
5pm, Sun 1-5pm.

Harlingen
* Gemeentemuseum Hannemahuis
Voorstraat 56
Open: Tues to Sat 10am-5pm; Good Fri,
Easter Mon, 5 May and Whit Mon 1.3-
5pm. Closed public holidays. After-
noons only in winter.

Heerenveen
Crackstate Mansion
Oude Koemarkt
Open: In use as town hall. May be seen
during office hours.

* Willem van Haren Museum
Van Harenspad 50-52
Open: Tues to Fri 10am-5pm, Mon 2-
5pm, Sat 11am-4pm. Closed Sun and
public holidays.

Hindeloopen
* Hidde Nijland Museum
Dijkweg 1
Open: Mar to Oct, Tues to Mon 10am-
5pm; Sun and public holidays 1.30-5pm.

Joure
* Johannes Hessel-Huis
Geelgieterstraat 1
Open: May to Sept Mon to Fri 10am-
5pm, Sat and Sun 2-5pm. Oct to Apr
Mon to Fri 10am-5pm. Closed Easter
Day, Whitsunday, Christmas Day.

Leeuwarden
* Gemeentelijkmuseum Het
  Princessehof
Grote Kerkstraat 9-15
Open: Mon to Sat 10am-5pm; Sun 2-
5pm.

* Fries Museum
Turfmarkt 24
Open: Tues to Sat 10am-5pm; Sun 1-
5pm.

Frysk Letterkundich Museum
Grote Kerkstraat 28
Open: Mon to Fri 9am-12.30pm and
1.30-5pm. Closed public holidays.

Makkum
Pottery Museum De Waag
Pruikmakershoek 2
Open: 1 May to 15 Sept, Mon to Sat
10am-5pm; Sun 1.30-5pm.

Tichelaars Koninklijke Makkumer
  Aardewerk en Tegelfabriek (ceramic
  factory)
Postbus 11
8754ZN Makkum
☎ 05158 1341
Guided tours: Mon to Thurs 10am-4pm.,
Fri 10am-3pm.
Showroom open Mon to Fri 9am-
5.30pm, Sat 9am-4pm.

Moddergat-Paesens
* Museum 't Fiskerhuske
Fiskerspad 4-8
Open: 1 Mar to 1 Nov, Mon to Sat 10am-
5pm; also on Easter Mon, Ascension
Day and Whit Mon.

Rijs
Sybrandy's Recreation and Bird Park
J. Schotanusweg 71
Open: Easter to Sept, daily, 9am-6pm.

Sneek
* Fries Scheepvaartmuseum
Kleinzand 14
Open: Mon to Sat 10am-noon and 1.30-
5pm.

Vlieland
Bezoekerscentrum Vlieland (natural
  history visitor centre)
Dorpsstraat 150
Open: Nov to Mar Tues and Wed 2-
4pm. Oct and Apr Mon to Sat 2-5pm.
May to Sept Mon to Sat 10am-12noon
and 2-5pm.

Municipal Museum Tromps Huys
Dorpsstraat 99
Open: May to Sept Mon to Fri 10am-
noon and 2-5pm. Oct and Apr Mon to
Sat 2-5pm.

West-Terschelling
Municipal Museum 't Behouden Huys
Commandeurstraat 30-32
Open: 1 Apr to 31 Dec, Mon to Fri 9am-
5pm. 15 July to 15 Sept, also open Sat
9am-5pm.

Ferry Services

Wadden Islands
(Service all year round)

Harlingen-Terschelling
Up to three times daily. Journey time: 1
hour. Reservation compulsory.
☎ 05620 6111

Holwerd-Ameland
Up to six times daily. Journey time: 45
minutes. Reservation compulsory.
☎ 05191 6111

Harlingen-Vlieland
Three times daily. Journey time: 1 hour.
No cars.
☎ 05620 6111

Lauwersoog-Schiermonnikoog
Four times daily. Journey time: 45
minutes. No cars.
☎ 05193 9050 or 05195 1210

North Holland-Friesland
(Service from early May to mid- Sept)

Enkhuizen-Stavoren
May to Sept only. Three times daily.
Journey time: 1 hour 20 minutes. No
cars, but cycles and mopeds allowed.
☎ 02990 23641.

8

GRONINGEN — THE MOST NORTHERLY PROVINCE

Groningen is seldom visited by overseas tourists from the West, perhaps because it has become associated with new industrial developments, or it appears to be isolated in the far north of the country.

The truth is that there are rolling farmlands with cattle breeding and agriculture based on ancient manor farms, old villages built on mounds called *wierden* (*terps* in Friesland), fenland showing the results of peat-cutting over hundreds of years, rolling woodland, and extensive lakes and waterways ideally suited to recreational sailing. All this, together with the country's third largest port, one of the largest deposits of natural gas in the world, and deposits of salt for industry, add up to a fascinating part of the country which has been neglected too long by the visitor.

Route 16: Groningen and Neighbourhood. Approx 35km

The city of **Groningen** is easily reached by two motorways, the A7 from the west and Amsterdam, and the A28 linking with the centre and south of the country. It lies at the centre of a network of trunk roads, and has good rail connections. It makes an ideal base from which to explore the province, and warrants some time spent looking around.

The city sprang up in 1040, as a trading settlement on the dividing line between the sandy country to the south and the claylands to the north, at a point where access to the sea was possible along the Reitdiep river. By the Middle Ages it had become a member of the Hanseatic League, and had extended its influence over the surrounding country, becoming an independent state. A university was established in 1614. Extensive damage occurred during the last days of World War II and, after rebuilding, much of the city centre has been pedestrianised.

Groningen now has its own casino, one of seven in Holland. There are also boat trips along the canals in season. The whole city centre is surrounded by water, showing how it was originally fortified, and parking is possible at places around the canal ring.

About 4km out of the city, south towards **Haren**, is the Hortus de Wolf, the botanical garden belonging to Groningen University. Of interest to

A WALK AROUND GRONINGEN

Start at the railway station, turn right and walk to the Herebrug. Cross the bridge to the Hereplein and then turn right along Heresingel as far as the crossroads. Turn left into Verlengde Oosterstraat, and continue into Rademarkt, passing the old St Anthony Gasthuis or almshouse on the left. This beautiful old building, dating from 1517, was once a hospital for plague victims, and in the last century was an asylum. At the top of Rademarkt, cross over into Gedempte Kattendiep, a filled-in canal, and a short way along, on the left, turn into Kleine Peperstraat, then almost immediately right again into Peperstraat, to the beautiful Pepergasthuis (1405) with its chapel. Go through here into an alley at the back called Achter de Muur, from which Poelestraat can be entered, and a left turn leads to the Grote Markt, where in the corner of the square is the huge Martinitoren. This may be climbed, and the effort is worth it for the view of the city and of the surrounding countryside on a clear day. The tower is almost 100m high, and dates back to 1469, although the top was destroyed by fire and rebuilt in the seventeenth century. The earliest record of a tower here is from 1215, and the present one belongs to the municipality. In the Martinikerk itself is an organ said to be one of the finest in Europe, and the choir dating from 1413 has some unique murals. Behind is the Martinikerkhof or former churchyard, a peaceful oasis surrounded by attractive old buildings of which the Provinciehuis, or seat of the Provincial Government, has parts dating from the sixteenth century.

Next to this is a house with a beautiful Renaissance façade of 1559. Go through the arched gateway in the corner of the churchyard into Turfstraat, then at the end turn left along Turfsingel to an ornate gateway into the Prinsenhof garden. On the arch over the gate is a remarkable sundial (1731), and the garden itself has been restored to its seventeenth-century state with clipped hedges, sheltered walks, roses and a herb garden. The Prinsenhof was a house for lay brothers in the fifteenth century, then became the bishop's home in 1568-76; now it is the site of the local radio station. From the garden, turn left and left again into Kattenhage, and into St Walburgstraat, with the Natural History Museum on the left. Ahead is a small square with restored houses. Turn right into Jacobijnerstraat leading to Oude Ebbingestraat, then left and right into Rode Weeshuisstraat; the carved doorway of the old orphanage is on the left.

Turn right into Oude Boteringestraat and on the left is the old city Kortegaard or watch house (1634), its name a corruption of the French *Corps de Garde*. Along this street are a number of elegant seventeenth-

and eighteenth-century houses, and at the end of the street, across the Boteringe bridge, is the 'new' town, built since 1625. The bridge leads towards the Ossenmarkt, with a number of attractive eighteenth-century houses. Walking westwards along Lopende Diep (north side), one can see high and low water quays; this was once the town moat and the link with the sea during the period of its membership of the Hanseatic League. The waters were tidal as far as the Spisluizen until 1877, when sea locks were built on the Reitdiep at Zoutkamp. Lopende Diep leads to the Kijk in 't Jatbrug. On a house at the south-east corner is a carving of a head of an old man 'peeping into the creek'. Once over the bridge, continue down Oude Kijk in 't Jatstraat past the tree-bordered forecourt of the former Harmonie building, once the home of the music society but now the University Law Faculty. Beyond here, on the right, is the fifteenth-century Mepschen almshouse, next door to one of the oldest houses in Groningen. Turn right through Kromme Elleboog and along Turftorenstraat to the Hoge der A. Many of the brick warehouses along the waterside have been converted into flats and apartments.

Turn left along the waterfront to Museumbrug where, on the left, is the Groningen Museum, with a large historical collection, fine silver and Chinese porcelain, and modern art. Return along the waterside to the A-brug, turn right into Brugstraat, where there are two more excellent museums: the Northern Shipping Museum, and Niemeijer's Dutch Tobacco Museum. Both are housed in restored medieval buildings, in one of which are the remains of the first stone house in the city. Further along is the lovely A-kerk, originally consecrated in 1247, added to at various times since, and restored in 1981. Through the A-kerkhof is the the Corn Exchange and the Vismarkt, and beyond, through Koude Gat, is the Grote Markt. The buildings here suffered much damage in 1945, the main survivors being the town hall, a neo-Classical building of 1793 to 1810, the Hotel de Doelen (1730) and the fine Goudkantoor from 1635, with the shell motif decoration that is typical of Groningen.

From the Goudkantoor, turn south along the pedestrian street of Herestraat, right into Kleine Pelsterstraat, and right again into Pelsterstraat. Here, on the left, is the oldest almshouse in Groningen, the Heilige Geest or Pelstergasthuis. Originally a shelter for the sick, poor, and travellers, this beautiful twelfth-century building has been an almshouse since the sixteenth century. It has its own church, and by walking through beside this, a second courtyard can be seen, with one of the remaining original town pumps. Return to Herestraat, and turn right to follow the road back to the station.

garden lovers, it contains many tropical plants in a huge glasshouse divided into sections according to climate. A short distance to the west, just across the motorway, is the Paterswoldse Meer, a lovely lake formed by generations of peat cutting, and now used for all kinds of watersports and recreation. A very picturesque road runs all round the lake, which is right on the border of the provinces of Groningen and Drenthe. Still on the provincial boundary, about 15km further to the west, is the small town of **Leek**, in the neighbourhood of which is the country park of Nienoord. Leek is easily reached along the A7 motorway, although a more pleasant route is along the road through Hoogkerk, Oostwold and Midwolde.

At **Midwolde** is an interesting brick-built twelfth-century church, which has close historical links with the estate of Nienoord. The mausoleum of the former occupants of Nienoord, made in 1664 by the Dutch sculptor Verhulst, is to be found here, as is a very rare organ and a fine carved pulpit. The estate has pleasant waymarked walks and cycle paths, together with many attractions including a children's farm, playground, miniature railway, mini golf and outdoor swimming pools. On the lake are facilities for model boat enthusiasts, and an extensive model railway system offers similar facilities to model railway fans.

In addition to all this, the buildings of the old manor house, which was founded about 1525 and rebuilt after a fire in the nineteenth century, now form part of the National Carriage Museum, the stable block accommodating a magnificent collection of historic coaches. In the house are children's carriages, dog-carts, horse-drawn sleighs, and many travelling accessories from former days, including dressing cases, drinks cabinets, carriage commodes, and so on. All give a real insight into the rigours and

The unique decorative sundial in the Prinsenhof garden, Groningen

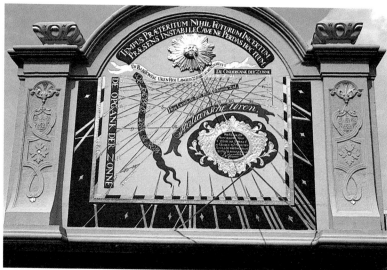

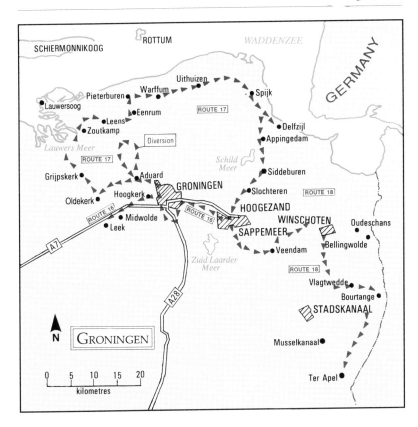

pleasures of travel before the days of trains and motor vehicles. Many of the children's carriages come from the Royal Family and belonged to Queen Wilhelmina. In the museum garden is a shell-grotto, its walls richly decorated with shells and pebbles from round the world.

On the estate there are plenty of refreshment facilities, an open-air theatre and a fully equipped campsite. From the lake, round trips by boat may be taken to the nearby Leekster Meer, where boats can also be hired.

Route 31: Around the North of Groningen Province

This route runs past some of the interesting old villages built on mounds and fortified manor houses, and into the little towns of Zoutkamp and Appingedam.

Leave Groningen via the ring road Friesestraatweg (N46) on the north-west side of the city, thence taking the N355 Zuidhorn road. At **Aduard**, about 5km out, is an old abbey church situated in the former refectory. Opposite the church, on the Kaakheem, is an old-fashioned post office, still in use. From the village, a diversion may be made northwards to

Feerwerd and Ezinge, where there is a good example of a manor house nearby, at **Allersma**. Continue along the main road towards Zuidhorn, then left (signed Zuidhorn, Niekerk and Drachten) to go under the railway and straight ahead to Niekerk. Follow the winding road through the village and the adjoining village of **Oldekerk**, then turn right just before the de-restriction sign. Follow this minor road for a short distance and on the left is a good example of a wooden bell tower. The route now follows the signed ANWB 'Ommelander Route' to Grijpskerk, over the van Starkenborgh Canal. Continue past the thatched mill and over the level crossing, then follow the signs through the town. Turn left at the main road by the high wooden mill and leave the signed Ommelander Route. In 2km turn right, signed Pieterzijl and Metslawier. After passing through Pieterzijl and crossing into the Province of Friesland, turn right towards Munnekezijl and Zoutkamp. Turn left at the Zoutkamp sign to the road along the old dyke, following the Ommelander Route signs again **Zoutkamp** was once a thriving fishing port, but since the closing of the Lauwersmeer in 1969 it now relies on the tourist industry. The newly-reclaimed land is being developed, and the new road across the Pampusplaat to Lauwersoog is particularly good for bird watchers.

Follow the signs out of the town to Lauwersoog, but instead of following the motor road straight ahead, turn left onto an unsigned road which runs beside the Zoutkamper ril, the estuary of the Riet Diep. This leads to a new main road, signposted Schiermonnikoog and Lauwersoog. Just before reaching a wind pump/generator turn left towards Ballastplaat, a picnic area, then immediately turn right again towards Nieuwe Robbegat. Turn left at the T-junction by a 'no lorries' sign and continue through the picnic and walking areas to Expo-Zee. This very good exhibition deals with the sea in general and the Wadden Shallows in particular. An explanatory video in English is available. Proposals for linking the chain of Wadden Islands by barrier dams, thus enclosing the Waddenzee, have now been rejected as environmentally unacceptable. After visiting the exhibition it is possible to drive along the enclosing dam to a car park and picnic area by the hugh sea locks and the ferry port for Schiermonnikoog before returning towards Zoutkamp. Here either take the old main road below the sea dyke, or the new main road which leads over the reclaimed land. Both meet near the village of Verhuizen.

Continue on the main road past Ulrum and then turn right into **Leens**. The church here is one of the oldest in the province, and has a very fine interior with a superb carved pulpit, pews and choir screen. The organ is an outstanding instrument, built in 1733. Just beyond the village is the mansion of Verhildersum, first inhabited in 1398, now owned by the local authority and open to the public. A permanent exhibition entitled 'Wad and Land' illustrates the way in which the land and sea have been formed and have changed over the centuries, and how man has adapted and occupied the land. Changing exhibitions are staged here, and the gardens, restored to their former style, are well worth seeing. North of Leens, in

Kloosterburen, is a new bulb-growing area, and the Kloostertuin (gardens) are worth a visit during the bulb season.

From Leens, continue through Wehe-den-Hoorn to **Eenrum**, which has the distinction of having the smallest five-star hotel in the world, with just one room. There is a very attractive arboretum with more than 500 types of tree and shrub, all suited to the sandy soil. Here too, next to the high windmill, is an interesting museum 'Abrahams Mosterdfabriek'. The buildings have been restored and opened as an old-fashioned mustard mill, where visitors can see mustard being made in the traditional way. There is a restaurant and a shop. From Eenrum follow the road towards **Pieterburen**, which has a world-renowned seal nursery. A small exhibition shows how sick, injured or orphaned seal pups are nursed back to health before being returned to the sea. Nearby is a path to the church and a small botanical garden with a collection of many wild flowers.

Pieterburen is the centre for *Wadlopen* or walking over the mudflats of the Waddenzee, and there is a small exhibition centre in the village about the walks. The region off the coast is unique in Europe, and the extensive areas of mud which are covered and uncovered twice every day by the tides stretch for over 10km offshore. They provide a feeding and resting place for birds and other creatures. However, it must be emphasised that walking out over the mud must not be undertaken without an experienced guide who knows the tides and the dangers, and who is trained and equipped to lead parties safely. A selection of walks is available, ranging from short introductory trips to long, strenuous walks to Ameland or Schiermonnikoog.

A long-distance footpath, the Pieterpad, starts at Pieterburen, and extends right through the east of the country to Maastricht in the extreme south, a total of 466km. Here it links up with the French GR5 via a connecting path through Belgium, so a continuous walk is possible from the Wadden Sea coast to the Mediterranean.

From Pieterburen, take the minor road past the windmill via Westernieland and Den Andel to **Warffum**, which is an outstanding mound village with an outdoor museum, 'Het Hogeland', depicting the way of life. From the church a network of small footpaths radiate out through the town to outlying farms. From Warffum the major road continues east to **Uithuizen**, on the outskirts of which is the beautiful moated manor house of Menkemaborg, with period rooms, and a park with a maze and lovely rose gardens, open to the public. The road continues through Uithuizermeeden and Roodeschool to **Spijk**, another outstanding mound village whose thirteenth-century church, stands in the centre of a moated mound, surrounded by a ring road from which the streets fan out.

Three kilometres to the south of Spijk, the road forks for Delfzijl to the left or Appingedam to the right. **Delfzijl** is the largest port in the north of the Netherlands, and the third largest in the whole country, having developed rapidly since the discovery of huge deposits of salt and natural gas in the area. Originally a fortified town on the river Eems, a windmill stands on the oldest bulwark, and on the sea dyke is a good sea-water aquarium and shell collection. **Appingedam**, 4km inland from Delfzijl, is much more interesting, being noted for its 'hanging kitchens', built out from the houses and overhanging the water of the Damsterdiep in the old town centre. Many of the narrow streets are restricted to pedestrians, and the fine seventeenth-century town hall, thirteenth-century St Nicolaikerk and the regional historical museum are all worth seeing. Almost absorbed by recent development are the old villages of Solwerd and Opwierde, whose churches still stand intact on their mounds.

The main N33 road from Appingedam runs south to Siddeburen, where by turning right, the road leads to **Slochteren**. This town is on the largest natural gas deposit in Europe, but the installations are not intrusive. Unlike the northern part of the province, whose villages are on mounds, set between large estates and farms linked by winding roads, the countryside around Slochteren is traversed by drainage ditches running either side of straight roads which follow sand ridges. Between these ditches lie narrow plots of land, sometimes as long as 2-3km.

On the edge of the town of Slochteren lies the sixteenth- century manor house and estate of Fraeylemaborg. Surrounded by a wide moat, the house contains various exhibitions of works of art, etc, and the grounds include stables and coach-house. The extensive wooded parkland is laid out in the nineteenth-century English style, while within the estate there is a very fine restaurant in the converted coachhouse.

A graceful period room at the manor house of Menkemaborg, near Uithuizen

Some 6 to 7km south-west of Slochteren is the large industrial area of **Hoogezand-Sappemeer** where, in spite of the industry, attempts have been made to provide some pleasant parks, recreation areas, and open spaces. In particular, there is the Zuidlaardermeer on the south of the town. This lake was originally constructed to act as an 'overflow' reservoir for when the river Hunze flooded, but it is now a very popular area for all watersports, with the Meerwijk recreation area at its northern end. The town has shipbuilding yards along the banks of the Winschoterdiep, which is so narrow that boats have to be launched sideways into the water.

The return to the city of Groningen may be made either by the A7 motorway, or along the old road which runs beside the Winschoterdiep.

Route 18: South-East Groningen. Approx 80km

This tour takes in the extensive peat area between the German frontier on the east, the border of Drenthe on the west, and the sandy ridge known as the Hondsrug which runs south from the city of Groningen, just to the west of the Zuidlaardermeer.

Hoogezand-Sappemeer was one of the first of the peat-cutting colonies in the province, and the road which runs south from the Hoogezand junction on the A7 motorway leads through typical peat-fen country.

A turning 7km south of the motorway leads left to **Veendam**, described as the garden city of the north because of its many parks and lakes. Formerly a ship-building centre, it has several houses which were once the homes of sea captains. The most interesting place is the Veenkoloniaal Museum, depicting the history of the Groningen peat-cutting industry. Leave the town to the east, joining the main N33 road, which should be followed north to Meeden, then turn right towards Winschoten, through typical ribbon development along the roads between the drainage canals.

Winschoten grew from the monastery in neighbouring Heiligerlee, and has three fine tower windmills. In the centre of an agricultural area, the town lies on top of a very rich deposit of salt which serves the industry of Delfzijl. There is an exceptionally fine rose garden in the town park, with over 100 different species. In **Heiligerelee** itself there is a bell musem situated in an old foundry building.

Take the road south to **Wedde**, where there is a fourteenth-century manor house (not open to the public) called Huis te Wedde or Wedderborg, and also a recreation park. From here follow the road to **Onstwedde**, on the edge of an area of sandy tracks, isolated farms and a network of winding waterways. The Saxon origin of the area can be seen in a number of early farmhouses to be found in the 'protected' hamlet of **Smeerling**, to the east of Onstwedde on the road to Vlagtwedde. In a countryside of heather, woods and wet grassland, an unusual feature is the tree-lined earth banks.

At Vlagtwedde, pass the village and continue on the minor road east-

❋   wards, to the fortified village of **Bourtange**. During the war with Spain, a road ran from Germany along a sandy ridge through the marshes towards Groningen, and in 1580 Prince William of Orange ordered an earthwork to defend this road, which was never taken. Bourtange was the only fortified place in the north to be built solely for military reasons. During the seventeenth century, the defences were strengthened and extended, and again withstood siege, thus contributing to the safety of Groningen which was also beseiged. In the eighteenth century the fortress had five bastions, connecting earth ramparts and other outworks, barracks, powder magazines and a radial street plan leading from the town centre to the bastions. Towards the end of the nineteenth century it had outlived its purpose, many of the ramparts were destroyed, and the moats filled in. Bourtange became a forgotten town; but in 1964 the fortifications were rebuild and restored, including the fine windmill on one of the five bastions. The whole complex forms a complete star-shaped pattern in the surrounding fields which now replace the former marshes.

From Bourtange, return to Vlagtwedde and follow the road south. Here the route runs almost parallel with the German frontier, through pleasant scenery with fine farmhouses and old oak woods, many of which are nature reserves, notably at Metbroek and 't Liefstinghsbroek. About 10km south of Vlagtwedde is the village of **Sellingen**, an area excellent for walking and cycling. The wooded land continues all the way to **Ter Apel**, in the extreme southerly corner of the province where it joins Germany to the east and Drenthe to the west; it also lies on the edge of the peat area, and owes its origin to the digging of canals in connection with the peat cutting industry.

Additional Information

Places of Interest

Appingehdam
* Gewestelijk Historisch Museum
Blankenstein 2
Open: Tues to Fri 1-5pm. Sat, Sun,
Easter Mon, 30Apr, Whit Mon. 26 and
31 Dec 2-5pm.

Delfzijl
Museum de Noordhoorn (aquarium)
Zeebadweg 7
Open: mid-May to mid-Sept Mon to Fri
7am-5.30pm, Sat and Sun 10am-6pm.
Mid-Sept to mid-May Mon to Fri 1-5pm,
Sat and Sun 1-6pm.

Eenrum
Abraham's Mosterdmakerij (mustard
  mill)
Molenweg 5
Open: Daily 10am-6pm.

Groningen
* Groninger Museum
Praediniussingel 59
Open: Tues to Sat 10am-5pm; Sunday1-
5pm. Closed 1 Jan and 25 Dec.

*Natuurmuseum Groningen
St Walburgstraat 9
Open: Tues to Fri 10am-5pm. Closed
weekends and holidays.

* Noordelijk Scheepvaartmuseum and Niemeyer's Tabakmuseum
Brugstraat 24-26
Open: Tues to Sat 10am-5pm; Sun and public holidays 1-5pm. Closed 1 Jan, 5 and 25 Dec.

Prinsenhof Garden
Turfsingel
Open: Mid-Mar to mid-Oct, Mon to Fri 9am-sunset, Sat and Sun, 10am-sunset.

Haren
* Hortus de Wolf (garden)
Kerlaan 30
Open: All year, daily 10am-4.45pm.

Heiligerlee
Klokkengieterijmuseum (bell museum)
Provincialeweg 46
Open: Tues to Fri 10am-5pm, Sat, Sun and holidays 1-5pm. Closed 1 Jan and 30 Apr.

Kloosterburen
Kloostertuin (garden)
Open: all year daily. Admission free.

Lauwersoog
* Expozee
Strandweg 1
Open: Apr to Oct Tues to Fri 10am-5pm. Sat, Sun and public holidays 2-5pm.

Leek
* Nationaal Rijtuigmuseum (carriage museum)
Huis Nienoord
Open: Apr to Sept, Mon to Sat 9am-5pm; Sun 1-5pm.

Leens
* Borg Verhildersum
Wierde 40
Open: Easter to Oct, Tues to Sun 10.30am-5.30pm.

Pieterburen
Bezoekerscentrum Ten Dijke (information centre)
Hoofdsstraat 83
Open: Daily all year 10am-noon, 1pm-5.30pm.

Seal Nursery
Hoofdstraat 94a
Open: Daily 8am-5pm.

Slochteren
Fraeylemaborg
Hoofdweg 32
Open: All year, daily except Mon, 10am-noon and 1-5pm. Closed 31 Dec, 1 Jan.

Uithuizen
* Menkemaborg
Menkemaweg 2
Open: Apr to Sept, daily 10am-noon, 1-5pm; Oct to Mar 10am-noon, 1-4pm; closed Jan.

Veendam
* Veenkoloniaal Museum
Krkstraat 18
Open: Sun to Fri 2-5pm. Closed Good Friday, 30 April, Ascension Day, 25 and 31Dec.

Warffum
Openluchtmuseum Het Hogeland
Schoolstraat 2
Open: Apr to Oct Tues to Sat 10am-5pm, Sun 1-5pm.

9

BEAUTIFUL DRENTHE

Drenthe is one of the earliest known settled areas in the Netherlands, as can be seen by the presence of more than fifty megalithic tombs or *hunebeds*. From north to south, right across the province, runs the sandy ridge known as the 'Hondsrug' (dog's back) where many of the tombs are to be found. For the traveller who enjoys beautiful country and peaceful surroundings, Drenthe has much to recommend it, with lovely moorland areas, small lakes, and many forests with miles of cycle paths and footpaths. The 'Pieterpad' runs the length of the Hondsrug, and it is possible to cycle for a whole day along secluded cycle routes with hardly another soul to be seen. For horse-riders there are plenty of special paths, and small horsedrawn covered wagons may be hired for the day to explore the sandy lanes through the woods and heathlands.

Apart from its natural attractions, Drenthe has a wide variety of museums, large and small, ranging from the huge peat colony village at Barger Compascuum to the musem of cut-paper art at Westerbork.

Large quantities of oil have been found in Drenthe, especially in the area around Schoonebeek, but the small pumps which bring the oil to the surface are far from intrusive, because of careful landscaping.

The provincial capital of Drenthe is Assen, which, with the towns of Emmen in the south-east and Meppel in the south-west, make good bases for touring.

Route 19: Assen and North-West Drenthe. Approx 75km

Assen, like many larger Dutch towns, has recently been redeveloped and a large, modern shopping complex has been built. However, the old town centre, which like in so many of the small villages in Drenthe is known as the *brink* or village green, remains unspoilt. The town was developed from this point, and around the Brink are some attractive old buildings, including the former chapel of a Cistercian nunnery founded in the thirteenth century, which now forms part of the group of buildings housing the Drents Museum. This includes one of the finest archaeological collections in the Netherlands, with the oldest vessel ever found, a wooden

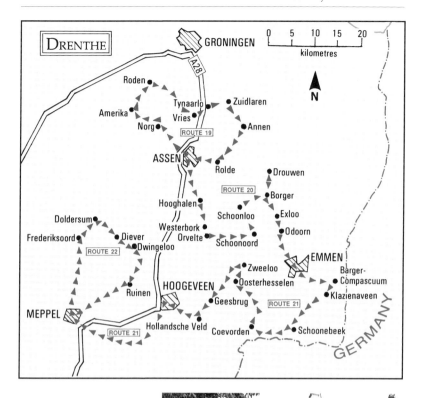

Ontvangers Huis, Assen, which houses part of the Drents Museum

canoe from Pesse, some 25km to the south of the town. Dated approximately 6,800BC, the canoe, like many other artefacts, had been preserved by the peat soil. Other exhibits include material found in *hunebeds*, such as Beaker pottery and Bronze Age jewellery, together with Roman treasures from Beilen and other sites. The museum also has a fine collection of traditional costumes, as well as ceramics, silver and glass. Also part of the museum is the Ontvangershuis (1650), formerly the official residence of the Receiver-General of Drenthe, are a number of beautiful period rooms, and nearby may be found remains of the thirteenth-century cloister, old convent wall and pump.

Motor-cycle enthusiasts will know that Assen is the home of the Dutch TT races, held on the circuit just off the motorway to the south of the town, but the young enthusiast is also catered for in the Jeugdverkeerspark (Young Peoples' Transport Park), located in the Asserbos near the town centre. This unique park contains roadways with all the appropriate traffic signs, on which children aged 6-12 may drive pedal cars and have great fun learning the rules of the road. For very young children there is a special bus, and a small playground exclusively for the under-fives.

The neighbouring Automuseum has a collection of vintage and veteran cars, including several Bugattis. There are also motor-cycles including a Royal Enfield from 1912, Indians from 1916 to 1942, and a Norton racing machine, plus a collection of mechanical toys.

Leave the town by the road leading west across the ring road and motorway, signed to Smilde. In about 2km, turn right in the direction of Norg and Roden. At **Norg** is a thirteenth-century 'saddle tower' church, with choir, in which there are some thirteenth-century paintings believed to be the oldest in Drenthe. Here, too, is an old village green. From Norg, take the road towards Haulerwijk and in about 4km turn right through the village of Een towards **Een-West**. On the right can be found the Zwartendijksterschans. This large earthworks is a four-sided fort with four star-shaped bastions on each corner, and was restored by volunteers in 1988. It is said to be the fortress on which Pieter Stuyvesant based his plans for New Amsterdam, now New York. Narrow lanes lead north through the appropriately named hamlet of **Amerika**, which is just a long lane with a few farms, where horse drawn wagons may be hired.

Continue through Nieuw-Roden into **Roden** itself. On the Brink is the Nederlands Museum Kinderwereld, an outstanding collection of all kinds of children's toys and games from the past 150 years. Here is everything from dolls and dolls' houses to toy soldiers and forts, from magic lanterns to model steam engines, a complete model railway layout, old spinning tops and hoops, and much more. Many of the toys and games can be tried by today's children; a day out not to be missed by any child — or its parents!

From the centre of Roden, take the road leading eastwards to Peize, go through the town past the windmill, and follow the minor picturesque road on the right to Donderen and **Vries**, where there is a beautiful twelfth-century Romanesque church with one of the finest towers in the province. From the church, cross over the main road and follow the road for Tynaarlo, which crosses over the Noord Willems canal and under the motorway. Through Tynaarlo the road continues to Zuidlaren, near the border with Groningen province.

Standing on the Hondsrug, **Zuidlaren** is one of the prettiest *brink* villages in Drenthe, but it is also an impressive place, noted for its horse market. A fine old oak tree stands on the *brink* , and the seventeenth-century manor house 'Laarwoud' is now used as the town hall. During the months of July and August, folklore markets are held, where local crafts and produce are on sale, demonstrations are given, folk dancing takes place and local costumes are worn. For the children there is the Sprookjes-hof fairy-tale park. The whole area is ideal for cycling, there being many cycle paths through lovely wooded countryside.

Equally attractive is the road south from Zuidlaren (signpost 228 by the church) to Annen and **Anloo**, the latter being another very old village with an ancient church, whose nave dates from the eleventh century. The little spire on top of the twelfth-century tower was added in 1757, and seems rather incongruous, but the nave is the oldest Romanesque building in Drenthe. The church contains wall paintings from three different periods.

Just to the south of Anloo, in the Boswachterij Anloo or Anloo Forest, is one of the many megalithic tombs to be seen in this locality, together with a pinetum. The tomb lies just to the west of a sandy cycle track, and consists of a total of eighteen stones. A minor road runs south from Anloo (*paddestoel* 21573) along the edge of the forest and a car park is located near the pinetum and tomb. Follow this winding road south, passing two more tombs, then turn left at the T-junction and sharp right at *paddestoel* 21571, on the edge of the village of **Eext**. Cross the main road N33, and at the next junction, near signpost 3364, is another tomb with thirty-nine stones. Turning right at this junction, follow the road through to **Rolde**, its fifteenth-century Gothic church with Drents-type tower being one of the finest in the province. It possesses a fine pulpit and stained glass windows by the artist Joep Nicolas (1964). Behind the church are two more tombs. To complete the route, return to Assen along the minor road past the church, or turn south past the mill and turn right along the main road N33.

Route 20: From Assen to Emmen. Approx 72km

This route goes past the largest radio telescope in Western Europe, and an old Saxon village where rural crafts are practised; to a museum which delves into the history of the tombs, and to a very fine modern zoo.

From Assen town centre, leave by the road running south past the railway station, Overcingellaan, and turn left at signpost 4022. This is not the motorway, but the road which runs parallel, between the motorway and the railway. After about 6km, in the village of **Hooghalen**, turn left

and follow a minor road north-east, towards Amen. In about 2km, is a car
✳ park at the end of Melkweg Pad ('Milky Way Path'). Leave the car and
walk along this path for about 2km, to the largest radio telescope in
Western Europe. Along the path are scale models of the solar system. Cars
are not allowed because of the risk of disturbing the sensitive electronic
equipment. Not far from here is a memorial marking the site of the
notorious Westerbork Transit Camp, used during World War II by the
Germans to send Dutch Jews to Germany and the concentration camp at
Auschwitz. By the car park a memorial centre records the transportation
of some 100,000 Dutch Jews and other refugees. It stands as a reminder of
the terrible effects of racial hatred and persecution. Ironically the camp
was originally built in 1939 by the Dutch Government to accommodate
many German Jews who had fled from Germany, to what they thought
would be freedom.

Return to Hooghalen, turn left again and continue along the road until
the next on the left which leads via a right fork through the hamlet of
Zwiggelte to **Westerbork**, where folklore markets are held some summer
🏛 evenings. A museum farm, 'In de Ar', has old rooms and antique implements, while the Nederlands Museum van de Knipkunst, illustrates the
art of paper-cutting from the seventeenth century to the present day.

✳ Continue in an easterly direction, to the next village of **Orvelte**, an old
Saxon villagewhich is maintained as a centre for traditional crafts such as
milling and baking, wood carving, pottery, clog-making, and the blacksmith's art. The old houses are the homes of the craftsmen, and the Saxon
origins of the village and its surrounding farmland are shown by means
of way-marked paths around the area. Visitors' cars are not allowed in the
village, but adequate free car parking is available. Several craft workshops may be visited. The farm is very interesting; by way of experiment,
old and new methods of farming are followed side by side. During
holiday times special demonstrations of cheese and butter-making are
given, and there is a very good restaurant in one of the enormous old
barns. The whole place is worth more than just a passing visit.

From the car park, return to the road from Westerbork, turn left, then
left again at signpost 1222, and then turn right towards **Schoonord**. At the
main road, turn left and in a short distance is the entrance to another open-
🏛 air museum, this time called 'De Zeven Marken'. Unlike Orvelte, which
is a living village community, De Zeven Marken is a museum showing the
life-style and work of a typical Drents farm and village at the turn of the
century. Demonstrations of wood carving, pottery, weaving and other
crafts are given at various times.

Some 4km south, along the road to Sleen, there is another megalithic
⊓ tomb, known as the 'Papeloze Kerk' or church without a Pope. There are
fifty-three stones, of which twenty-eight form a kidney-shaped outline.

Visiting this tomb is a diversion, because from Schoonoord, the route
continues north through peaceful forests along the Hondsrug, and at
Schoonloo turns right towards **Borger**, an interesting village with plenty

Hand loom weaving at 'De Zeven Marken' open-air museum, Schoonoord

Cycling, as here in the woods near Schoonloo, is a popular recreation in Holland

of scope for walking and riding in the neighbouring forests. Guided walks are organised during the summer by the State Forestry Service. However, perhaps the most interesting sight is the largest megalithic tomb in the Netherlands, one of the most concentrated group of such ancient monuments in the country, to be found on the minor road leading to Bronneger. The museum t' Flint 'n Hoes is housed in the former workhouse, and has an exhibition of finds, displays about the Beaker Culture and how the tombs were built. The tombs themselves are made from huge boulders which were carried to Drenthe by glaciers during the Ice Ages. The original cap and roof stones have now collapsed in most instances, and many stones have long been removed. The tomb by the museum has forty-seven stones and is 21m long, with many of the capstones in position.

The church in Borger was built in the ninteenth century, but its stone tower is from the fourteenth century. About 4km to the north, along the road to Gasselte, is a natural history museum, at **Drouwenerzand**, which has many exhibits concerning underwater aquaria, both fresh and salt water. There are also two recreation and amusement centres in the neighbourhood, although they seem out of place in the countryside.

From Borger itself, leave by the road which runs parallel to the main road, going south through Ees to **Exloo**, where there is a small children's farm and museum-farm. An unusual feature of this village is the daily departure of a flock of sheep from a sheep barn in the main street to the heathlands beyond the village. They leave at about 12.30pm and return for the night about 5pm. On leaving the village, take the road to **Odoorn** where the church, originally built in the twelfth century, has evidence to suggest that stones from tombs were used for the choir. The major road south from Odoorn forks in about 4km, and the left fork is taken into the town of Emmen.

Emmen is first mentioned in 1137 as a village lying on a spur of the 'Hondsrug'. However, men lived in the area long before that, and hunters from about 6,000BC must have used the stag-horn harpoon, the oldest find in Holland, which was excavated from the peat just to the south. The town lies right on the edge of extensive peat countryside, with its network of small canals and drainage ditches dividing the land into square plots, so unlike the neighbouring Hondsrug with its forest and heath. Since World War II, much light industry has been established here, and Emmen has grown rapidly into a modern but pleasant town.

One of the most interesting attractions is the Noorder Dierenpark, which has recently been completely reorganised into one of the most modern zoos of its kind, re-creating African savannah in which the animals roam freely. The zoo is also well known for its large pool for sea-lions, and a walk-through cage with over two hundred free-flying birds. The latest addition is an enormous covered enclosure with free-flying butterflies from all over the world, among which visitors may walk.

Of more local interest is the small museum 'De Hondsrug', which illustrates the history and prehistory of Emmen and district. In direct contrast is the 'Radiotron', a permanent exhibition of radio, gramophone and telephone equipment and apparatus from 1880 to the present day.

Emmen is one of the centres for the annual four-day Drenthe cycle rides, arranged so that participants may ride at their own speed and enjoy the beautiful countryside. A glance at the area touring map will show just how much of this there is, and it is possible to cycle from Emmen to Roden along the Hondsrug, or from Emmen to Assen, along special cycle paths, most of which run through State Forestry areas (*Boswachterij*).

Route 21: From Emmen to Meppel. Approx 107km

This route takes the visitor to some rather unusual attractions through the countryside in the south of the province. Leave Emmen in the direction of Klazienaveen, to the south-east of the town, and turn off at Nieuwe Dordrecht in the direction of **Barger-Compascuum**. Here can be found the open-air museum National Veenpark, devoted to the history of peat-cutting. The industry originated around 1850, when peat workers and their families from the Frisian fenlands and from neighbouring Germany came here to work. This living museum has reconstructions of original turf huts and the later brick cottages of the early 1930s. School, church, bakery, windmill — all are here in their original or reconstructed form. There are old turf-cutting implements, photographs, and a horsedrawn barge, once used to move the peat blocks, now carries visitors around the site. A light railway, also used to move the hand-cut peat now carries visitors to see the old workings, as well as to areas where peat is still cut. On certain days, steam cutting machines are in operation, and the whole picture of formation, cutting, drying and land restoration can be seen. The original churchyard with its simple graves still exists, and the old bakery is used to bake currant buns in a turf oven. An exhibition hall is used for films and slide presentations, which include commentary in English. Refreshments and meals are available. During the year, the site is used for events such as folk-dance festivals, and various other exhibitions.

From the museum village, take the road south to Zwartemeer, through Klazienaveen to **Schoonebeek**. The first references to Schoonebeek date from the fourteenth century, and in the area there are a number of old Saxon farmhouses; in the town, opposite the town hall, is a magnificent example, fully restored and open to the public. Inside is an example of an old 'sand carpet', made by spreading fine sand on the floor to create patterns, which were changed as required for such purposes as to encourage a good harvest, etc. Near the town are two unique huts, one just near the frontier south of Nieuw-Schoonebeek and the other actually in the town, where it has been rebuilt. These huts are known as *boeen*, or cattle-herder's huts, which in former times were built some distance from the main farm; the cattle-herder lived there to look after the calves in winter. These are the only ones in the Netherlands, although once there were some thirty or forty in the Dutch-German frontier region.

Today things have changed for Schoonebeek, with the discovery of oil. Since 1943, when the first well was sunk, some 600 wells have been drilled, about half of which are in production. The operation is largely screened by trees to minimise the effect on the landscape. Guided tours around the installations are possible, for groups, by arrangement with the VVV.

From Schoonebeek, the road westwards, parallel with the German frontier, leads to the border town of **Coevorden**, with its restored twelfth-century castle, open to visitors at certain times. The municipal museum is located in the magnificently restored musket and cannonball armoury of the old Arsenal, which is currently used to house the public library, and the old fortifications on the northern side of the town are now a garden. Exhibits in the museum include two silver chalices from 1672, and a model of the fortifications, together with maps, plans and photographs from around 1550 to the present day. Old photographs of the town during the late nineteenth and early twentieth centuries are also on view.

Other places of interest in the town include a fine seventeenth-century house in Friesestraat, a seventeenth-century Greek church with a magnificent pulpit, and an eighteenth-century synagogue, now used as a music school. In the town centre is an attractive statue of the Goose Girl; a goose market is still held here every November.

From Coevorden take the road north towards Dalen, then turn left to cross the main road in the direction of Oosterhesselen. The road bypasses

The Goose Girl statue in the main square, Coevorden

the village and continues through the villages of Meppen and Oud-Aalden, with their attractive old Saxon farmhouses, to **Zweeloo** with its interesting thirteenth-century church and unusual pagan altar. Return towards Oosterhesselen, bearing right through Meppen and continuing along the road towards Mantinge for about 3km. Take the narrow lane through the woods (Boswachterij Gees) for about 2km and turn left at a T-junction towards Gees. This is a particularly attractive area for walks, both through the woods and across the heathlands of the Hoge Stoep.

At **Gees**, where there is a large 35 ton ice-bourne boulder, turn right and continue to Geesbrug. Go through the village and fork left, then left again to cross the main road in the direction of **Schoonhaven** recreation area, which is open all the time and has unrestricted access. This is a well laid out country park with swimming facilities, beaches, woodlands and a good restaurant. The spoil obtained from excavating the lake was used to construct a hill from which there is a good view. From the park follow signs to the village of Hollandscheveld, and thence to **Hoogeveen**, a modern town where traditions die hard. Every Sunday morning at 9.30am, the people of the town are called to church by a drum beat, rather than by the sound of church bells, a 300-year-old tradition. The museum 'Venendal' is located in a seventeenth-century gentleman's house, and contains period rooms, costumes, ornaments and other items relating to the region. Built on top of an old fen, the wide streets follow the lines of old drainage canals. The earliest of these was filled up in the seventeenth century, thus laying the foundations of the modern town.

From Hoogeveen take the road south to **Zuidwolde**, another village with many attractive recreation areas and a museum with a collection of handcarts and stone and mineral collections. Also in the village is a cheese farm and a tinsmith/pewterer's workshop where demonstrations may be seen. By keeping to secondary roads instead of the motorway the route passes through **De Wijk**, a centre renowned for the storks which nest there. From De Wijk continue along minor roads past the estates of Havixhorst and Schiphorst to Meppel.

Route 22: Meppel and the Villages of South-West Drenthe. Approx 63km

Lying as it does in the extreme corner of Drenthe, **Meppel** makes a convenient base for excursions into parts of Overijssel. The town is dominated by the impressive tower of the fifteenth-century church. There are some attractive seventeenth-century houses, and an interesting printing museum. As it is the main shopping centre for the area it is often possible to see women wearing the unusual local costume from Staphorst. In the summer boat trips may be taken to the 'broads' of north-west Overijssel.

Leave the town by way of Steenwijklaan, which runs beside the railway, then at the major road junction on the north-east of the town, take the minor road across the N32 motor road towards **Ruinerwold**. Here is a museum farm dating from 1680, with seventeenth-century wall cupboards and tile pictures. Continue along the same road for about 10km to the village of **Ruinen**, whose fifteenth-century church on the *brink* contains some sixteenth-century wall paintings. During the summer, a folklore evening is held each week, with demonstrations of old crafts.

On the outskirts of the village to the north is a sheep-fold, a very large shelter into which the flocks of sheep are herded for the night. At around 5-6pm every evening the sheep may be seen being driven in from the heathlands to the fold. In the summer months a visitor centre is opened here with information on the Drents heathlands, the flora and fauna.

From Ruinen, cyclists have an advantage over cars because they can ride through the woods and over the heath to Dwingeloo. Cars will have to continue through Ruinen to Eursinge, then follow the minor road beside the motorway, which is crossed to Pesse. The road then runs north to Spier, then left again, back across the motorway and through the woods to Lhee, and so to **Dwingeloo**. The village centre, the *brink*, is very attractive, with a number of cafés and restaurants, all overlooked by the church, a fourteenth-century Gothic building with an unusual onion-shaped tower. On summer evenings on the *brink*, demonstrations of old crafts and old-style harvesting methods are given.

The next village is **Diever**, reached by crossing the canal, the Drentse Hoofdvaart, at Dieverbrug. On the *brink* at Diever is the Schultehuis, built in 1604, and now a small museum of household goods and furniture. The Glass Museum, 'De Spiraal', shows how glass is worked and has been used through the centuries. A modern studio has been added, and in summer demonstrations of traditional glass-blowing are given. There is also a small museum 'd'Olde Radio', which has a collection of historic radios, televisions, gramophones, lighting and electrical apparatus. The village also has a potter and a blacksmith, who give demonstrations in season. Diever is ideal for walking and cycling. Horsedrawn wagons may be hired nearby at Vledder, Doldersum and Zorgvlied.

The route continues along the road to **Vledder**, where there is a fifteenth-century church with a fourteenth-century 'saddle-roof' tower. The road turns left in Vledder, coming to **Frederiksoord**, where there is a museum with a collection of clocks and watches made between 1500 to 1900. The horticultural school in the village has a garden which may be visited in summer, with a variety of roses, shrubs and trees. In the neighbourhood are a number of Saxon farmhouses, as well as tumuli.

The road running south leads towards **Havelte**, past two megalithic tombs on the left side of the road. These were completely destroyed during World War II, during the construction of an airfield by the German forces, but fortunately a local archaeologist had made a scale model of them, so they have now been restored exactly to their former state. Havelte has a fifteenth-century church with a Drents tower.

Leaving the town, the road runs south from the land of woods and heath, joining the main road where it crosses the Drentse Hoofdvaart or canal, and in 7km Meppel is reached at the end of the tour.

Additional Information

Places of Interest

Assen
*Automuseum Assen
De Haar 1a
Open: Apr to mid-Sept Mon to Fri 9am-5pm, Sat and Sun 10am-5pm.

* Drents Museum
Brink 1-5
Open: July and Aug, Mon to Fri 9.30am-5pm, Sat and Sun 1-5pm. Sept to July, Tues to Fri 9.30-5pm, Sat and Sun 1-5pm. Closed 1 Jan and 25 Dec.

Jeugdverkeerspark Assen (transport park)
Haarweg 1
Open: Easter to mid-Sept, Mon to Fri 9am-5pm, Sat and Sun 10am-5pm.

Barger-Compascuum
* Nationaal Veenpark (peat industry museum)
Berkenrode 4
Open: Mid-Mar to Oct, daily 9am-6pm.

Borger
* Museum 't Flint'n Hoes
Bronnegerstraat 12
Open: Easter to Sept Mon to Fri 10am-5pm. Sat Sun and public holidays 1-5pm.

Coevorden
* Gemeentemuseum Drenthe's Veste
Haven 5
Open: Mon to Fri 10am-12.30pm and 1.30-5pm, Sat and Sun 2-5pm. Oct to Apr, Mon to Fri 10am-12.30pm and 1.30-5pm. Closed first Mon in month and public holidays.

Het Kasteel
Kasteel 31
Open: During VVV opening hours.

Diever
Glasmuseum De Spiraal
Moleneinde 6
Open: July and Aug, Mon to Fri 10am-noon and 1.30- 5.30pm, Sat 10am-5pm. Sept to Dec and Feb to July, Tues to Fri 1.30-5.30pm, Sat 10am-5pm.

* Museum d'Olde Radio
Achterstraat 9
Open: May to Oct Tues to Sat 1-5.30pm. July and Aug Tues to Sat 11am-5.30pm. July and Aug special tour and demon- strations Mon, Tues and Fri at 2pm.

Schultehuis
Brink 7
Open: May to Sept mon, Tues, Thurs to Sat 10am-12noon and 2-5pm. Closed public holidays.

Drouwen
Natuurhistorisch Museum Het Drouwenerzand
Gasselterstraat 5a
Open: April to Nov 10am-5pm.

Emmen
Nooder Dierenpark (zoo)
Hoofdstraat 18
Open: Mar to Oct 9am-5pm daily (July and Aug to 6pm), Nov to Feb 9am-4.30pm daily.

* Oudheidkamer De Hondsrug
Marktplein 17
Open: Apr to June and Sept, Wed to Sat 10am- noon and 1-5pm, Sun and public holidays 1-5pm. June to Aug Mon to Sat 10am-noon and 1-5pm, Sun and public holidays 1-5pm.

* Radiotron
Marktplein 17
Open: April to Sept Wed to Fri 10am-12noon and 1.30-5pm, Sat, Sun and holidays 1.30-5pm. June to Aug also Mon and Tues 10am-12noon and 1.30-5pm.

Exloo
Museumboerderij Bebinghehoes (mu- seum farm)
Kinderboerderij (children's farm)
Zuiderhoofdstraat 6
Open: June to Sept Mon to Fri 10am-5pm, Sat 12noon-4pm. Sept to May Mon to Fri 12noon-4pm (subject to change).

Frederiksoord
Horticultural School Garden
Maj van Swietenlaan 15
Open: May to Sept daily 10am-4.30pm.

* Klokkenmuseum
Maj van Swietenlaan 17
Open: May to Sept, Mon to Fri 10am-5pm, Sun 2- 5pm.

Hoogeveen
* Museum Venendal
Hoofdstraat 9
Open: Mon to Fri 10am-noon and 2-4.30pm, Sat 2- 4.30pm.

Orvelte Saxon Village
Dorpstraat 3
Open: Apr to mid-Oct, Mon to Fri 9.30am-5pm; Sat and Sun 11am-5pm.

Meppel
* Graphisch Museum Drenthe (printing museum)
Kleine Oever 11
Open: Tues to Sat 1-5pm. Closed 1 Jan 30 April, Ascension Day, 25-6 and 31 Dec.

Roden
* Nederlandsmuseum Kinderwereld
Brink 31
Open: Mar to Sept, Mon to Sat and public holidays 10am-noon and 2- 5pm, Sun 2-5pm.

Ruinerwolde
Museumboerderij (museum farm)
Doctor Larijweg 21-21a
Open: Mon to Sat 9-5pm. Closed public holidays.

Schoonebeek
Museumboerderij 'Zwaantje Hans-Stokman's Hof'
Burg. Osselaan 5
Open: July to Aug Mon to Fri 10am-5pm. May to June Mon to Fri 1-5pm.

Schoonoord
Openlucht museum 'De Zeven Marken'
Tramstraat 73
Open: Apr to Oct, daily 9am-6pm.

Westerbork
Museumboerderij In De Ar
Hoofdstraat 42-44
Open: May to Sept Mon to Sat 9-5pm, Sun 1-5pm.

Nederlands Museum van de Knipkunst (art of paper cutting)
Hoofdtstraat 16
Open: May to Sept Mon to Fri 10am-5pm, Sat 10am-2pm.

Zuidlaren
De Sprookjeshof (fairytale park)
Groningerstraat 10
Open: Easter to mid-Oct, daily, 9am-6pm.

Zuidwolde
Museum De Wemme (handcart museum)
Burgemeester Tonckenstraat 49
Open: Easter to mid-Sept Mon 1-5pm, Tues to Fri 10am-5pm. (Pewter workshop open Tues to Sat 10am-5pm.)

10

AROUND HILVERSUM AND AMERSFOORT

The two towns of Hilversum and Amersfoort, although in different provinces, are linked by beautiful heaths and woodland extending from the shores of the Gooimeer and Eemmeer in the north, to the Utrechtse Heuvelrug in the south. North of Amersfoort lies the Eemland polder and the old twin villages of Bunschoten/Spakenburg, and to the east is the Gelderse Vallei. Many historic buildings, including castles and palaces, are to be seen, also the best-preserved fortress town in Holland and Napoleon's pyramid at Austerlitz. The region is particularly pleasant for cycling along the paths which criss-cross the heathland of 't Gooi, north and east of Hilversum, and the State Forest area of Vuursche to the south and east, linked through quiet minor roads and paths to Amersfoort and the extensive heath and wooded areas south of the town.

Route 23: Around Hilversum. Approx 63km

Hilversum was originally a poor heathland village, until the coming of the railway from Amsterdam to Amersfoort, and the growth of the textile industry. The present town is relatively modern, and most of the buildings are nineteenth century. The St Vitus Church, with its 98m tower, was designed by the architect who was also responsible for both the Centraal Station and the Rijksmuseum in Amsterdam. A good example of twentieth-century design is the fine town hall, built in 1931 to a design far ahead of its time. The VVV in Hilversum can supply a leaflet describing the buildings and the many sculptures around the town. Hilversum is best known as the centre of Dutch radio and television broadcasting. Other interests are catered for by the Pinetum Blijdenstein, with 450 species of conifer, and the Dr Costerus botanical garden specialising in wild plants and herbs.

Owing to a complicated one-way system, follow local signs from the town centre along 's Gravelandse Weg, in the general direction of Weesp and Amsterdam. On approaching 's Graveland, turn right beside the canal and take the next turning to the left across the canal towards Ankeveen, where the road bears right alongside the lake, joining the main road at signpost 942, and turning left to Weesp. Cyclists may follow a winding route across the lakes from Ankeveen to **Weesp**. This village is now much industrialised, but the little eighteenth-century town hall contains an exhibition of Weesp porcelain dating from the eighteenth century. Follow the road beside the river, under the railway by the station, and follow signs to **Muiden**, going under the motorway. Cyclists may cross the river Vecht in Weesp and follow the river to Muiden. The locks here date back to 1694, and are still in use, with many boats passing through on their way from the IJ-meer to the lakes along the Vecht. The narrow streets of Muiden make parking difficult. The most interesting sight here is the castle or Muiderslot, a medieval brick building at the mouth of the river. It was rebuilt in the fourteenth century on the original foundations. Fully restored in 1948, it is now open to the public.

Return to the locks in Muiden, turn left and follow the narrow road alongside the canal, the Naarder Trekvaart, keeping the canal on the left. On reaching the Hakkelaarsbrug (about 2km) cyclists should cross the bridge and continue on the other side of the canal, then follow signs for Naarden-Vesting, otherwise a long diversion is necessary. Motorists should rejoin the main road, as the canal road is not a through road for cars. Follow signs for Naarden-Vesting, then, after leaving the main road, Parking-Centrum, crossing the bridge over the moats. Visitors arriving at about 1pm may be startled by a loud report, as a gun is fired daily .

Naarden-Vesting (Fortress Naarden) is a perfect example of a seventeenth-century fortified town, but with an even older history. The present layout evolved with streets in an oval shape with a church in the centre , so that by 1560 the usual walls with gates, towers and moat existed. In 1572 the town was completely destroyed by the Spanish, but rebuilt 24 years later with six bastions, five gates and an artificial harbour, and was captured by the French in 1672. Retaken by William III, the whole system was rebuilt in 1688. Finally, during World War I, the fortress was again put on a war footing even though Holland was neutral.

In one of the casemates there is the Vestingmuseum which shows these developments and military methods, as well as an exhibition dealing with the experiences of Naarden in World War II. Because of the double ring of moats and the star-shaped fortifications, access to the town is limited, but once inside explore the narrow cobbled streets of the town and the paths along the ramparts between the double moats.

The fifteenth-century St Vitus or Grote Kerk, stands in the centre of the town. There is a sixteenth-century choir screen inside, and the tower may be climbed for a fine view, across to Flevoland, and over the town fortifications below. In Turfpoortstraat, in a house built in 1615, is the Comenius Museum. This commemorates the seventeenth-century philosopher who advocated the use of illustrations in childrens' school books, and who lived and is buried here in Naarden.

Leaving the fortress by the exit towards the south-east, turn left along Huizer Straatweg, under the motorway and follow Naarder Straat through an area of country estates to the centre of **Huizen**, then turn left along Karel Doormanlaan to the harbour area. Formerly an old fishing port on the shore of the Zuiderzee, this is now a rapidly developing yachting marina and centre for watersports.

Cyclists from Naarden may leave the fortress via the ramparts and along Oostdijk, under the motorway, then follow cycle routes along the coast of the Gooimeer all the way to Huizen harbour. The eastern part of Huizen is being developed very rapidly and it is very difficult to find the way, because maps cannot keep up with the pace of road building!

South of Huizen is an area of heathland crossed by a number of foot and cycle paths, and from Huizen cars can follow Ceintuur Baan and Blaricummer Straat to **Blaricum**, and the twin village of **Laren**. These are rather exclusive, pleasant residential areas, with shady roads lined with holly hedges, and old farm houses situated between large and small villas.

Entering Laren via Toren Laan, on reaching the *brink*, turn right down Naarder Straat, and on the left at the cross-roads at Oude Drift is the Singer Museum, a cultural and art centre with collections of paintings by nineteenth- and twentieth-century French and Dutch Impressionists, and by the founder W.H. Singer (1868-1943). Returning to the town centre, bear right along Sevenaarstraat into Hilversumse Weg which leads to the motorway junction. Join the motorway A1 in the direction of Amersfoort, and be prepared to leave it again at the turn-off for Soest, in about 4km. This leads along the N221 road, which runs through some very pleasant wooded country with fine estates.

Just near the motorway turn-off is the mansion of Groeneveld, now the National Forest Centre. Its park is open to the public, and various exhibitions are arranged and regular concerts are held in the house. At **Soestdijk** (signpost 850) turn right; at this junction, on the right of the road, is the Soestdijk Palace, which until 1980 was the home of the Queen of the Netherlands. Built originally as a hunting lodge for the regent Willem III, it is not open to the public, but a very fine view of the front of the building may be obtained from the road.

In the area around Soest there are plenty of opportunities for horse riding, with many stables and equestrian centres.

Continue along the road from the palace, and take the right turn at signpost 860 towards Maartensdijk. At the next cross-roads a diversion to the right leads to Kasteel Drakensteyn, the country house of Queen Beatrix, but it is not open to the public. From the crossroads continue to Maartensdijk, then turn right to Hollandsche Rading and Hilversum.

South-west of Amersfoort the large area of heathland known as the Leusder-Heide is a military training ground, and at **Soesterberg**, about 7km out of Amersfoort on the road to Utrecht, is the Air Force Museum, with aircraft and other material showing the history of the Dutch air force.

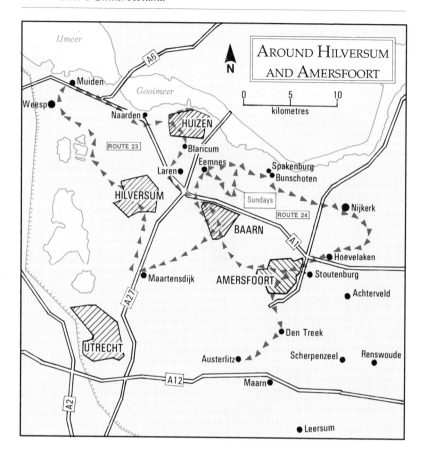

Route 24: The Eemland Polder. Approx 50km

Amersfoort makes a good centre for exploring the Eemland Polder. Leave the town in the direction of Soest, and just after crossing the railway near Soestdijk station, turn off the main road, on to Stadhouders Laan and Toren Laan, into the centre of **Baarn**. This was once described as a 'fashionable village' and the description could still apply, particularly as regards the surroundings and the Baarnse Bos. On the *brink* is a fifteenth-century Dutch Reformed Church with a fourteenth-century tower, and in nearby Java Laan, are the Peking Garden and the Hortus Botanicus (the botanical garden of Utrecht University), both open to the public. From the town centre, follow Eemnesser Weg towards the motorway junction, then turn right, under the motorway and along Wakkeren Dijk to **Eemnes**, passing a number of old farms along the way. The village is situated on the edge of the polder, in pleasant surroundings, and has a fifteenth-century church with tower, dating from the time when this was a much larger community. The road now runs on as Meentweg, still going past old farms. A short way past the village, is a turning on the right which runs out across the polder to a small ferry across the river Eem to Eemdijk. This ferry does not run after dusk or on Sundays, when Eemdijk may be reached by way of Baarn and Eembrugge.

The road to Eemdijk, along the other side of the river, will bring you back to the ferry landing, from where the straight road to Bunschoten/ Spakenburg can be followed across the polder. On reaching the main road, follow signs for 'Centrum'. These lead to **Spakenburg**, a very old fishing village with narrow streets and an inner harbour where traditional boats may be seen, often with eel nets hanging from their masts to dry. The dyke at the entrance to the harbour gives good views across the Eemmeer, and there is a fine new marina. The fishing village of Spakenburg is joined to the twin village of **Bunschoten**, an agricultural community, where old farmhouses stand close together on either side of the long street.

The most notable feature of these twin villages is the unique traditional

The Koppelpoort spanning the river Eem at Amersfoort

A Walk Through Old Amersfoort

Long before receiving its first charter in 1259, the lovely medieval town of Amersfoort originated as a settlement on a ford on the river Amer, now called the Eem. It is the only European town whose centre is surrounded by a double ring of canals, and it has many exceptionally fine historic buildings. The walk here takes in those buildings of greatest interest. Many of the sights are widely scattered, and those with more time can obtain a booklet in English from the VVV with a detailed longer town walk.

Parking in the town is not easy, so park at the railway station, near the VVV office (P+R car park), and take a local bus from the station to Hellestraat near the modern town hall. With this on the left, walk across Westsingel and cross the canal, turning right into Breestraat. Ahead is the great Onze Lieve Vrouwe Toren, all that is left of the former church, built in the fifteenth century and blown up accidentally in 1787 when used as an ammunition store. According to legend, the church was built as a place of pilgrimage after miracles occurred as a result of a simple peasant girl's action in throwing a statuette of the Virgin Mary into the canal. The remains of the statuette are now kept in the old Catholic Church in 't Zand, on the north of the inner town. From the tower, walk across the churchyard to the Visbank, still in regular use on Friday mornings by fishmongers from nearby Spakenburg. On the corner of the churchyard is the Kapelhuis, once used for the administration of the church, and now used as a gallery. On the other side turn right along Lieve Vrouwestraat, cross over Langestraat, and continue opposite along Scherbierstraat, at the end of which is Muurhuizen. These unique 'wall-houses' almost completely encircle the inner town, and are built on the town walls.

Turn left along Muurhuizen to Korte Gracht, where across the canal, on the right, is the house Tinnenburg, a beautiful wall house, the oldest known such building, dating from before 1414. At the side of the house are the remains of the old water gate. Also, by looking down past Tinnenburg to the next canal bridge, under Zuid Singel, the so-called 'house with the purple window panes' may be seen. The glass has not been painted, but has changed colour with age. Just beyond the trees, further along the same canal, may be seen the pointed turrets of the Monnikendam, a water gate on the second town wall, built in 1380-1450. Although the walls were demolished during the last century, the gate was preserved, and it stands at the confluence of a number of small streams from the Gelderse Vallei which flows into the river Eem.

Continue to walk along Muurhuizen, and on the right is the tower known as the Plompe or Dieventoren, built in the thirteenth century as part of the first town wall, and used as the town prison for many years. The little steeple on top was placed there in 1860, having been taken from the old Latin School. The passage through the base of the tower was made in 1942. There are many other fine old houses along this part of the wall, and at the far end of Langestraat is the Kamperbinnenpoort, all that remains of a much larger gate in the first town wall. A pewter workshop nearby may be visited.

From the gate, continue again along Muurhuizen to Kerkstraat, on the left, and through here to the Appelmarkt, where the beautiful 'Onder de Linde' is situated. Dating from the sixteenth century, this building with its lovely stepped gable and attractive windows is now used as a bar, a quite different use from its original purpose as a home for the canons from the nearby church of St Joris. The tower dates from the thirteenth century, and the main building was completed in 1534; it contains a lovely sixteenth-century rood screen and a very fine organ. The outside of the south porch, built around 1500, is particularly beautiful, with much carved stonework around the windows. Nestling against the wall of the church is the little seventeenth-century Botermarkt where butter was weighed and sold.

The large square known as the Hof is surrounded by old houses with attractive gables. From the corner of Hof, follow Lavendelstraat to Havik, site of the town docks in the Middle Ages. Looking to the right provides one of the most attractive views of Muurhuizen, with the sluice where the canal water ran below the houses into the harbour. Turn left along Havik, cross over the bridge into Nieuweweg and along to 't Zand, turn left again, and on the left, on Westsingel, are the three old wall-houses which now house the Museum Flehite which deals with the history of the town. One of the houses is original, while the others had neo-Renaissance gables added in the nineteenth century.

From the museum return towards 't Zand and turn left along Kleine Spui towards the imposing Koppelpoort, a combined land and water gate built over the river Eem around 1427. Two arches span the roads and a central arch over the water has a wooden gate lowered by means of two treadmills which still exist. The town centre may be reached again along Westsingel. From here, either return to the station by bus, or look around the shops in the pedestrianised Varkensmarkt and Utrechtse-straat. Amersfoort is known for its jewellery shops, which sell beautiful traditional silver ornaments. From the Varkensmarkt (Pig Market) walk down Arnhemse-straat to the wide ring road, and on the left is a huge Ice Age boulder, mounted on a plinth. This is the famous 'Amersfoortse Kei', weighing some 9 tons.

The wide road where the boulder stands is known as Stads-ring, and was once the outer moat which ran around the south and east of the town. To the north the moat is still in existence and the whole ring has been landscaped for most of its length, with trees and small parks making it very attractive. The town is a garrison town, and some old barracks still exist, some being classified as listed buildings.

Traditional sailing boats in the harbour at Spakenburg

costume worn by many of the women as a matter of course, not as a tourist attraction, and remarkable for their preservation of details from late-medieval dress. The outstanding feature is a huge shoulder-piece made from brightly-coloured cloth sewn onto a special linen, then starched to make it stand out. Some are hand-painted, and it is possible to see them being made. During the summer an exhibition of historical costumes, model boats, furniture, etc is held behind the Noorderkerk.

Returning along the main street of Bunschoten, turn left at signpost 3016 and go across the polder, cross the motorway bridge to **Nijkerk**, an attractive town on the edge of the Gelderse Vallei. The beautiful eighteenth-century organ in the the Grote or Catharinakerk is used for recitals during the summer months, and on Thursday evenings in summer the carillon is played. Exhibitions about the old town are held in the Waag, which also houses the Netherlands Electricity Museum. The view along the canal (the Arker-vaart) from near the town hall, towards the Nijkerkernauw is very attractive, and the canal is often busy with pleasure craft.

The return to Amersfoort may be made by leaving Nijkerk along the road running south through **Driedorp**. Just past the windmill 'De Hoop', turn right and follow the road through Zwartebroek to **Hoevelaken**. This is a prosperous village on the outskirts of Amersfoort. The manor Huis te Hoevelaken houses art exhibitions. Continue under the motorway junctions back into Amersfoort.

South and south-west of Amersfoort is a very attractive area of wooded and park-like country with big estates, stretching across to the Utrechtse Heuvelrug. The area is particularly suited to exploring by bicycle, and a circular, signed route known as the 'UMO Route' takes in part of it; but take care as in places the cycle paths are rather sandy.

Also to the south is the large estate known as 'Den Treek'. Near the mansion is a little shop belonging to a wood carver, where a wide variety of craftwork is sold. Not far from here is **Austerlitz** where an artificial hill was built in 1804 by French soldiers encamped nearby, and was named after the Battle of Austerlitz in Czechoslovakia, where the French gained a victory over Russian and Austrian troops. Now 20m high, the pyramid had a tower added in 1894, and an access stairway built. A small fee is charged for ascending to the balcony on the mound, but the view on a clear day is worth the effort. Those who think Holland is flat are in for a surprise.

Additional Information

Places of Interest

Amersfoort
* Museum Flehite
Westsingel 50
Open: Tues to Fri 10am-5pm; Sat, Sun 2-5pm. Closed public holidays.

Baarn
National Forest Centre
Kasteel Groeneveld
Open: Mid-Jan to Nov, Tues, Wed to Fri 10am-5pm, Sat and Sun, noon-5pm.

Canton Park and Peking Garden
Faas Eliaslaan 49-51
Open: All year, Mon to Fri 8.30am until $^1/_2$ hour before sunset.

Hilversum
Blijdenstein Pinetum
van der Lindenlaan 125
Open: All year, Mon to Fri 10am-4pm. Also second Sat each month 10am-4pm.

Dr Costerus Botanical Garden
Zonnelaan 2a
Open: All year, daily sunrise to sunset.

Hoevelaken
Huis te Hoevelaken
Changing art exhibitions. Enquire locally for opening times.

Laren
* Singer Museum
Oude Drift 1
Open: Tues to Sat 11am-5pm, Sun and public holidays noon-5pm. Closed 1 Jan, Good Fri, Easter, Whitsun, 30 Apr, 25 Dec.

Muiden
* Muiderslot (castle)
Herengracht 1
Open: All year, Mon to Fri 10am-4pm; Sun and public holidays 1-4pm. May-Oct open until 5pm. Guided tours.

Naarden
Comenius Museum
Turfpoortstraat 27
Open: Jan to mid-Dec Tues to Sun 2-5pm. 30 April 1-5pm. Closed Easter Monday and Whit Monday.

* Vestingmuseum
Westwalstraat 6
Open: Easter to Oct, Mon to Fri 10am-4.30pm; Sat, Sun and public holidays noon-5pm.

Nijkerk
Nederlands Elektriciteits Museum
Waagplein 2a
Open: Apr to Oct, Tues to Sat 9.30am-5pm, Sun 2-5pm.

Soesterberg
Airforce Museum Kamp van Zeist
Kampweg
Open: 1 Apr to 30 Dec, Tues to Fri 10am-4.30pm; Sun, Easter Mon and Whit Mon noon-4.30pm. Closed Christmas.

Weesp
Gemeentemuseum
Nieuwstraat 41
Open: Mid-Jun to mid-Sept Mon to Fri 9.30am-12.30pm, Sat 2-5pm.

11

THE VELUWE

The Veluwe is one of the largest areas of open countryside in Western Europe, being some 50km from north to south and about the same wide. It is one of three regions in the Province of Gelderland, and is mainly parkland, woods and heath. Bounded on the north by the Veluwemeer, by the rivers IJssel and Rhine to the east and south, and by the Gelderse Vallei on the west, the largest towns are Arnhem and Apeldoorn. However, there are a number of other interesting towns and villages, mainly around the edges. The region is divided by an east-west motorway passing by Apeldoorn, to the south of which are two national parks.

Route 25: Through the North of the Veluwe. Approx 100km

On the northern perimeter of the Veluwe, on the coast of the IJsselmeer, lie the old sea ports of Harderwijk and Elburg. To the east is the old Hanseatic town of Hattem on the western bank of the river IJssel, and to the south are the towns of Heerde and Epe. Crossing back towards Harderwijk, across woods and heathland, the route passes through Vierhouten, Elspeet and Uddel.

Harderwijk may be reached from Amersfoort via Nijkerk and the motorway, or from Flevoland across the Harderbrug. An old Zuiderzee and Hanseatic port dating from 1231, and the departure point for many ships sailing to the East Indies, the port was no longer able to flourish due to the silting up of the Zuiderzee in the eighteenth century. Remains of the medieval ramparts may be seen at the Vispoort on the Strand Boulevard, and in Smeepoortstraat near the *Kazerne* (barracks), originally a convent and later converted to accommodate colonial troops. The Veluws Museum, in an eighteenth-century gentleman's house in Donkerstraat, has displays of local history and geology, and the former town hall (1727) in the Markt is now a music school. Near the old harbour is the Dolphinarium, one of the biggest in Europe.

Leave Harderwijk by the old road past the approach to the Harderbrug, towards **Nunspeet**, a popular seaside and country holiday resort. Next the road passes through **Doornspijk**, one of the oldest villages in the

THE VELUWE

North-West Veluwe, before reaching Elburg.

❄   **Elburg** is a beautiful thirteenth-century town on the former Zuiderzee, planned in an almost perfect square surrounded by moat, ramparts, dry moat and walls. Parking is strictly controlled, and a notice at the approach to the town advises motorists to 'go further on foot'! There is a car park near the harbour, approached from the road leading into the town from the Elburgerbrug. From here, the town is entered via the old Vispoort-

🏰   brug, a lovely square tower with turrets at the corners and an ornate spire. The town centre still retains much of its old character, with old brick walls, round bastion towers and casemates between the outer ramparts. The inner moat is now dry in most places, and is used for car parking, gardens, allotments, etc. As the town is entered, through the Vispoort, a beautiful stepped gable may be seen on the left, on the corner of Ellestraat. Vispoortstraat leads straight ahead, to cross Beekstraat into Jufferenstraat. Beekstraat is a wide tree-lined street with a small canal running through the centre. In this street are several beautifully restored stepped- and bell-shaped gables. Continue into Jufferenstraat and take the first turning on the left (Schapensteeg), at the end of which, on the left, is an old decorated door. Turn right into Van Kinsbergenstraat. On the corner is the fourteenth-century castle, and next door is the former town hall.

The VVV (in Jufferenstraat opposite the abbey), can supply a detailed

The Vispoort rising above Elburg's tiled roofs

town walk with map, which is especially interesting to those who like old architectural monuments. Most visitors will, however, prefer to wander at leisure through this lovely little town, where all the streets except one, the Krommesteeg (Crooked Alley), are completely straight. A walk round the ramparts gives good views of the historic buildings. Of special interest are the old abbey buildings, containing the town museum. An annexe of the museum is housed in the Vispoort, where it is also possible to visit the casemates under the town walls. In Ledigestede is the impressive Feithenhof, built in 1740 as an almshouse for twenty-four elderly people. Along Noorderwalstraat and Oosterwalstraat are old houses built into the walls themselves, best seen from the ramparts on the east of the town. Near the Vispoort, in the dry moat on the west side, is an open-air rope-walk. The fascinating craft of ropemaking is rarely seen these days, and visitors are welcome to watch.

Leaving Elburg, the road swings away from the shore past **Oldebroek**, an old farming village with eighteenth and nineteenth-century farm-houses along the road. Here it is possible to see the old Veluwse costume being worn. The church tower dates from 1200, and inside are some painted ceilings in the choir vaults, an old oak pulpit and some seven-teenth-century silver. The local museum is in the town hall. In this part of the country the farmhouses are quite different from those in the north, being smaller, often completely thatched, with roofs coming very low at the sides. The living area is at the front, and the animals are kept in the rear and side parts, all under one roof.

Keep to the main road, continuing to Wezep, then turn to the left through Hattemerbroek to **Hattem**, an old fortress town on the boundary between North Veluwe and the IJssel Valley. The VVV can supply a plan and notes, but the walk decribed here covers most points of interest.

From Hattem rejoin the main road near the river, and continue south through the hilly wooded country around **Heerde**, which is a centre for tree and rose nurseries, and on to Epe after passing under the motorway. **Epe** is a popular holiday resort which also has a district museum with an exhibition of the local costumes from the Eastern Veluwe area.

Beyond Epe, to the south, is Emst and **Vaassen**, where a turning on the right leads to Kasteel de Cannenburgh, a very fine moated castle built in 1543, and enlarged in later years. It has been lived in continuously through the centuries, and is now cared for by a foundation which preserves castles in Gelderland. Both the castle and its grounds are open.

The route now leaves the main road and heads across the heath and forest areas to the east. Much of this is Crown Land, and at certain times some roads are closed to cars, so watch for closure and diversion signs. The route here avoids these problems. From the castle take the road east past a water mill and church to *paddestoel* 21088, turn right and go straight on for $2\frac{1}{2}$km. Turn right at *paddestoel* 20177, and bear right (20176) at Niersen. Continue along this road to Gortel. Here, turn sharply back to the left at signpost 2870, crossing some lovely heathland and wooded country

A Walk in Hattem

Of the four town gates in this ancient town, only the fourteenth-century Dijkpoort remains. The walk starts from this gate, a fairy-tale-like tower with four corner turrets. Through the archway, Kruisstraat leads to the Markt, dominated by the church, a six-teenth-century basilica now the Reformed Church. In the square is the large Stadhuis, built in 1619, with ornate decorated gables, and a pump dated 1776. Between the Stadhuis and the church is Kerk-hofstraat, at the end of which is the beautiful sixteenth-century Daendelshuis. Turning left, on the corner of Ridderstraat is a bakery museum where bread is baked in the traditional medieval manner. Continue across Kruisstraat into Achterstraat, at the end of which is the Regional Museum, incorporating the Anton Pieck museum and the Voermanhuis. At the end of the street, where it joins Molen-belt on the right and Zuiderwal on the left, is the original town pump, erected in 1733. Looking to the right, the huge tower mill will be seen. Built in 1852 and recently restored, it is still in working order. Walk back along Kerkstraat to the Markt, to an old seven-teenth-century house on the right. Opposite is Korte Kerkstraat, a small street with attractive old houses, looking almost like a village street in the middle of the town. At the end is the Hoge Huis, built on the town walls in 1580. If time permits, walk along the footpath beside the town walls and the moat, then return along Kruisstraat.

to **Vierhouten**, a very popular country holiday resort with almost unlim-ited opportunities for walking and cycling. At Vierhouten, turn left and pass signpost 6918 in the direction of Elspeet. The road passes between the Vierhouter Bos on the left and the Elspeeter Heide on the right, part of the latter being a military training area.

Elspeet is another village in the middle of a very pleasant area for walking and cycling, and all these roads are picturesque. There are fre-quent parking places, with walks along the many paths, and deer and wild pigs roam freely, although one is lucky to see them.

At Elspeet, continue south at signpost 196, to the village of Uddel, where the road bears right, passing Uddelermeer (swimming is possible here) and on to **Garderen**. The church tower dates from the eleventh century, and was once used as a beacon for fishing boats on the Zuiderzee. In the village is a farmstead originally dating from 1326, although now with a nineteenth-century appearance. At signpost 3030, take the road for Putten, and in the town centre (signpost 2939) turn right and follow signs to Ermelo and so back to Harderwijk.

From Harderwijk, a drive of some 30km leads to **Apeldoorn**. Well situated and with first-class facilities, it is a holiday and congress town in the centre of an area of beautiful natural scenery. The town itself, although very pleasant and with good shops, is used as a starting point for tours in the surrounding countryside, details of which may be obtained from the VVV office by the railway station. Some of these tours, which last about $2^1/_2$ to 3 hours, go through the State Game Reserve, where wild animals may be seen. Cars are not allowed, and booking on the tours is essential.

On the northern edge of the town centre is the Royal Park of the palace *Het Loo*. From the station follow Nieuwstraat, Loo Laan and into Amersfoortseweg, where the park, palace entrance and free car park, can be found. Originally, William III, Prince of Orange, purchased a small medieval manor house for use as a hunting lodge, then in 1684 it was established as a palace. The English Princess (afterwards Queen) Mary Stuart, wife of William III, laid the foundation stone, in 1685, of a new palace, the gardens of which were even finer than those of Versailles. Members of the House of Orange inhabited the palace from the time of William III to Queen Wilhelmina, who ruled for 57 years until her abdication in 1948. It is no longer used by the Royal Family, and has been fully restored, following the seventeenth-century plans. Together with the restored gardens, it is now a national museum. Visitors can see how the Royal Family lived here during three centuries, and how the House of Orange Nassau was linked to the Netherlands. The Royal Mews are also open, and house a collection of carriages, coaches and sledges. The park

The gardens of the Royal Palace Het Loo at Apeldoorn

is open to pedestrians only, with several waymarked routes. The old castle is in the park, but only the exterior may be seen.

In and around Apeldoorn are many reminders and memorials to those lost, both at home and abroad, during World War II, including the many resistance fighters who operated in and around the countryside here.

On the outskirts of the town to the west is the large recreation park 'Berg en Bos', with both natural and man-made attractions. Within its boundaries is the 'Apenheul', where apes of many kinds are free to move among the trees and among the visitors. A group of gorillas live on an island within the park. At the nearby Julianatoren there is a playground offering many attractions for children.

Another way of spending a day is to take the steam train from Apeldoorn south along the eastern edge of the Veluwe to Dieren. During the summer a combined excursion trip may be taken on the train, continuing with a 3 hour horse-drawn wagon ride through the beautiful forest scenery. Another trip combines the steam train ride with a boat trip from Dieren up the river IJssel to Zutphen, returning to Apeldoorn by normal train service. Both are available as day-trips from any station in Holland.

The Veluwe is not only one of the largest areas of open countryside in Western Europe, but it is unique for its variety of scenery and wildlife. Within this large area are two national parks, the National Park De Hoge Veluwe and the National Park Veluwezoom. The former is the most famous of the two, and from Apeldoorn a very pleasant circular drive may be made to include a visit to the park, within whose boundaries is a well known museum of modern art.

Route 26: A Drive Around the Hoge Veluwe. Approx 67km

Leave Apeldoorn by Arnhemseweg, under the motorway, and at Beekbergen turn left at signpost 216, and follow signs for **Loenen**. About 1km after crossing over the motorway, there is a car park on the left, near Holland's highest waterfall. This is 15m high in total, and there are three falls which cascade through the woods, with broad flights of steps on either side leading to pleasant woodland paths. Continue along the road to Loenen, and turn right at signpost 2454, taking the road across heathland towards the A50 motorway to Arnhem. Near the junction is a memorial to 117 Dutchmen who were shot in 1945 at Woeste Hoeve in retaliation for an attempt on the life of a German SS officer.

Cross the motorway and follow a narrow road winding through the forest to **Hoenderloo**, where there is one of the entrances to the National Park De Hoge Veluwe. Having paid the entrance fee, which covers all the exhibitions within the park, drive straight to the visitors' centre (*Bezoekerscentrum*). Maps, explanations and other exhibits will repay some study before setting off to explore the park, which covers a total of over 13,500 acres. About one half of this is heath, grassland and shifting sand. One quarter is planted woodland and the remainder is naturally-seeded Scots Pine. The woodland is mixed, and as far as possible the original character of the Veluwe landscape has been retained. Wildlife includes sparrowhawks, kestrels, woodpeckers, foxes, badgers, pine martens, weasels, together with deer, wild boar and mouflons, the longhaired sheep imported from Corsica.

Fences in certain parts of the park divide off areas where the larger and wilder animals roam freely, but normally cars can drive through about 32km of road, subject to a speed limit of 50kph (30mph). Certain roads are one-way, so watch for signs. There are also about 40km of cycle paths, together with extensive footpaths, all waymarked or signed. At the restaurant near the visitor centre are 'white bikes', which may be borrowed free of charge. The park is open all the year, from 8am to sunset, although some of the facilities might be closed in winter.

Within the park is the State Museum Kroller-Muller, a modern purpose-built complex which houses the world-famous collection of works by modern artists, including the renowned Van Gogh collection of 276 works. Adjacent is a sculpture garden with works by the world's best-known modern sculptors. Near the northern boundary of the park is the 'St Hubertus' hunting lodge with a splendid garden, open all year round.

A leaflet in English gives general information about the park and the best places to see the wildlife. However, the captions on exhibits in the visitor centre are only in Dutch, although brief descriptions in four languages are available. Likewise, walks through the park are only described in Dutch, although the maps are easy to follow, with coloured spots corresponding with coloured posts on the ground.

After exploring the park, leave by the Otterlo gate on the west side. In **Otterlo** is a tile museum with a unique collection of 7,000 tiles from the thirteenth century to the present day.

Take the road south along the edge of the national park, to Schaarsbergen and keep to this road as far as signpost 4716, turn left, and continue through **Deelen** to Hoenderloo. Turn right through the village, and at signpost 3239 take the road on the left which leads through the forest to Beekbergen, where a left turn will lead along the main road back to Apeldoorn. An alternative route from Hoenderloo is to continue ahead to the N304 road, turn right and follow this road along the edge of Ugchelse Bos back to Apeldoorn. Although a main road, this is a very pleasant route through attractive countryside.

Either from Apeldoorn, or after leaving the Hoge Veluwe National Park, there are good motorway routes to Arnhem.

Route 27: In and Around Arnhem

Arnhem is the capital of the Province of Gelderland, and the geography of the area shows why it grew in importance. Built on the north bank of the river Rhine and backed by steeply rising hills of the Veluwe, it is halfway between the densely-populated western part of Holland and the industrial Ruhr area of Germany, with the river providing a natural highway. With its motorway and rail links, Arnhem has become an important centre for industry and business.

Its bridge, as a major crossing of the Rhine, was of great importance during the final stages of World War II. The hilly wooded country north of the river and the flat country with open roads along dykes to the south explains the failure of the Allied forces to relieve their airbourne colleagues trying to hold the bridge intact. One wonders how the airborne troops managed to achieve what they did, when everything was clearly against them. During and after the unsuccessful airborne operation, until its eventual liberation after bitter fighting in April 1945, Arnhem was subjected to heavy shelling from across the Rhine, and the present town has been almost completely rebuilt since then.

Arnhem has seen much conflict during its long history and the town ramparts were not finally levelled until 1853, being replaced by boulevards. The bridge to the west is a modern structure, while that to the east, the former Rijnbrug, is now renamed John Frost Bridge after the British Parachute Brigade commander who held it during the fighting in 1944.

The older buildings have all been restored or rebuilt since the damage done during the war, and include the oldest building, St Pieters Gasthuis (1407) in Rijnstraat. The Grote or Eusebius Kerk was built between 1452 and 1650, the 98m high tower being a replacement for that destroyed in 1944. Nearby is the former Stadhuis, originally built in 1545 as the mansion of Maarten van Rossum, also called the Duivelshuis on account of the carvings on the front. In the Markt is the eighteenth-century Waag, near to the Huis der Provincie, the first public building to be erected after the war (1954). The Sabelspoort is the only remnant of the fortifications of 1440. Near the Stadhuis is the Gothic Walburgiskerk (1422), the oldest church in Arnhem. Just to the east is Airborneplein, a sunken garden in the centre of a busy roundabout, in which is a broken column from the ruins of Arnhem, bearing the date 17 September 1944.

In the immediate vicinity of Arnhem are several museums and attractions which should not be missed. West of the town, towards Oosterbeek is the Electrum, a museum of the electrical power and engineering industry. In **Oosterbeek** is the Airborne Museum, housed in the old Hotel Hartenstein, the headquarters of the 1st British Airborne Division during the operations of 1944. There are displays of equipment used here at the time, models, photographs and dioramas which, with spoken commentaries, explain the operation and its consequences. The conditions within the command post in the cellars have been reproduced with life-sized models of the people involved. Opposite the museum is the airborne memorial, while a short distance away, in a select residential suburb, is the beautifully landscaped and maintained war cemetary, resting place for nearly two thousand British and Allied soldiers.

By contrast a short distance along the river to the west is the Rhine Terrace Westerbouwing, a leisure park with children's playground, scooter tracks, cable cars, etc. Further west is the thirteenth-century Kasteel Doorwerth which houses the Netherlands Hunting Museum.

At **Bennekom**, north-west of Doorwerth, is the small museum 'Kijk en

One of the different types of Dutch windmill at the Arnhem Open Air Museum

Luister' (Look and Listen), with an interesting collections of old costumes, tools and mechanical musical instruments. North of here is the Ginkelse Heide, where many of the airbourne forces were dropped in 1944 before trying to reach the Arnhem Bridges.

Back in Arnhem, north of the town, is the famous Open Air Museum, set in a lovely park. Dozens of farmhouses, cottages, mills and houses have been moved to here from their original locations and equipped with authentic articles. Here are the different styles of farmhouse from the various regions of Holland. In addition there is an example of every type of Dutch windmill, a boatyard from Marken, old craft workshops where demonstrations are given and a very fine costume collection. Although the museum grounds are open daily, many of the buildings, such as the costume hall, are closed on Monday.

Next to the Open Air Museum is Burgers Safari Park, one of the best zoos in Europe, with animals in as natural an environment as possible, yet visitors can watch them in safety.

Those who think that Holland is flat should travel east from the museum and drive round the narrow lanes of the Nationaal Park Veluwezoom. Kasteel Rosendael, with its lovely gardens and famous shell gallery stands near the bottom of the winding road, with steep gradients and hairpin bends, leading to **Posbank**, where there are superb views and good walking. It is forbidden to drive or cycle after dusk.

Additional Information

Places of Interest

Apeldoorn
*Paleis Het Loo (Royal Palace)
Amersfoortseweg
Open: Tues to Sun 10am-5pm. Closed 25 Dec.

Park Berg en Bos
Apenheul
J. C. Wilslaan 21
Open: Apr to June 9.30am-5pm, July and Aug 9.30am-6pm, Sept and Oct 10am-5pm.

Arnhem
Burghers Dieren and Safari Park
Schelmseweg 85
Open: Daily 9am-8pm, Safari Park closes 5pm.

*Het Nederlands Openlucht Museum
Haeferlaan
Open: Apr to Oct daily 9am-5pm. Many buildings closed Mon.

*Elektrum Museum
Klingelbeekseweg 45
Open: Mon to Fri 2-5pm. Closed public holidays.

Bennekom, near Ede
Kijk en Luister Museum
Kerkstraat 1
Open: May to mid-Sept, Tues to Sat 2-5pm; mid-Sept to Apr Wed and Fri 2-5pm. Closed on public holidays.

Doorwerth
Kasteel Doorwerth
Fonteinallee 4
Open: April to Oct Tue to Fri, Easter Mon, 5 May, Whit Mon 10am-5pm. Sat, Sun and 30 April 1-5pm.

Netherlands Hunting Museum
Kasteel Doorwerth
Fonteinallee 4
Open: April to Oct Tue to Fri 10an-5pm. Sat, Sun and holidays 1-5pm. Nov to Mar Sat, Sun and holidays 1-5pm. Also

open Mon in school holidays 10am-5pm.
Admission charge in summer includes
entrance to castle.

Elburg

Gemeentemuseum
Jufferenstraat 8
Open: Tues to Fri 9.30am-noon and 2-
5pm. Mon 2-5.

Epe

Veluws Klederdrachten Museum
Markt 5
Open: Mon to Fri May to Sept 1.30-
4.30pm.

Harderwijk

Dolfinarium Harderwijk
Strandboulevard Oost 1
Open: Early Mar to Oct daily 9am-5pm.

* Veluws Museum
Donkerstraat 4
Open: May to Sept, Mon to Fri 10am-
5pm, Sat 1-4pm. Oct to May, Mon to Fri
10am-5pm. Closed public holidays.

Hattem

Museum Hattem and Anton Pieck
  Museum
Achterstraat 46-48
Open: July and Aug, daily except Sun
10am-4.30pm; Sept to June, Tues to Sat
10am-4.30pm.

Hoenderloo

* Bakkerijmuseum Het Warme Land
  (bakery museum)
Kerkhofstraat 13
Open: May to Sept Tues to Sat 9.30am-
4pm. Oct to April Wed and Sat 9.30am-
4pm. Closed Jan, Feb and public holidays.

St Hubertus Hunting Lodge
Hoge Veluwe National Park
Open: May to Oct, Mon to Fri 10am-
5pm.

Oldebroek

Oudeheidkame Oldebroek
Zuiderzeestraaatweg 139
Open: Mar to 20 Dec Tues and Fri 2-
5pm.

Oosterbeek

Airborne Museum
Utrechtseweg 232

Open: Mon to Sat 11am-5pm, Sun and
public holidays noon-5pm. Closed 1 Jan
and 25 Dec.

De Westerbouwing Rhine Terrace
Open: May to Sept, daily, 10am-6pm.

Otterlo

Hoge Veluwe National Park, Visitor
  Centre and Kröller-Müller Museum
  (modern art)
Entrances also at Hoenderloo and
Schaarsbergen.
Open: Park daily 8am to sunset. Mu-
seum Apr to Nov, Tues to Sat 10am-
5pm, Sun and public holidays 11am-
5pm (Easter Day 1-5pm). Nov to Mar,
Tues to Sat 10am-5pm, Sun 1-5pm.

* It Noflik Ste (tile museum)
Eikenzoom 10
Open: Tues to Sat 10am-noon and 2-
5pm; Sun and public holidays 2-4pm.

Rozendaal

Kasteel Rosendael
Kerklaan
Open: Mid-May to mid-Sept, Tues to Sat
10am-5pm; Sun 1pm-5pm.

Vaassen

Kasteel de Cannenburg
Maarten van Rossumplein 4
Open: Apr to Oct, Tues to Sat 10am-
5pm; Sun and 30 Apr 1pm-5pm. Last
entry 4pm.

Boat Trips

Arnhem

Rederij Heymen
Kantoorschip
Rijnkade
Arnhem
☎ 085 515181
Various cruises in summer, including a
cruise on the Rhine and IJssel rivers.

Steam Train Lines

Apeldoorn-Dieren

July and Aug, daily except Sat.
NS Stations, Apeldoorn and Dieren.
Enquire from VVV.
☎ 055 788421

12

WEST AND CENTRAL OVERIJSSEL
AND THE IJSSEL VALLEY

The very large province of Overijssel is divided into three administrative areas, namely West Overijssel, Salland and Twente. In this chapter we cover West Overijssel and the whole of the IJssel Valley, including that part which lies in the province of Gelderland.

Route 28: The Old Coastline and The Broads. Approx 100km

The old sea-dyke of the former Zuiderzee still exists, and it is possible to drive along the road on top of the dyke all the way from Vollenhove in the south to Lemmer in the north. Our route takes in a large part of the dyke, passes through the reed-fens of the Weerribben to Steenwijk, then to the broadlands around Giethoorn. The area around Staphorst is then explored before returning to the starting place at Hasselt which is conveniently accessible from Zwolle, the provincial capital. Part of this route follows the ANWB signed 'North-West Overijssel Route'.

Hasselt is an old fortified Hanseatic town on the Zwarte Water, chartered in 1252. Scattered throughout the town but particularly along the picturesque tree-lined Herengracht and in the Hoogstraat, are attractive seventeenth-century houses, and the Waterpoortje in Ridderstraat is a remnant of the fourteenth-century town walls. In the Markt is the Stadhuis, parts of which date back to 1500, with a fine collection of old weapons and paintings, and archives relating to the history of the town. Nearby is the Grote or St Stephanuskerk, with a massive tower, dating from 1466. There is an early sixteenth-century wall painting of St Christopher on one of the supporting pillars of the tower. An attractive park along the Zwarte Water contains a corn windmill dated 1784; it stands at the beginning of a stone dyke built in the eighteenth century against the onslaught of the water from the former Zuiderzee.

Leave Hasselt in the direction of Genemuiden. It is best to follow the signed ANWB route at this point, because there is a double bridge leading out of the town and it is easy to lose the way. Cyclists have separately signed routes where roads are for motor vehicles only.

Genemuiden, a town dating from 1275, lies on the Zwolse Diep, and its

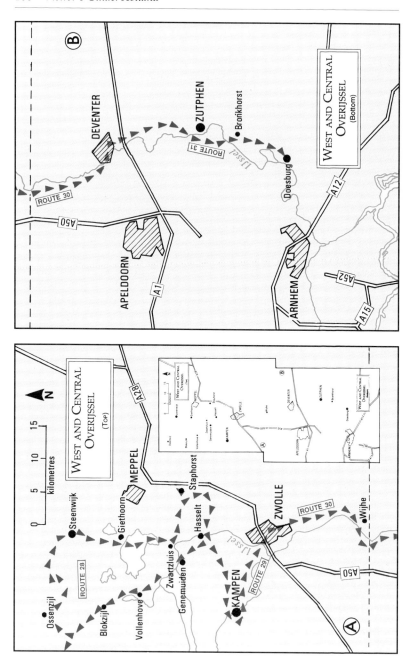

inhabitants have for centuries made their living from the rushes used for making high-quality rush matting. This cottage industry is now mechanised. From Genemuiden, cross the Zwolse Diep by ferry and continue left along the dyke road towards **Vollenhove**, an old fishing port first mentioned in 944, and known for its fine old buildings and picturesque harbours. The old town hall (1621) near the inner harbour is now a restaurant, and next to it is the Grote or St Nicolaaskerk dating from the end of the fifteenth century. Inside is an organ dated 1686, and many monuments to the noble families who came to the town in the fourteenth century when it was the country seat of the Bishops of Utrecht. Opposite the church is the seventeenth-century Latin School building with a lovely stepped gable and high arched windows. The former French School building next door is now a hotel.

On the east side of the town, follow the ANWB signs north along the former sea dyke to **Blokzijl**, an old fortress town established in the fifteenth century by Dutch merchants, which still retains its character. Since the enclosing of the Zuiderzee, the trading vessels have changed to pleasure cruisers. The harbour basin lies in the centre of the town, where there is an old 'high water' cannon which used to be fired as a warning against floods, and last used after the disastrous floods of 1825 when a vast area of Overijssel was under water. Take a short walk through the narrow streets to see the beautiful old merchants' houses with their high decorated gables. The old orphanage, Prins Maurits Weeshuis in Brouwersstraat, is now an exhibition centre. Inside the fine seventeenth-century church is a model of the armed merchant ship *De Zeven Provincien*.

A small windmill of the type known as a tjasker on the Weeribben at Ossenzijl

From Blokzijl, continue along the dyke road following ANWB signs. Small ponds to the right show where the sea has broken through in the past. Beyond the hamlet of Blankenham, continue to Luttelgeest orchid farm, then return to the signed route. Follow the signed route to the left then right, along to the Kuinder Bos picnic and recreation area. Way-marked footpaths wander through the woods. The road junction on the old dyke may be regained by going through the tiny township of **Kuinre**, which originally consisted of just one street with fortified houses.

From signpost 333 on the dyke road, turn towards **Ossenzijl**, where a visitor centre provides information about a very extensive and interesting nature reserve, with fenland, reed beds and small waterways. Many species of bird, including a colony of blue herons, breed here, and old fen-workers' cottages and a type of small windmill known as a *tjasker* can be seen.

Drive through the Wieribben to a small road on the left in about $3^1/_2$km, and follow the signs to **Paasloo**, a very small village with one of the oldest churches in Overijseel. Dating from 1336, the nave bears a striking re-semblance to an Overijssel farmhouse and the door is Norman.

From Paasloo, follow the road to the old fortress town of **Steenwijk**, where a large part of the old town wall and moats remain, forming a pleasant walk. One of the most interesting buildings in the town is the old Boterwaag (1642) in Waagstraat, and there is an interesting circus mu-seum and local museum in the Markt. Just outside the walls is the park and nineteenth-century villa of Rams-Woerthe, now the town hall.

Leave Steenwijk by the road running south, turning right at the T-junction on the edge of the town, then in 2km turn left (signpost 4367) towards **Giethoorn**. Park at the northern end of the village and walk through to the pretty paths running beside the waterways. Peat-digging, and storm floods, in particular the disastrous break-through of the Zuiderzee in 1776-7, formed many ponds and lakes which today give the area its characteristic appearance. The waterways were originally dug to transport peat, and now the whole village is intersected by these canals, crossed by numerous little bridges to give access to the houses. It is now a tourist attraction, with reed-thatched houses open as gift shops. One small museum, the 'Oude Aarde', includes a collection of precious and semi-precious stones and minerals, while the Histo Mobil, has a superb collection of farm carts, cars, cycles and other vehicles. The best way to see the village — known in Holland as the Venice of the North — is to hire a small boat. The whole area resembles the East Anglian Broads, and that name is given to many of the stretches of water in this area. The large lake nearest the village is called the Bovenwijde (*wijde* means broad). On this broad is the large 'Smits Paviljoen', with pleasant terraces and a restaurant with superb views over the water. Most of the small roadways between the canals are closed to motor vehicles, although cycles are permitted on some paths. Naturally the area is a paradise for pleasure boating.

From Giethoorn, do not follow the ANWB route, but continue south , along Beulakerweg, passing on the right a wooden bell tower dating from 1633 beside the church. After leaving the village, the road crosses the beautiful Beulakerwijde and Belterwijde, where the scenery of the broads and the water birds which breed here may be admired from parking bays.

Passing Schutsloterwijde on the right, the road bears right at signpost 6070, and heads towards **Zwartsluis**. This former fortress town came into prominence during the eighty-years' war, and was known as the 'Poort naar het Noorden', or gateway to the north. Situated on the Zwarte Water, where two waterways, the Meppelerdiep and the Arembergergracht joined to run into the Zuiderzee, it still provides the gateway for pleasure and other craft to enter the extensive recreation areas of the broads.

Leave the town by the road to Hasselt, turn left then right, taking the road across the polder which in about 7km reaches the Staphorst to Rouveen road. **Staphorst** and **Rouveen** form one municipality. The village street, the Diek, is about 12km long, and on each side are fine farmhouses, painted traditionally in green and blue, with reed-thatched roofs. Of the 1,100 or so farmhouses in the whole parish, some 300 are listed buildings. Formerly this area was quite isolated and the traditional local costumes have been retained to the present day. Most of the women still wear the unique dress, but visitors are asked not to take photographs without permission, and not on Sundays. In Staphorst itself there is a ban on photography. Although the essential character of the village is being preserved as much as possible, it is nevertheless developing, with new housing and some industry coming into the area. One of the 150-year-old farmhouses has been restored and houses a museum, open during the summer, showing in detail the life and work of the inhabitants. An exhibition has costumes from Staphorst, Rouveen and nearby IJhorst, and in the rear of the farmhouse is a hand-weaving workshop. The road through Staphorst is closed to through traffic on Sundays during the times of church service.

East of Staphorst is 'Zwarte Dennen', a recreation area with parking, picnic tables, lake and walks.

Go south to Rouveen to the junction with the A28 motorway, then turn right along the minor road beside the canal towards Hasselt, the starting point of this route. Follow the start of the route again to signpost 11359, go under the main road bridge and turn left towards Mastenbroek and IJsselmuiden, finally crossing the bridge into Kampen.

The 50km-long river IJssel is the only major river in Holland which runs from south to north. It connects the river Rhine at Arnhem with the IJsselmeer near Kampen. The river crosses Gelderland from Arnhem to Deventer, the country to the east of the river being known as the Achterhoek. North of Deventer the river forms the boundary between Gelderland and Overijssel. Our journey along the IJssel valley will be described from north to south in three sections. It forms an ideal link route between north-east Holland and the great river plains of the south, and passes through a number of interesting towns.

Route 29: Kampen and Zwolle. Approx 12km

Kampen is an old Hanseatic town at the mouth of the IJssel. The quayside is always busy and a number of traditional Dutch sailing vessels are based here, many being available for hire. The most interesting of the three town gates is the fourteenth-century Koornmarktspoort, on IJsselkade, its twin towers with steeples standing on either side of a tall central building.

The spires and towers of the other gates, the Broederpoort and the Cellebroederspoort, may be seen from the streets in the town. Kampen lost its importance when the river silted up in the seventeenth century, but now, because of its position in relation to the new polders, it has regained its place as a centre for trade and communications.

The old town is confined on the west side by a moat and on the east by the river. In Oudestraat there are narrow alleys with buildings on either side which lean towards each other and are prevented from collapse by buttresses of wood or steel. At the northern end of Oudestraat is the town hall, consisting of the Oude Raadhuis (sixteenth century) and the Nieuwe Raadhuis (eighteenth century). The adjoining 'Gotische Huis' houses the district museum. Nearby stands the beautiful seventeenth-century

---

A Walk Around Zwolle

Zwolle has an exceptionally well-preserved town centre and fortifications, originally from about 1250, but strengthened in 1621 with a star-shaped perimeter and moat, most of which still exists. The street plan is exactly as originally laid out with parking only outside the walls.

The Grote or St Michaelskerk is early sixteenth century, and the organ, dating from 1721, is one of the finest in Holland. On the side of the church in the Grote Markt stands the guardhouse of the town, built in 1615. Over the doors are carved the words *'Vigilate et Orate'* ('Watch and Pray'). Behind the church, in Grote Kerkplein, is the VVV office. From here, walk between the old Stadhuis, and the Wheeme, originally the clergy house of the Grote Kerk, into Lombaardstraat and then to Goudsteeg, where on the left is the Huis met de Hoofden, a fifteenth-century residence now a music school. The Gothic building takes its name from the 'heads' on top of the brick supports on the gables. Goudsteeg leads to Koestraat where, by turning left, the turreted Sassenpoort is seen. This is the only remaining town gate from 1408, and bears a tablet commemorating 700 years of the town's existence. From the gate, walk up Sassenstraat, to Nieuwe Markt and on the left is the refectory of the former Bethlehem monastery. Continue ahead to the Bethlehemskerk (1308), also part of the monastery.

Sassenstraat winds to right, and then left. On the right there is a house, known as Karel V Huis, on account of a medallion bearing his

Nieuwe Toren, with a carillon. By way of contrast, in Botermarkt is the Kampen Tobacco Museum, with an exhibition of cigar-making tools and machines, and a 5m long cigar, the largest in the world.

Leave the town by the old the bridge to **IJsselmuiden**, where there is a fine view of the waterside, and follow the road to **Zwolle,** another Hanseatic town and capital of the province of Overijssel. There is now a new motorway fom Kampen to Zwolle on the opposite side of the river.

Route 30: The IJssel Valley to Deventer. Approx 35km

Leave Zwolle on the N337 road signed to Ittersum and Wijhe. This road runs parallel with the river and the railway, which it crosses about 10km south of Ittersum. After another 3km, the small riverside town of **Wijhe** is reached, situated in an ideal area for walking and cycletouring. At this point, cross the IJssel by car ferry, to continue along the other side of the river, which is a more pleasant road. The road runs south through **Veessen**, where there is an eighteenth-century windmill and good views over the river. Continue along the river valley to Welsum, and Terwolde.

As the road comes opposite **Deventer**, a fine view of the town can be

head dated 1571 on the Renaissance gable. Just beyond, on the right, a small street, Rode Eeuw Straat, leads into Oude Vismarkt, where a left turn leads across Grote Markt into Voorstraat. Along this street, on the left, is Drostenstraat which leads to Ossenmarkt and the church of OLV ten Hemelopneming (Our Lady of Heaven) with its distinctive 'pepper-pot' tower.

Cross back over Voorstraat, along Melkmarktstraat and into Melkmarkt. Turn left, and on the left, at No 41, is the provincial museum, with period rooms and exhibits relating to the province. It has an eighteenth-century façade but dates back to the sixteenth century, the back of the building being particularly attractive. The nearby Vrouwenhuis (No 53 Melkmarkt) has an interesting frontage. At the end of Melkmarkt turn right to Rodetorenplein. Standing on its own here is a fine seventeenth-century building, the 'Hopmanshuis', this was once known locally as the house with ninety-nine windows.

Continue along Buitenkant beside the moat, where remains of the thirteenth-century town walls may be seen. Cross the Stadsgracht by the bridge, turn right into Thorbeckegracht and look back over the water to the old defence towers between the walls, each with three weapon slits and various lookout openings. The walls of the towers are more than 1m thick. Continue on to the footbridge, where an excellent view can be obtained of the Broerenklooster and Broerenkerk (1465), owned since the Reformation by the Dutch Reformed Church.

A Walk in Deventer

Start at the *brink*, a large open space in the town centre. At the end is the magnificent Waag, dated 1528. This now houses the local history museum, with old bicycles, a typical Salland kitchen, and furnishings from the old Burgerweeshuis (orphanage). The fine merchant's house behind the Waag, on the left, is known as De Drie Haringen. Built in 1575, it is now the VVV office. Further along, at Brink 47, is an excellent toy museum, with one of the largest public collections in existence.

Beyond the Waag at the far end of the square is a fine old building known as the Penninckshuis, with statues on the façade representing Faith, Hope, Love, Prudence, Strength and Modesty. Outside is a statue of Albert Schweitzer. Continue around the *brink* and turn into Bergstraat, which leads through the old Bergkwartier to the twelfth-century Bergkerk, the 'Church on the Hill', its twin spires standing high over the town. On the Bergkerkplein are lovely old Overijssel façades. At the end of Bergkerkplein, near where Bergstraat enters the square, is a steep alley, Kerksteeg, on one of the walls of which is a stone with an iron ring, placed there in the sixteenth century. Iron chains were fastened to the ring and hung low over the street in times of war. Continue ahead into Bergschild, then right into Rijkmanstraat.

Turn left into Achter de Muuren which leads to a small square. Through a gate in the wall is a yard in front of the Muntentoren, where Deventer's coins were minted in the seventeenth and eighteenth centuries, now used as a church. Continue through the passages back into Rijkmanstraat, turn left to the *brink*. Cross over into Kleine Overstraat and turn left into Vleeshouwersstraat, crossing into Grote Poot then into Kleine Poot by the church entrance. The Grote or Lebuinuskerk is the oldest church in Deventer, with a fine carillon in the cupola-topped tower. Across the square is the unusual Botermarkt, its roof supported by a cast-iron colonnade. Returning along Kleine Poot to Grote Kerkhof, the Stadhuis is ahead. Walk to the end of the square, around the end of the church and turn left down Vispoort to the waterfront.

For a good panoramic view of the town cross on the small pedestrian ferry to the opposite bank of the river, where there is a small park. On the town waterfront near Vispoort is a round brick building, part of the restored town defences. Returning on the ferry, go up IJsselstraat into Achter de Muuren with remains of the town walls, and characteristic old houses. In the old Buyskensklooster nearby is the Athenaeumbibliotheek, the oldest municipal library in Western Europe.

obtained over the river to the left. Take the road into the town over the Wilhelminabrug. Another old Hanseatic town with a well preserved centre, its importance derives from its position on the river, a major trade route, and the fact that a bridge has been here since the fifteenth century.

Route 31: The IJssell Valley to Zutphen and Doesburg. Approx 33km

Leave Deventer by following signs for Gorssel and Zutphen, which leads to the main N48 road. About 2km south of the town, this road crosses under the A1 motorway at the boundary between Overijssel and Gelderland. The river IJssel winds through a broad flood plain to the right of the road, and in the neighbourhood of **Gorssel** there is plenty of scope for cycling or walking. At Eelde, the road crosses the Twente Canal, a major and very busy waterway, then crosses a railway to enter the town of **Zutphen**, standing at the confluence of the Berkel and the IJssel rivers. It owes its importance as a trading centre to the communication by water with France, Germany and Scandinavia during the Middle Ages.

Confined on the west by the river IJssel, and on the north and west by the river Berkel, the inner or old town is bounded on the remaining sides by canals and fortifications, many of which remain.

To leave Zutphen, drive north along IJsselkade, towards the railway, then turn left across the IJsselbrug, left again on to the main N345 road. This gives a fine view back across the river to the town. About 2km from the IJsselbrug take a left turn along a minor road leading eventually to the ferry at **Bronkhorst**. Cross the IJssel into the town, which is officially the smallest in Holland, although it is barely the size of a village. It has a chapel dating from 1344 which was once part of the castle. The Hoge Huis, a seventeenth-century manor house, is best seen from the dyke after leaving the ferry. In Bronkhorst, turn right and go towards Steenderen, passing a windmill (1844) on the right then follow minor roads to Does- burg. The road runs very near to the river on a big loop, and joins the main road on the edge of Doesburg.

Doesburg demonstrates, once again, how an early settlement at a strategic river position grew into an important fortified trading centre. Originally the river IJssel ran from Germany through Doetinchem in eastern Gelderland, turning north to run via Zutphen and Deventer to the Zuiderzee. At the point where it turned north, an early settlement arose. By AD1000 a permanent settlement existed by the river IJssel, at the place now known as Doesburg. Although the whole system of major rivers in Holland is very complicated, it is unclear when and how the connection between the Oude IJssel and the Rijn was made. One suggestion is that the Roman General Drusus built a canal link from the IJssel at Doesburg to the Rijn near Arnhem. Such a link exists, but evidence for Roman involvement has yet to be found.

Doesburg was later fortified with walls, gates and canals, and joined the Hanseatic League in 1447. At the end of the fifteenth century, wars and silting of the river IJssel began a decline in the town's importance as a trading centre, since when farming, cattle-raising and industrial develop-

The statue of Albert Schweitzer standing before the Penninckshuis, Deventer

A Walk in Zutphen

Start in Kerkhof, by the Grote or St Walburgskerk with its magnificent tower. Inside are some beautiful wall paintings and a fine organ on which recitals are given. The chapter house adjoining the church contains a very rare chained library from 1561, unique in Western Europe, with over 400 old hand-written books and manuscripts.

Opposite the church is the oldest square in Zutphen, where the outlines of the original castle around which the town developed, are incorporated in the pavement. Around the corner, in Waterstraat, is the Bourgonjetoren, part of the town's medieval defences, whose walls are 4m thick. Return through 's Gravenhof and walk along Martinetsingel, to the Drogenapstoren, built in 1446 as the Saltpoort, one of the town gates. The building was also the first water tower for the town. Walk through Drogenapssteeg into Zaadmarkt, and on the right, a short way along, is the Bornhof, a fourteenth-century hospice for elderly poor people. Further along on the other side, in one of a number of houses in this street with attractive façades, is the Museum 'Henriette Polak' of modern art.

Continue on into Houtmarkt, and across Lange Hofstraat into Groenmarkt. On the corner to the left is the Wijnhuistoren containing a carillon dated 1648. Badly damaged in the fighting during the last days of World War II, it has now been restored and houses the VVV office. Walk up Korte Hofstraat, bear right along Turfstraat, then right again into Oude Wand. On the left is the entrance to the fourteenth-century Agnietenhof, formerly a nunnery, now almshouses. At the end, turn left along Komsteeg to the Hagepoortplein, on the other side of which is the fifteenth-century Berkelpoort over the water, with its turrets. In times of war gates were lowered to prevent shipping from passing through, and defenders could drop pitch and boiling oil from the battlements.

Cross over the river Berkel and along Isendoornstraat; at the end on the right, is the Nieuwstadspoort, through which the town was invaded by the Spanish in 1572. Returning left and back over the Berkel and right into Rozengracht, where there is a museum dealing with the history of the town and district. Ahead and over the water on to Berkelkade, a right turn to Stationsplein will reveal the old mid-fourteenth-century powder tower, part of the old town defence works, which now houses a very large collection of lead toy soldiers, mostly in original colours, set out in parade and battle formations. The tower forms the north-west corner of the town walls. From here, return across the bridge, right along Barlheze, past some more fine façades, and left into Groenmarkt. At the end, turn right at the Wijnhuistoren, down Lange Hofstraat, where the fifteenth-century Stadhuis is on the left. Next to it is the Burgerzaal (1452) with a very fine oak roof. The walk ends back at the Grote Kerk.

ment arrived, although not affecting the character of the town. Serious damage occurred during World War II, but this has now been repaired.

The layout of the town centre depends on the star-shaped fortifications of the early eighteenth century, much of which still survive. On entering the town, keep straight ahead to 'Centrum',which leads to the Markt in the oldest part of the town. The tower of the Grote or St Martinikerk, one of the tallest in Holland, was destroyed by German forces in1945, but it has now been rebuilt, and the original carved seventeenth-century pulpit was rescued from the ruins. Beyond the church, in Roggestraat is the Roode Toren, built in 1789 and now a museum, illustrating the history and development of the town. At the corner of Roggestraat and Koepoortstraat is the town hall, which now occupies a group of buildings dating from the fourteenth to the seventeenth centuries. In Koepoortstraat is the Waag, another impressive building, dating from the sixteenth century. Along this street are a number of dignified and elegant houses. In Gasthuisstraat, leading from the junction of Kerkstraat and Koepoortstraat, are sixteenth-century almshouses.

There are many other interesting buildings to be seen and a leaflet in English is obtainable from the local VVV. Many of the eighteenth-century fortifications have been restored and laid out as a park, on the south and north-east of the town.

Exits from the town towards Arnhem are via the Coehoornsingel, the ring road around the north of the town which crosses the IJssel to join the A48 and N48 roads.

Additional Information

Places of Interest

Deventer
* De Waag Museum
Brink 57
Open: Tues to Sat 10am-5pm. Sun and public holidays 2-5pm. Closed Easter Sun, Whitsun, 1 Jan and 25 Dec.

* Speelgoed en Blik Museum (toy museum)
Brink 47
Open: Tues to Sat 10am-12.30pm and 2-5pm, Sun and public holidays 2-5pm. Closed Easter Sun, Whitsun, 1 Jan and 25 Dec.

Doesburg
*De Roode Toren
Roggestraat 9-11
Open: May to Aug, Tues to Fri 10am-noon and 1.30- 4.30pm, Sat and Sun 1.30-4.30pm. Sept to May, Tues to Fri 10am-noon and 1.30-4.30pm, Sat 1.30-4.30pm.

Giethoorn
Histo-Mobil
Cornelisgracht 42
Open: May to mid-Oct daily 10am-6pm.

* De Oude Aarde
Binnenpad 43
Open: Mar to Oct 10am-6pm daily. Nov to Feb Sat, Sun and school holidays 10am-6pm. Closed 1 Jan, 25 Dec.

Hasselt
De Zwaluw windmill
Stenen Dijk
To view enquire at VVV.

Kampen
*Stedelijk Museum Kampen
Oudestraat 158
Open: Tues to Sat 11am-12.30pm and
1.30-5pm.

Kamper Tabaksmuseum
Botermarkt 3
Open: July and Aug Thurs 9am-noon
and 2-5pm, other times by appointment.

Ossenzijl
De Weerribben Visitor Centre
Hoogeweg
Open: Wed to Fri 10am-4.30pm, Sat to
Tues 1.30-4.30pm.

Staphorst
* Museumboerderij Staphorst
Gemeenteweg 67
Open: 1 Apr to 31 Oct, Mon to Sat 10am-
5pm. Closed on public holidays.

Steenwijk
Kermis en Circusmuseum
Markt 64
Open: Tues to Fri 10am-noon and 2-
5pm. Also July and Aug Sat 2-5pm.

Zutphen
* Musem Henriette Polak
Zaadmarkt 88
Open: Tues to Fri 11am-5pm. Sat, Sun
1.30-5pm. Good Friday, 31 Dec 11am-
4pm. Easter Mon, Ascension Day, Whit
Mon, 26 Dec 1.30-5pm. Closed 1 Jan,
Easter Day, 30 Apr, 5 May, Whit Sun
and 25 Dec.

Kruittoren (museum with toy soldiers)
Stationsplein 1
Open: Easter to mid-Sept Wed, Sat and
Sun 1.30-4.30pm. School holidays daily
1.30-4.30pm.

* Stedelijk Museum voor Zutphen
Rozengracht 3
Open: Tues to Fri 11am-5pm. Sat, Sun
1.30-5pm. Good Friday, 31 Dec 11am-
4pm. Easter Mon, Ascension Day, Whit
Mon, 26 Dec 1.30-5pm. Closed 1 Jan,
Easter Day, 30 Apr, 5 May, Whit Sun
and 25 Dec.

Zwolle
* Provincial Overijssels Museum
Melkmarkt 41 and Voorstraat 34
Open: Tues to Sat 10am-5pm, Sun and
public holidays 2-5pm. Closed 1 Jan,
Easter, Whitsun and 25 Dec.

13

Salland, Twente
and Achterhoek

To the east of the IJssel Valley, stretching to the frontier with Germany,
lie parts of the provinces of Overijssel and Gelderland collectively
known as Twente and Achterhoek. Twente is the most easterly of the three
regions of Overijssel while the Achterhoek, or 'back corner', is the eastern
region of Gelderland. We also include parts of the central Salland region.
Ideal for walking and cycling, at the same time there are industrial towns
which have developed rapidly since World War II. This is 'old' land, away
from the low-lying polders, and has its own particular attraction.

In the north, Ommen lies half-way between Zwolle and the German
frontier, and makes a good centre for the first route.

Route 32: Ommen and Hardenberg. Approx 52km

In **Ommen** there are three old windmills, one, 'De Oordt', together with
a former toll house, contains the municipal museum which has prehistoric
finds and other items relating to the town's history.

Around the town are many picturesque roads, cycle tracks and footpaths, those to the east being especially attractive.

At the main N34/N347 cross roads take the road south over the bridge,
then turn left through woods to **Beerze**, a very attractive hamlet with old
thatched houses typical of this region. Continue ahead to cross the main
N36 road, then take the next turning left towards Diffelen, crossing the
river Vecht at the sluice to the Boswachterij Hardenberg, where there are
plenty of cyclepaths, footpaths and recreation areas. Take any of the quiet
roads through the woods and heathland to Heemse and into **Hardenberg**.
Very little of the old town survives, most of it having been destroyed
during World War II but part of the town wall remains, and a windmill
stands high above the town. A small historical museum is housed in the
old town hall. About 7km north of the town is Slagharen Ponypark, a large
amusement park. From nearby Lutten, take the road to **Dedemsvaart**,
known principally for Tuinen Mien Ruys, twenty beautiful gardens
within an area of 5 acres, each illustrating a different type of plant or
flower. From here continue to **Balkbrug**, site of one of Europe's most

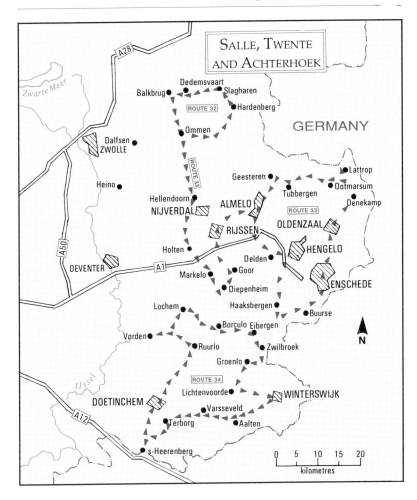

modern cheese factories, turn left and take the minor road to Ommen.

Route 33: The Sallandse Heuvelrug and Twente. Approx 157km

Immediately south of Ommen a belt of small hills known as the Sallandse Heuvelrug stretches towards Gelderland. This route follows the ridge, then makes a circuit of Twente, the eastern region of the province of Overijssel.

From Ommen, cross the river and follow the road south to **Hellendoorn**. There are two windmills and a historical museum situated in a centuries-old Saxon farmhouse. In the neighbourhood, on the road to Luttenberg, is the Hellendoorn Avonturenpark, with many attractions for all ages. South of the town, the road crosses the railway and the main N35 road into **Nijverdal**. Unlike Hellendoorn with its 900-year history, Nijverdal was only established in 1836. From here go west along the main road for a short distance, then turn left along the road through the forest to the visitor centre, 'Bezoekerscentrum Noetselerberg'. This gives information about the Sallandse Heuvelrug and the State Forestry Service, together with details of all the walking routes in the area. The road south follows a beautiful route through the forest to 'Bos Dierenwereld', a natural history museum with displays and dioramas telling the story of European wildlife.

South of Holten the main road runs south-east to **Markelo**. This has one of the oldest villages in Twente , with three typical Twents farm taverns with antique interiors. Take the road south via Beusbergen and Stokkumto the little rural town of **Diepenheim**. Nearby is the Rosarium De Broenshof, with more than 1,000 varieties; it is open to visitors free of charge. Around the neighbourhood are other castles and estates, including Huis te Diepenheim, Het Nijenhuis, and Huize Warmelo, whose grounds are open to walkers. An old Saxon farmhouse from 1475, 'Erve Broaks', is of interest. To the south-east of the village, on the road to Markvelde, is a thirteenth-century watermill, 'Den Haller', which is still in use.

From Diepenheim take the road to **Goor**, another old town, surrounded by pleasant woods and heath, with many large estates. In the churchyard is a family vault and memorial to an Englishman, Thomas Ainsworth of Lancashire, who died in 1841 in Nijverdal. Ainsworth introduced the English power-loom system and taught young workers how to to treble the output from their existing hand-thrown shuttles, thus revolutionising the important textile industry of Twente.

From Goor, take the road towards Markelo, and outside the town at signpost 2960 turn right and follow the pleasant road to **Rijssen**, a little town dating back to 1243. The twelfth century church has a sandstone font from about 1200. A large oil windmill stands by the river Regge on the north-east side of the town.

The main road north-east is now followed via Wierden to **Almelo**, the third largest town in Twente. The town has a good shopping centre, and the Grote Kerk has a crypt dating from 1236, bells from the seventeenth and eighteenth centuries, and Venetian glass chandeliers. A number of small old streets and houses, combined with open parks and modern buildings, create a lively and growing town. The former town hall in Grote Straat, with a cupola, is now a restaurant. The Waaggebouw, built in 1914 in Oudhollandse style as a market hall, is used as an exhibition centre. The moated Huise Almelo, begun in 1135, the property of the Count of Rechteren Limpurg stands in a tree-lined park near the town centre, but is not open to the public.

Leave the town and take the road south through Bornerbroek towards **Delden** passing through more very pleasant wooded country with typical Twickelse farm houses with black and white shutters. Just the north of the town follow signs to Kasteel Twickel, dating from 1347. The castle is not open, but the extensive park, with a French garden laid out by the famous designer Marot in 1690, later extended with an English garden and orangery, may be viewed during the summer.

The road from Delden leads into **Hengelo**, a modern town and industrial centre. The central shopping area is pedestrianised. Some eighteenth-century town houses exist, not far from the Stadhuis, a modern building with a carillon of forty-seven bells, one of the largest in Holland. There are some old salt boreholes with towers in the industrial area south of the town. On nearby Twekkelerweg, is the recreation park 'De Waarbeek', alongside the Twente Kanaal.

To the south is **Haaksbergen**, another pleasant town well situated for a holiday centre in beautiful countryside. The old railway station has been purchased by the Museum Buurt Spoorweg (MBS), a railway preservation society, and has been restored to the style of 1900. The goods shed houses a museum, and work is in progress to restore to working order one of the very few remaining Dutch State Railways steam locomotives. Meanwhile, a steam service is operated on certain days during the summer from Haaksbergen to Boekelo, a distance of 7km.

From Haaksbergen take the main road leading to **Enchede**, the largest town in Overijssel. An important industrial and cultural centre and still largely concerned with textiles it is now also a leading centre for the microelectronics industry.

A disastrous fire in 1862 destroyed almost everything in the town, and the only building which survives is Het Elderinkshuis, built in 1783. The Grote Kerk was rebuilt, a fine organ installed in 1893 and the beautiful stained glass windows made in Delft were fitted in 1928. The eleventh-century Romanesque font is its most important possession. The impressive town hall was built in 1930–3. In the Markt stands a monument commemorating the great fire, while in the public park near the railway is a memorial to victims of World War II.

In Enschede are several outstanding museums. The Rijksmuseum Twente is the largest museum in eastern Holland; in the garden is a farmhouse of the eighteenth-century 'Los Hoes' type from Twente. The Textielindustriemuseum deals with the Twente and Achterhoek textile industry, with demonstrations of weaving, linen production and lacemaking. In the same building is the DAF Automobile Museum.

Leave the town centre following signs for **Oldenzaal** the oldest town in Twente, which is busy with traffic into Germany. The St Plechelmusbasiliek has a huge thirteenth-century tower with a carillon of forty-six bells hung in a so-called floating belfry. The bell tower is the largest in Europe, and the church itself, built of sandstone in the twelfth century, has many treasures, including an early sixteenth-century monstrance and a beautiful baroque pulpit. In Marktstraat is the seventeenth-century 'Het Palthehuis', a historical museum with typical Twentse interiors, an old pharmacy and library. West of the town is a recreation park, Het Hulsbeek, while to the east, towards the frontier, there are many footpaths and cycle tracks worth exploring.

The main N342 road leads north to **Denekamp**, whose massive sandstone church tower dates from the thirteenth century. In the town is an old shop and house from 1880, fitted and stocked in the original style. The Maria Kloeze is a small Saxon half-timbered house, formerly the home of the old women who, at the time of the Reformation, roused or knocked up the Catholics so they could attend secret services during the night.

The twin-wheeled water mill in the grounds of Kasteel Singraven, near Denekamp

About 2km west of the town is Kasteel Singraven partly dating from about 1415. The house has a fine collection of seventeenth-century paintings, furniture, Chinese porcelain and Gobelin tapestries, and guided tours are possible. An interesting double watermill dating from 1448, and still in use as a sawmill and corn mill stands in the grounds. Entrance tickets for the castle may be obtained at the restaurant by the mill.

From Denekamp the road runs north for about 6km through pleasant scenery to **Lattrop** and Brecklenkamp, a beautiful moated manor house from 1635.

From the village of Lattrop follow signs to **Ootmarsum**, a small town surrounded by pleasant woods and heathland. The town itself is very old, and the thirteenth-century Roman Catholic church is the only one of the so-called Westphalian 'hall' type in Holland. Its treasures include a fifteenth-century monstrance, a huge organ (nineteenth-century) and a lovely carved nineteenth-century pulpit and canopy. Some handsome half-timbered houses with gables, and a town hall from 1778 with a gable decorated in rococo style and stained glass windows, can be seen. A farm museum, 'Het Los Hoes', shows the lifestyle of former times, with exhibits of spinning and weaving, agricultural implements and machines. Outside the town, on the Almelo, road is the Kuiperberg (70m above sea-level) the highest point in Twente, with a direction indicator and fine views over the surrounding countryside of Twente and Germany.

Take the road to **Tubbergen** where there are several tumuli, half-timbered farmhouse and in Grotestraat, an interesting sundial. From the town centre take the road to the right towards **Geesteren,** where there is a large farmstead, the 'Erve Brager', with two barns, and a bakehouse and granary with plastered walls. From here take the road via Harbrinkhoek and Mariaparochie back to Almelo.

Route 34: The Achterhoek. Approx 129km

A convenient starting point to explore the Achterhoek is the town of **Lochem** on the south bank of the Twente Canal. It may be reached quite easily from Almelo via the motorway A35 south, then on to the A1 west to the junction signed Lochem, which is 12km to the south. The town lies in pleasant farming country, and has a town hall built in 1634 and a late-Gothic church with carillon. In the church tower is a brass-rubbing centre (enquire at the local VVV for opening times). Leave the town by the minor road leading east to **Zwiep**, a village which has one of the few herds of Scottish Highland Cattle in the Netherlands; also a fine corn windmill, and a restaurant with gardens, known as the 'Witte Wieven' or White Women. From Zwiep, the road swings south to **Barchem**, with the woods on the right offering very good walking. Turn left in the village to **Borculo**, a small town on the river Berkel. An old gate from 1598, and an old lock and weir from 1628, recall the former barge traffic on the river. There is also an old undershot watermill from 1628, with mill pool and two waterwheels. A terrible cyclone caused much destruction in the town in 1925, and a museum commemorating the occasion is annexed to a Fire Service Museum with an interesting collection of old fire pumps, the oldest from 1670.

To the south-west towards Ruurlo, is a farming museum, 'De Lebbenbrugge', with an old farm hostel, kitchen, dairy, weaving shop, baking oven, stable, barns and other interesting items. There are plenty of recreation facilities around Borculo. From the town, take the road to **Eibergen**, also on the river Berkel, with an old watermill the 'Mallumsche Molen', sluice gate and mill house, dating from 1753.

To the east of the town, on the major road, at signpost 2163, take the minor road signed for Zwilbroek and Winterswijk via Meddo, and where it crosses the road from Groenlo towards the German town of Vreden signs for the Natuurpark 'De Leemputten' will be seen. This landscape was formed from century-old clay pits which have now been abandoned to nature. A unique and attractive area has been created for walking or sitting watching the wildlife.

From the claypits, take the road towards **Groenlo**, an old walled town with moats and ramparts, on which stands a captured Spanish cannon of 1627. The old St Callixtuskerk contains remains of wall paintings from about 1400, and the font is dated about 1200. The Grolsch Museum is situated in a seventeenth-century farmhouse, and contains local historical and folklore material and works of religious art. Somewhat different is the Stoomhoutzagerij 'Nahuis' on the Winterswijkseweg. This is a working museum located in an old steam sawmill. An engine dated 1897 is supplied with steam from a wood-fired boiler to drive sixteen saws. A smaller steam engine, of a unique type, is coupled to a 100 volt dynamo to supply light to the factory and dwelling house.

Leave Groenlo by the minor road running south-west signed for Lievelde, and watch for signs to 'Erve Kots' an open-air museum illustrating the life of farmers and peasants in the Achterhoek in former times. Back on the road continue into **Lichtenvoorde**, then from signpost 9385 along the minor road to Vragender and Winterswijk.

• On the right in **Vragender** is the windmill, 'De Vier Winden', and to the left of the village are ruins of St Janskapel dating from 1444. The road enters the outskirts of **Winterswijk**, a town lying at the centre of an area of quiet meadows, woods and small rivers near the water tower. There is a network of footpaths and cycle tracks, and no less than seventy-two estates in the area which permit free walking. An unusual feature is the stone quarry, about 3km to the east, where fossils can be found. In the town, the district museum Huize Freriks in Groenloseweg has departments of history, natural history and geology.

Leave the town and take the road to Bredevoort and **Aalten**. The fifteenth-century church has a twelfth-century Romanesque tower and a beautifully-restored organ. Behind the district museum Frederikshuus is

De Freriksschure, an old Saxon farm with wooden façade.

The road from Aalten to **Varsseveld** runs between the railway and the small river Slingerbeek, through pasture and woodland. Through Varsseveld the road swings slightly to the south to **Terborg**, where it crosses the Oude IJssel river to **Etten**, then continues to the junction with the road from Doetinchem to Emmerich, in Germany.

At the junction turn left to the old frontier town of **'s-Heerenberg**. The castle, Huis Bergh, is one of the largest and finest in Holland. The earliest parts date from the thirteenth century, with the finest parts from the fifteenth and seventeenth centuries. The castle contains furniture and art treasures, and is now a historic monument. The ramparts are almost complete and a 20 minute walk round them gives good views of the castle, passing old guard houses and cottages. Near the castle entrance is the old mint, where coins can still be produced. The wooded estate is a nature reserve. On the south of the town, on Emmerikseweg, is the Recreation Centre Gouden Handen, an exhibition of works by artists and craftsmen in an old monastery building which also includes an exhibition of dolls, sculpture, models, childrens' attractions and dioramas. The Dutch describe it as the world's greatest leisure garden.

's-Heerenberg lies within an area known as Montferland, consisting of the extensive woods of the Bergher Bos on the German frontier. This hilly ground was formerly a coniferous forest used for timber, but is now a nature reserve, open to walkers.

Returning north through the town, the road leads to **Zeddam**, with its very fine old brick windmill dating from about 1450 opposite the 'Rosmolen', a corn mill driven by a horse. Built in 1546, it has been restored as a museum. The road continues north towards **Doetinchem**, the principal town in the Achterhoek. The Grote or Catharinakerk, has a choir dating from the fourteenth century and a modern carillon. In the town is a music school with one of the most modern purpose-built premises in Europe, and a good district museum.

Leave the town towards the east and follow signs for Ruurlo and the road through Zelhem. Approaching **Ruurlo** Kasteel Ruurlo, first mentioned in 1326, is on the right and is now used as the municipal offices. It can be visited on request, while the gardens and the extensive wooded estate are freely accessible to the public. In the town centre stands a seven-branched oak tree several hundred years old. To the north of the town is a windmill driving a sawmill, dating from 1851, and the Kaasboerderij 'n Ibbink shows visitors how genuine farmhouse cheese is made.

The main road, N319, leads west to **Vorden** a town ringed by eight castles, the oldest, Kasteel Vorden, dating from 1208. Many of the parks, gardens and woods are open to walkers and cyclists, with varying restrictions.

From Vorden take the main road back across the railway, and turn left at signpost 3457 to follow the pleasant road back to Lochem.

Additional Information

Places of Interest

Aalten
Museum Frederikshuus
Markt 14-16
Open: Mid-May to mid-Sept Mon to Sat
2-5pm, Tues to Fri 10am-12noon and 2-
5pm. Mid-Sept to mid-May Mon, Wed
and Fri 2-5pm. Ascension Day and Whit
Mon 10am-4pm, Closed other holidays
and for three weeks in July; enquire
locally for exact dates.

Borculo
Het Eiland (watermill)
Burg
Bloemersstraat
Now a restaurant, open all week.

Stormramp Museum and Brandweer
 Museum (cyclone and fire service
 museum)
Hofstraat 5
Open: Mon to Fri 10am-noon and 2-5pm,
Sat and Sun 2-5pm. Closed public holidays.

Tolboerderij De Lebbenbrugge (farming
 museum)
Lebbenbruggedijk 25
Open: Mid-June to end Oct, Tues to Sat
10am-noon and 2-5pm. Sun 2-5pm.

Dedemsvaart
Tuinen Mien Ruys
Moerheimstraat 78
Open: Apr to Oct, Mon to Sat 10am-
5pm, Sun 1- 5pm.

Delden
Kasteel Twickel (gardens only)
Open: Wed and Sat in summer 1.30-
5pm. Enquire locally for exact dates.

Denekamp
Huis Singraven
Molendijk 37
Open: Mid-Apr to Oct, Tues to Fri.
Tours only at 11am, 2pm, 3pm and 4pm.

Singraven watermill
Schiphorstdijk
Open: Apr to Nov, Tues to Sat 10.30-
11.30am, 2-4pm.

Diepenheim
Den Haller (watermill)

Watermolenweg 32
Open: Tues and Thurs, 2-5pm.

Rosarium de Broenshof (garden)
Grotestraat
Open: All year, daily until sunset.

Doetinchem
* Stadsmuseum Doetinchem
Grutstraat 27
Open: Tues to Fri 10am-5pm, Sat and
Sun 2-5pm. Good Fri 10am-5pm.

Eibergen
Mallum watermill and miller's house.
Working Sat 2-5pm.

Enschede
* Rijksmuseum Twente
Lasondersingel 129
Open: Tues to Fri 10am-5pm; Sat, Sun
and public holidays 1-5pm. Closed 1
Jan.

* Textielindustriemuseum
Industriestraat 2
Open: Tues to Fri 10am-5pm, Sat, Sun 2-
5pm. Closed public holidays, but open
Easter Mon, Whit Mon and 25 Dec 1-5pm.

DAF-Automobielmuseum
Bentstraat 43
Glanerbrug
Open: Tues to Sat 10am-5pm, Sun 2-5pm.

Groenlo
Grotsch Museum
Notenboomstraat 15
Open: Mon to Fri 2-5pm. Closed public
holidays.

Stoomhoutzagerij Nahuis
Winterswijkseweg 49
Open: June to Sept Wed to Sat 10am-
noon and 2- 4pm.

Hardenberg
* Oudheidkamer
Voorstraat 34
Open: End May to Sept. Mon, Wed to
Fri 1.30-5pm.

's-Heerenberg
Gouden Handen Exhibition Centre
Emmerikseweg 13
Open: Apr to Oct daily 10am-6pm.

Huis Bergh
Hof van Bergh 8
Open: July to Oct Mon to Fri conducted
tours at 2.30pm, Sat and Sun at 2pm and
3pm). Mar to June and Oct to Nov, Sun
conducted tours at 2pm. and 3pm.

Hellendoorn
Hellendoorn Avonturenpark (recreation
  and fairytale park)
Luttenbergerweg 22
Open: End Mar to first week in Oct,
daily 9.30am-6pm.

* Oudheidkamer *Oald Heldern*
Reggeweg 1
Open: May to Sept, Mon to Fri 10-11am
and 2-4pm.

Hellendoorn-Nijverdal
Noetselerberg Visitor Centre
Nijverdalsebergweg 5
Open: Daily except Mon May to Aug
10am-5pm; Sept to Apr 10am-4.30pm.

Hengelo
De Waarbeek Recreation Park
Twekkelerweg 327
Open: Apr to first week in Sept daily
10am-5.45pm.

Holten
Bos Dierenwereld
Holterbergweg 12
Open: Apr to Oct Mon to Sat 9am-6pm,
Sun 11am-6pm.

Lichtenvoorde
Openluchtmuseum *Erve Kots*
Eimersweg 4
Lievelde
Open: May to Oct, daily 9am-5.30pm;
Oct to May, daily except Mon, 9am-
5.30pm.

Oldenzaal
Het Palthehuis
Marktstraat 13
Open: Tues to Fri 10am-noon and 2-
5pm; Sat 2-4pm.

Ommen
Oudheidkamer *de Oordt*
Den Oordt 7

Open: Mid-June to 31 Aug, Mon to Fri
10am-noon and 2- 5pm, Sat 2-4pm.

Ootmarsum
* Los Hoes Boerderijmuseum
Smithuisstraat 2b
Open: Apr to Nov, daily except Mon
10am-5pm.

Ruurlo
Kaasboerderij 'n Ibbink (farmhouse
  cheese)
Arfmanssteeg 1
Open: Daily 10am-12pm. Shop open
8.30am-6pm, Sun 10am-5pm.

Kasteel Ruurlo
Open: In use as town hall. May be
viewed during summer afternoons.

Slagharen
Shetland Pony Recreation Park
Zwartedijk 39
Open: Easter to mid-Sept, daily, 9.30am-
5.30pm; mid-Sept to mid-Oct, Sat and
Sun 9.30am-5.30pm.

Winterswijk
Streekmuseum Huize Freriks
Groenloseweg 86
Open: July to Sept Mon to Fri 9am-noon
and 2-5pm, Sat and Sun 2-5pm. Oct to
June Tues to Fri 9am-noon and 2-5pm,
Sat, Sun, Easter Mon, 30 Apr, Ascension
Day, Whit Mon and 26 Dec 2-5pm.
Closed 25 Aug.

Zeddam
Rosmolen
Bovendorpstraat 5
Open: May to mid-Oct Sat 11am-5pm,
Whitsun 10am-5pm, Ascension Day
10am-1pm. Demonstrations of working
horse-drawn mill once a month, enquire
at VVV Zeddam.

Steam Train Lines

Haaksbergen-Boekelo
Trains run July and Aug. Times from
Museum Buurtspoorweg,
Stationstraat 3,
Haaksbergen
☎ 05427 11516

14
ALONG THE GREAT RIVERS

The busiest waterways in Europe, the Rhine, the Waal and the Maas, stretch across the centre of the Netherlands from the German frontier in the east to the great delta area of the west. However the situation is complicated by the fact that they follow very winding courses, divide and join, and even change names at various points along their routes. The Rhine changes its name to Waal as it enters the Netherlands and continues westwards until just before it reaches Dordrecht. At the same point it connects by a canal to the IJssel near Arnhem, then flows as the Rhine towards Rotterdam, changing its name to Lek at Wijk bij Duurstede. The southernmost of the three, the Maas, has the longest route in Dutch territory of any river, flowing from the extreme south in Limburg parallel with the German frontier, turning west at Grave, south of Nijmegen, eventually coming to the sea south of Dordrecht. Even this is an over-simplification, because there are cross-linking canals, divisions in the rivers themselves, and smaller tributaries. Despite the fact that the great rivers carry large amounts of freight traffic, the whole area is extremely interesting and attractive, including as it does the fruit-growing district of the Netherlands. The country between the rivers lies mainly in Gelder-land, with parts in South Holland, North Brabant and Utrecht provinces.

The most important towns are Nijmegen, Tiel and Gorinchem, all lying along the Waal, the widest of the rivers. In late springtime the area is particularly attractive when the fruit trees are in blossom, but at other times the wide water meadows and twisting dyke roads, with old houses tucked behind, make ideal subjects for the photographer or painter. Many ferries cross the rivers, taking the visitor to fascinating places which would be missed if the motorways and main roads are followed over the bridges which now cross the area.

Europe's largest inland locks, the historic city of Nijmegen, and many smaller towns with interesting medieval buildings and castles lie 'along the Great Rivers'.

Nijmegen is one of the two oldest towns in the Netherlands, with a history going back to Roman times. Because of its strategic position and economic importance on a bend of the river Waal, Nijmegen has often been the scene of sieges and battles, culminating in the well-known action

A WALK IN NIJMEGEN

Start at the VVV office, situated in St Jorisstraat, near Keizer Traianusplein. Cross the road to the small wooden kiosk and walk to the remains of the fifteenth-century town walls to the left. Walk along the wall to the Belvedere, an old wall tower (now a restaurant), which gives a wonderful panorama of the river, the bridge and the surrounding countryside.

From the Belvedere, go down the path, across a stone bridge leading to the high ground of the Valkhof, where the original settlement was situated. Here, Charlemagne built a palace, later made into a fortress by Barbarossa, but demolished in 1796. The only remaining fragments are the ruined twelfth-century 'apse' and the lovely octagonal Carolingian Chapel — Nijmegen's oldest building, dating from the eleventh century and now used for small exhibitions.

From near the chapel a flight of steps leads down to the Waalkade, where the Velorama is situated. Walk along the quay beside the river to the Lage Markt. Along here are seventeenth and eighteenth-century dwellings and warehouses. From Lage Markt turn left into Priemstraat and on to Ganzenheuval, where steps on the left lead to St Stevenskerk. The main parts date from the fourteenth and fifteenth centuries, but almost complete reconstruction was needed after war damage in 1944-5.

Between the church and the Grote Markt is the Commanderie van St Jan, the twelfth-century hospital of the Knights of Malta. Later used for the first University of Nijmegen, then as a church it is now the City Historical Museum. From the Commanderie go through the double archway into the Grote Markt. The old Boterwaag, now a restaurant, dominates the square, and the old Laeckenhal, or cloth hall is also here.

From the Grote Markt continue straight along Burchtstraat past the town hall which has stood on the same site for six centuries then ahead along St Jorisstraat back to the start of the walk.

to secure the vital river crossing during 1944 as a prelude to the abortive attempt to seize the bridge at Arnhem, about 15km to the north.

During the fighting in 1944-5 much of the town centre was destroyed, but it has now been rebuilt in modern style, with many well-kept parks and gardens. The original fortifications, demolished in 1878, are marked by a boulevard linking two large roundabouts, the Keizer Karelplein on the south-west of the town centre and the Keizer Traianusplein to the east.

Nijmegen is now famous for its 'International Four Day Walks' held in July, associated with the town's annual summer festival, when the city is busy and accommodation may be difficult to find. There are plenty of museums, including the Velorama Bicycle Museum on Waalkade, Natural History Museum, City Historical Museum and the Museum G. M. Kam devoted to archaeology.

South of Nijmegen are two open air museums, Heiligland Stichting devoted to the Holy Land and the story of the Bible, with village and town buildings and other exhibits depicting life in the Middle East, and the Afrika Museum, which includes a reconstruction of an African village, and indoor exhibitions of African life, work and culture.

In the village of **Groesbeek**, where American airbourne forces landed prior to their capture of the bridge at Nijmegen in 1944, is the Bevrijdingsmuseum (Liberation Museum), dedicated to Operation 'Market Garden'.

Route 35: A Tour in the Betuwe. Approx 190km

The Betuwe is that part of Gelderland which lies north of the river Waal. Betuwe means 'good land' with rich vegetable and fruit growing areas, in contrast to the Veluwe, which is 'bad land', agriculturally speaking. Part

De Waag, now a restaurant, in the Grote Markt, Nijmegen

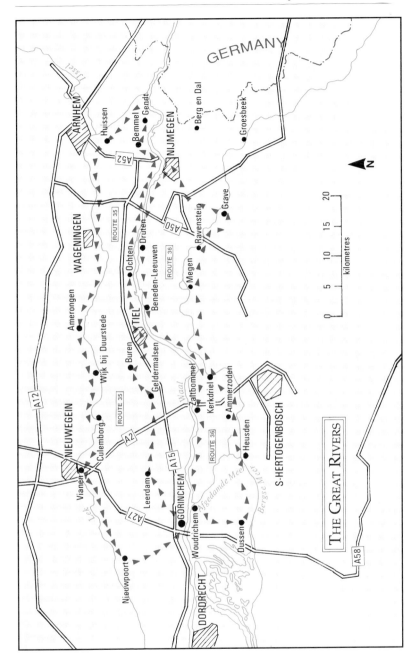

of South Holland Province bordering the rivers is also included here.

Starting from Nijmegen, cross the river by the Waalbrug and immediately turn off the main road to the right to Bemmel, then follow the road to Gendt and **Doornenburg**. Kasteel De Doornenburg lies on the point of land where the rivers Rhine and Waal divide. The castle was built mainly in the fourteenth and fifteenth centuries, but was completely destroyed in 1945 by German commandos. It was rebuilt and is now open for guided tours. It is also available for conferences and receptions, while a collection of weapons is on display in one of the towers.

From the castle, follow minor roads north to Angeren and **Huissen**, which belonged to Cleve in Germany until 1816. Formerly the river Rhine ran past the town walls — now it is about 1km away. Take the minor road north-west to Elden and follow the road alongside the river to **Driel**. This small town on the south bank of the Rhine, opposite Oosterbeek, is where the 1st Polish Parachute Brigade was dropped during the operations to capture the bridge at Arnhem, and is the point to which the remaining forces were withdrawn across the river when the action was abandoned.

Continue along the river dyke, towards Heteren; there are fine views across the river towards **Doorwerth** with its imposing castle. Further along the dyke road is Randwijk and the ferry to Wageningen. Cross the river and turn left at the main N225 road and continue to **Rhenen**. A white tower windmill stands high above the houses on one of the old walls, and nearby is the district museum containing many prehistoric and Roman finds. The Cunerakerk has a fine tower, the top of which provides a fantastic view over the river and surrounding countryside.

Continue along the N225 through Elst to **Amerongen**. Kasteel Amerongen's original castle was burned down in 1672 and rebuilt in the Dutch Classical style. It was at Amerongen that the exiled Kaiser Wilhelm of Germany signed the act to give up the German throne. The castle contains a large collection of works of art, porcelain, silver, glass and tapestry.

Continue along the road past the castle, cross straight ahead and follow the dyke road towards Wijk bij Duurstede. On the left, in about 4km is the strange shape of the sluice to control the flow of water, together with locks to allow passage of shipping.

Wijk bij Duurstede is a fascinating old town. The original town of Dorestad probably arose from a Roman settlement at the point where the rivers Kromme Rijn and Lek divided. It was once one of the largest trading towns in Europe and was, for a short time, the capital of the Norse Kingdom of Frisia. Interesting buildings include Kasteel Duurstede, whose eleventh-century keep stands within a park and has now been restored. In the Markt stands the Grote or St Janskerk, with a massive tower, built to rival the Dom in Utrecht, but never completed owing to lack of funds. Old pumps, the town hall (seventeenth century) and many fine old houses may be seen, and of special interest is the windmill 'Rijn and Lek', which stands over one of the town gates.

Beyond the town, the dyke road swings to the right towards the massive Prinses Irene locks, where the Amsterdam-Rijn Kanaal crosses the river Lek, at what is perhaps the busiest point on the European waterways system. The road crosses the canal near the locks, where a side road gives a view of the complex structure and the passage of shipping. Continue along the dyke road past Den Oord until, just before the railway, turn left to the ferry across the river to Culemborg.

Typical of so many of the old towns along the lines of the great rivers, **Culemborg** is another fortified town, whose centre is encircled by a canal. At one end of the Markt stands the town hall (1534-9), while at the other end is the Binnenpoort. The Grote or St Barbarakerk is mainly fifteenth century. The local museum is in the Elizabeth Weeshuis and of interest is the former home of Jan van Riebeek (1617-77) who founded the colony which became Cape Town.

From Culemborg, continue westwards along the river dyke, where there are fine views over the river to the right and over the surrounding countryside to the left. Just before passing under the end of the motorway bridge over the river, another lock and sluice complex will be seen on the right, all part of the extensive system for controlling water traffic and regulating the flow of flood water.

Beyond the bridge the road becomes very narrow and crosses the canal by the locks, at **Vianen**, situated at another major waterway junction. A broad main street runs from the turreted fifteenth-century Lekpoort past the Stadhuis, a fifteenth-century building housing a local museum, to the fourteen-century church. The town sits in a triangle formed by the river Lek and two motorways, which join at a massive junction south of the town. Leave the main street by passing through the Lekpoort, turn left, under the second (west) motorway, then follow the dyke road running parallel to the main road, to Lexmond. The dyke road continues close to the river to cross a small canal at Sluis. Immediately over the canal, turn right through the small town of **Ameide** with pleasant seventeenth and eighteenth-century gentlemen's houses at the foot of the dyke.

Continue alongside the river to Tienhoven, then a long stretch of dyke road leads into **Nieuwpoort**, a particularly attractive small fortified town lying directly opposite the town of Schoonhoven. Nieuwpoort has a Stadhuis (1697) built over the canal which runs through the town centre, forming a water gate, and is surrounded by old ramparts which are planted with trees.

Take the main road south and follow the road into **Gorinchem**, which lies on the north bank of the river Waal at the point where it is joined by a branch of the Maas, to become the Merwede. Most of the existing town walls and moats date from the sixteenth century, including the only surviving gate, the Dalempoort. St Janskerk has an impressive fifteenth- century tower. From the waterfront near the Dalempoort a fine view over the river towards Slot Loevestein may be obtained. At Gorinchem, the river Linge runs into the Waal, having followed a parallel winding course through the Betuwe from Doornenburg. Follow the road through Gorinchem, under the A15 motorway, to the town of Arkel then turn right along the picturesque high dyke road beside the river Linge to **Leerdam**. Since 1765 this has been a centre of the glassmaking industry and is the location of the National Glass Museum on Lingedijk. Remains of the walls and towers from the Middle Ages stand along the riverside, and the local museum, in 't Poorthuis, is in Kerkstraat, the former dwelling attached to the Veerpoort (1600).

From Leerdam take the road past the railway station to Geldermalsen, then follow signs to **Buren** and park just outside. Walk through the arched gateway into this completely enclosed town with its ramparts still intact, on which stands the town mill. This is a small gem of a town with a fourteenth-century church, early sixteenth-century Stadhuis, many fine wall houses and a magnificent former Weeshuis (1613) housing the

The old smithy at Buren

Marechaussee Museum. Culemborgsepoorthuis is the Gelders Boeren-
wagen Museum, a museum of farm wagons and other items from the past.

From Buren follow signs to **Tiel**, the centre of the fruit growing industry
of the Betuwe, situated in an area of beautiful villages and fruit farms and
site of an important fruit market. It is one of the earliest market towns in
Holland, having a harbour as early as AD435. It was fortified in the twelfth
century, had its own mint and became a member of the Hanseatic League.
Today the town has a large industrial area, and the largest inland locks in
the world where the Amsterdam-Rijn Kanaal joins the river. The Prins
Willem Alexanderbrug, to the east of the town, is one of the few toll
brigdes in Holland. Along the quay a length of the medieval town wall can
be seen, as well as the attractive seventeenth-century Waterpoort, completely restored after severe damage during World War II. There is an
interesting district museum nearby.

Leave the town in the direction of Amerongen and cross the canal by the
Prince Bernhard Sluice to avoid using the motorway. Once across the
canal continue straight ahead, turning right under the motorway, then
immediately left again, passing under the end of the toll bridge to Ochten.
Continue along the river bank to pass the twelfth-century church at
Dodewaard, and then by complete contrast, a nuclear power station.
Follow the dyke road back to Lent and cross the Waal to Nijmegen.

Route 36: Along the Waal and Maas from Nijmegen.
Approx 145km

This route covers the southern part of Gelderland between the Waal in the
north and the Maas to the south. The river Maas forms the border between
Gelderland and Noord Brabant, and the area is divided into two. On the
east is the so-called 'Land van Maas en Waal', and to the west the
'Bommeler Waard'. It is an area of pleasant and fertile farmland, with old
towns and castles, and quiet roads, set between two major rivers.

Starting from Nijmegen, cross under the railway on the north side of the
station, along Weurtseweg, and in Weurt turn right just past the church
to follow the dyke near the river, passing beneath the big new motorway
bridge, built in 1974. Follow the dyke road past Deest and **Druten,** beyond
which is Huis te Leeuwen, the gatehouse of a seventeenth-century castle
At **Beneden Leeuwen** there is a memorial to members of the Dutch Resistance army. Still keeping to the dyke road, pass under the end of the
Prins Willem Alexanderbrug.

From this point good views can be obtained from the dyke road through
Wamel and Dreumel; beyond the rivers Maas and Waal approach to
within 1km of each other. The road eventually arrives at the locks at St
Andries, where a canal was first cut in 1599 to connect the two rivers.

Across the locks is **Rossum**, an old Hanseatic town on the bend of the
Waal. Slot Rossum, an eleventh-century castle subsequently destroyed

and rebuilt in Tudor style in the nineteenth century, is now the town hall. Beyond this point the main road should be taken into **Zaltbommel**, an old Hanseatic town and the chief town of the Bommelerwaard, whose defence works still retain much of their original structure. The fifteenth century tower of the Grote or St Maartenskerk stands high over the town. In the Markt the Stadhuis and the Waag both date from about 1762, while a short distance to the north is the fourteenth-century Waterpoort. To the east of the Markt the fifteenth-century Gasthuistoren, restored in 1958, has a clock with moving figures. The local museum is situated in the Huis van Maarten van Rossum, south from the Markt.

From Zaltbommel, another dyke road leads west through Zuilichem to **Brakel**, site of a ruined fifteenth-century castle. The ruins lie in the park of the Huis te Brakel and may only be seen across the moat.

Beyond Brakel the dyke road is closed off, so drive south out of the town and turn right along the major road to signpost 5983, then follow signs to Slot Loevestein. This is a moated castle, standing on the point of land between the Waal and the Maas. The existing earth ramparts were built about 1576, but the only remaining tower from the original fourteenth-century building is the round shot tower. A small ferry (no cars) runs to and from Woudrichem, across the Maas. Motorists must return to the road junction at signpost 5983, then turn right across the river, and right again into **Woudrichem**. Because of its strategic position trade, industry and fishery thrived, and the town was fortified in the seventeenth century. In the old Arsenal is a fishery museum, and in the town are other interesting old buildings, including the St Maartenskerk (fifteenth century) and the Water or Gevangenpoort.

South of the town take the road towards Almkerk and **Dussen**. The town lies in an area where is a number of old Hollandse farms, and an eighteenth-century windmill used for pumping. On the east side of the town is Kasteel Dussen, a sixteenth-century moated castle with gate towers, part of which is now the town hall. From the castle, go through the town to the main road, turn left and follow the road via Genderen to cross the river Maas into **Heusden**, an old fortress town. In the sixteenth century ramparts with eight bastions surrounded by moats were constructed. During the nineteenth century the fortifications were demolished, but in 1968 they were restored and rebuilt, and now the town has regained much of its old appearance, with three windmills on the ramparts. Much wartime damage has also been repaired, including the building of a new town hall to replace the one blown up by German forces in 1944. A local museum is in the Gouverneurshuis, in Putterstraat.

Take the road to Herpt and follow the road towards the river. Cross by the ferry, and turn right along the dyke road to **Ammerzoden**. Kasteel Ammersoyen, a moated stronghold with round towers, was rebuilt after a fire in 1644. Damage from World War II has repaired and the castle is now open to visitors. The next village is **Hedel**, where only the remains of the castle walls exist. A local museum contains much interesting material found in the neighbourhood. Continue to Kerkdriel and along the dyke road to a roundabout, then right to the hamlet of Alem, from where the road runs towards the river and a ferry. After disembarking ferry signs direct cars to the right up the dyke to the road, while cyclists must use a steep flight of steps.

From the ferry turn left and follow through Maren-Kessel to **Lith**, an attractive rural village in an area of open river landscape with high banks and inner dykes, small villages and dyke farms. Along here the river meanders a great deal and there are ox-bow lakes, many of which form ideal places for wildlife or water sports. Continue from Lith to the main road, then turn left to Macheren and **Megen**, a small walled town with a fourteenth-century *Gevangentoren*. A number of old dwellings have been restored and the seventeenth-century church and Franciscanen-klooster reflect the importance of the town as a religious centre during the seventeenth century. From Megen take the road through Haren to **Ravenstein** with its castle on the river Maas. A moat still surrounds the town and the gates date from the renewal of the fortifications in 1522. Restoration has brought back much of the old appearance of the town, which was a centre for many religious establishments.

The dyke road now follows a winding course via Neerloon and Overlangel to **Grave**, another fortress town. There are a number of interesting old buildings, including the thirteenth-century Elisabethkerk restored in 1981. Owing to the flooding of the Maas in former times, the town was often cut off from the rest of the country, so the canalisation of the river and installation of sluices and locks to control the water was started in 1929. The dykes were made higher in the 1940s, so the danger to the town and surrounding countryside is now removed.

During the operations to capture the bridges across the major rivers in 1944, the Maasbrug at **Grave** was the first of the three bridges required to permit the advance overland from the south. The speed with which American Airborne troops were dropped in the area enabled this bridge to be taken quickly, unlike the bridges at Nijmegen and Arnhem, where the element of surprise had been reduced. Because of this, the town of Grave was undamaged, and the bridge taken intact. The route concludes by going across this bridge and returning to Nijmegen.

Additional Information

Places of Interest

Amerongen
Kasteel Amerongen
Drostestraat 20
Open: Apr to Oct, Tues to Fri 10am-5pm; Sat, Sun and holidays1- 5pm. (Good Fri 1-5pm).

Ammerzoden
Kasteel Amersoyen
Kasteellaan 7
Open: Apr to Oct, Tues to Sat 10am-5pm, Sun 1-5pm. Easter Mon, Ascension Day and Whit Mon 10am-5pm.

Berg en Dal, near Nijmegen
Afrika Museum
Postweg 6
Open: Apr to Oct daily 10am-5pm; Nov
to Mar Tues to Fri 10am-5pm, Sat, Sun
and public holidays 1-5pm but outdoor
museum closed. Closed 1 Jan and 25 Dec.

Buren
De Prins van Oranje windmill (1716)
Molenwal
In use Sat.

* Museum Koninklijke Marechaussee
  (royal constabulary museum)
Weeshuiswal 9
Open: May to Sept, Tues to Fri 10am-
noon and 1.30- 4pm, Sat, Sun and public
holidays 1.30-5pm.

Het Boerenwagenmuseum (farm wagon
  museum)
Achter Bonenburg 1
Open: May to Sept, Tues to Sun 1.30-
5.30pm.

Culemborg
*Museum Elisabeth Weeshuis
Herenstraat 29
Open: Tues to Fri 10am-noon and 2-
5pm, Sat, Easter Mon, Whit Mon, 26 Dec
and 30 Apr 2-5pm. Closed 1 Jan, Good
Fri, 5 May, Easter Day, Ascension Day,
Whit Sun and 25 Dec.

Doornenburg
Kasteel Doornenburg
Kerkstraat 27
Open: Apr to Sept guided tours only, Sun

The impressive tower windmill near the church at Ravenstein

2.30pm and 4pm. July and Aug also open Tues to Thurs tours at 11am, 1.30pm and 3pm, Fri and Sat 2.30pm and 3pm. Closed 30 Apr, 5 May and Easter Sun.

Groesbeek
* Bevrijdingsmuseum 1944 (liberation museum)
Wijlerbaan 4
Open: Mon to Sat 10am-5pm, Sun and public holidays 12noon-5pm. Closed 1 Jan and 25 Dec.

Hedel
Historisch Museum Hedel
Voorstraat 2
Open: Sat 2-5pm.

Heusden
* Het Gouverneurshuis
Putterstraat 14
Open: April to Sept every day 2-5pm. Closed Easter Day.

Leerdam
* Nationaal Glasmuseum
Lingedijk 28
Open: Tues to Fri 10am-1pm and 2-5pm, also Apr to Octoberr Sat and Sun 1-5pm.

*Museum 't Poorthuis
Kerkstraat 91
Open: Tues 1.30-4.30pm, Wed and Sat 11am-4.30pm.

Nijmegen
Natuurmuseum Nijmegen en Omstreken
Gerard Noodtstraat 21
Open: Mon to Fri 10.30am-5pm, Sun 1-5pm. Closed 1 Jan, Carnaval Monday, Easter Day, Whit Sun, Fri of 'Four Day Festival' and 25-6 Dec.

Nijmeegs Museum Commanderie van St Jan
Franse Plaats 3
Open: Mon to Sat 10am-5pm, Sun and public holidays 1-5pm. Admission free.

* Provinciaal Museum G. M. Kam (archaeology)
Museum Kamstraat 45
Open: Tues to Sat 10am-5pm, Sun and public holidays 1-5pm. Closed 25 Dec.

Stichting Velorama (bicycle museum)
Waalkade 107
Open: Mon to Sat 10am-5pm, Sun and public holidays 1-5pm. Closed 25 Dec.

*Rijksmuseum G. M. Kam
Museum Kamstraat 45
Open: Tues to Sat 10am-5pm, Sun and public holidays 1-5pm. Closed 25 Dec.

Bijbels Openluchtmuseum Heiligland-Stichting (Holy Land museum)
Profetenlaan 2
Open: Easter to Oct, daily 9am-5.30pm.

Tiel
Streekmuseum Groote Societeit
Plein 48
Open: Mon, Wed to Fri, Easter Mon, Whit Mon, 26 Dec and 31 Dec, 2-5pm. Saturday2.30-4.30pm.

Vianen
Stedelijk Museum
Voorstraat 103
Open: Tues to Fri 1.30-5pm, Sat 10am-4pm. Closed public holidays.

Wijk bij Duurstede
Kasteel Duurstede
Open: By appointment with VVV.

Rijn and Lek windmill
Leuterpoort.
Built on one of the town gates.
To visit apply VVV

Woudrichem
Slot Loevenstein
Open: All year Sat and Sun 12.45-4.30pm. Last tour 3.45pm. Closed Christmas and New Year.

Visserijmuseum (fishery museum)
Kerkstraat 41
Open: May to Sept, Mon to Fri 10.30am-noon, 1.30-4.30pm. Sun 1-4.30pm.

Zaltbommel
* Maarten van Rossummuseum
Nonnenstraat 5
Open: Tues to Fri 10am-12.30pm and 1.30-4.30pm, Sat and Sun 2-4pm. Closed Sat Oct to Mar, Easter Day, Whit Sun, 1 Jan and 25 Dec.

15

NOORD BRABANT — DEN BOSCH AND EINDHOVEN

Noord Brabant is the largest province in the Netherlands, stretching from the river Maas in the north to Belgium in the south, and from Germany and Limburg Province in the east to the Zeeland delta in the west. The greater part of the province is made up of woodland, heath and peat fen, and is largely 'old' land, not polder. Much of the land is recreational, with several nature reserves, yet some of the most historic towns and modern industrial developments are here. This chapter looks at the eastern part of the province known as the 'Meijerij', north-east and south-east Brabant, and the extreme northern tip of Limburg.

Route 37: Around Den Bosch. Approx 90km

To the west and south of Den Bosch is an area of dunes, heath and woods, pleasant for motoring or cyling. Leave Den Bosch by taking the Konings-weg south from Stationsplein, turning left across the river then bearing right along Wilhelminaplein. Immediately over the water, take the turning on the right which leads under the railway with the canal on the right. After passing the remains of Fort Isabella, turn right across the canal at a T-junction, then straight ahead for 2km. Turn left at the next T-junction, and follow minor roads to **Drunen**. Cyclists should turn left after crossing the canal near the old fort, and follow the cycle route for about 8km, then continue into Drunen. Go through the town, a fast-growing place with various industries including shoemaking and leather goods.

Continue into **Waalwijk**, the centre of the shoemaking industry. The National Shoe and Leather Museum is housed in the former home of a wealthy tanner.

From Waalwijk take the road towards Loon op Zand and Tilburg. In about 3km at Kaatsheuvel is 'Efteling', a well-known recreation park. Fairy-tale figures, a steam train running through the park, spectacular displays and many other attractions, are enjoyed by thousands of Dutch families every year.

From Efteling, continue south to **Loon op Zand** where there is a moated mansion house with outbuildings on the foundations of an old castle.

The Town of Den Bosch

Den Bosch is the official abbreviation for 's-Hertogenbosch, the historical and cultural centre and capital of Noord Brabant. The triangular centre of the town is confined by the rivers Dommel and Aa and on the south by moats along the town walls. Most of the massive ramparts from the seventeenth century still exist.

A walk starts from its oldest brick building, the thirteenth-century 'De Moriaan', now the VVV office, in the Markt opposite the Stad-huis, rebuilt in 1670 in Classical style. The Raadskelder (council cellar) beneath the town hall is now a restaurant. Adjoining the Markt the streets have modern shops and many are pedestrianised, but the actual buildings are quite old, with some fine upper façades and gables. Near the south-eastern corner of the Markt, Kerkstraat leads down towards the early thirteenth-century St Janskathedraal, said to be the most beautiful church in the Netherlands. The six-teenth-century tower is 137m high. The carillon of fifty bells, the majority of which were cast in England, is played every Wednesday morning. To celebrate the town's 800 years' existence in 1985, when Pope John Paul II visited, the cathedral was superbly restored.

The fifteenth-century Zwanenbroedershuis in Hinthamerstraat contains collections of religious antiques and art and music books. Opposite, the Kerkhof leads to the Museum Slager, devoted to the artistic family of that name. In Bethaniestraat is the Noordbrabants Museum, concerned with the art and culture of the province. At the end of the street, turn right along Hekellaan to Zuidwal, on the old town ramparts. On one of the bastions is a cannon dated 1511, with a barrel 6m long, which was never fired because it was unsafe. At this point Zuidwal becomes Spinhuiswal. Turn right into St Joris-straat; on the left is the sixteenth-century Refugiehuis, once a home for religious refugees, and now an arts and crafts centre. At the far end of the street, turn left and immediately right into Postelstraat then turn into Vughterstraat and Schapenmarkt. Turn right and left into Rozemarijnstraat. This narrow alley leads to the river Binnen-dieze, part of the waterway network which provided the main transport system of the medieval town. At the end of the alley, the river disappears underneath an old warehouse. Turn left along Burgemeester Loeff-Plein, then right into Tolbrugstraat. At the end, turn left alongside the Zuid Willemsvaart then right, across the canal on Citadellaan. On the right is the Kruithuis, built in 1621 as a store for ammunition and gunpowder outside the town walls. Its walls are 1m thick and it now houses the Museum of Modern Art.

An interesting way of seeing parts of the old town and its water-ways is to take a boat tour from the landing stage on St Janssingel, near the bridge over to Stationsweg leading to the railway station.

NOORD BRABANT–
DEN BOSCH AND EINDHOVEN

From the town centre follow the road east towards Udenout, turning left at a T-junction (signpost 5012) then right towards the car park at 'De Rustende Jager'. This is a good place to explore the extensive Loonse en Drunense Duinen, an area of sandy heathland and coniferous woods. The area is open to the public and is ideal for watching birds and other wildlife, or just for enjoying the peace and quiet of the countryside.

From here continue along the road in the same direction, looking out for signs to Helvoirt, where there is a farm, 'De Putakker', dating from 1540, with an old well in the yard. The church dates from the fifteenth century, and concerts of vocal and instrumental music are held here.

On the south side of the town, cross the main N65 road at signpost 1026 and take the road to Haaren, in what has been called the 'garden of Brabant'. Continue to the pleasant town of **Oisterwijk**. The oldest surviving house, originally a brewery, was built in 1633. To the south-east, on the road towards Spoordonk and Oirschot, is the Vogelpark, home of some 3,000 birds from all over the world. To the south of the town are extensive areas of heath and fen, with paths through the woods and beside the water. There are a number of nature reserves, some requiring entry permits. A pleasant drive through the countryside can be taken by taking minor roads to **Boxtel**, where St Petruskerk, has been a place of pilgrimage for 600 years, commemorating the miracle of the Holy Blood. The town was the scene of Wellington's first experience of action against the French, as an officer in the unsuccessful operations by the Duke of York in 1795.

Take the road to **Sint-Oedenrode**, a rural town in an area with thousands of poplar trees, used for making *klompen* or wooden shoes. The National Klompen Exhibition is held here every year. The present town hall occupies the former Slot Dommelrode, built in 1605, and used as a monastery between 1819 and 1954. On the south side of the town is Kasteel Henkenshage, dating from 1840 but with some medieval sections. In Kerkstraat is the Museum St Paulusgasthuis with a large collection of Brabant country-women's caps and bonnets and local historical items.

A straight road runs north through typical scenery, with fields and meadows, oak trees, conifers, and the ever-present poplars to **Schijndel**, a town noted for brewing, hop-growing, clog-making and hoop making, using the poplar wood. There is an old church, St Servatiuskerk, with a fifteenth-century tower, standing in the market place near a modern town hall. A windmill, 'De Pegstukken', is open to visitors.

A road to the east leads across the canal to the twin villages of **Heeswijk-Dinther,** where the Abbey van Berne in Dinther is the setting for organ concerts. In Heeswijk is the Meierijsche Museumboerderij, or farm museum, in a 250-year-old Saxon farm with authentic interior from the turn of this century. Just outside, at Muggenhoek, tours are possible in a horse-drawn wagon with driver. Along the road running north, parallel with the canal, is Kasteel Heeswijk, an impressive fourteenth-century building with paintings, porcelain, antique furniture, and wrought ironwork. Apart from the castle's immediate surroundings, the estate is open to the public, and there are a number of other woods and open spaces in the area with picnic places and paths for walking.

From here the road runs through Middelrode, and continues into **Berlicum**, with a fifteenth-century brick-built church restored after war damage. Along the road called Loofaert are several fine old farmhouses, the most outstanding of which is Eikenlust, dating from the sixteenth century, with a hexagonal tower and bakehouse. About 1km beyond the town on the right, is Huize te Wamberg, originating in 1620 and standing in its own estate. Signs direct you back into Den Bosch from just beyond the estate.

The road now leads to **Rosmalen** to the east of Den Bosch, where the Autotron, or National Transport Theme Park, with its exhibition of 250 veteran cars, aircraft and many other 'transports of delight' for young and old alike.

Route 38: Eindhoven and The Peel Country. Approx 155km

Eindhoven lies in South-East Brabant, in an area of sandy heaths and small streams known as Kempenland. Close by is Peelland, where peat has been dug for many centuries, leaving large areas of moorland and fen. Both districts have much to offer the naturalist, rambler and cyclist, and there are a number of natural recreation areas for visitors to enjoy.

Eindhoven, the largest town in the south of Holland and an important commercial and transport centre is easily reached by motorway from Den Bosch. The growth of the town accelerated with the growth of the now international firm of Philips, started in 1891 by Anton Philips (whose statue stands outside the railway station) and Gerard Philips who originally made electric lamps. The town's virtual dependence on one company was reduced in 1928 when the DAF automobile factory was built. Because of the presence of important international companies the town has a cosmopolitan character, with excellent shopping facilities and a large variety of restaurants and hotels.

Perhaps the most famous building in the town is the Evoluon, a futuristic structure on the ring road west of the town. Owned by the Philips company, it once housed a superb technological museum, but it is now closed and the building is a congress centre. Museums in Eindhoven include the famous Van Abbemuseum of modern art and the Museum Kempenland, housed in the former Antonius van Paduakerk, known locally as the Steentjeskerk, or little stone church. On the ring road to the south is an interesting open-air museum depicting a typical Iron Age settlement of the region.

The river Dommel, which runs through the town, has two watermills on its banks: a double watermill on Collesweg and a restored mill in parkland on Genneperweg near the ring road. Another mill is further south at Dommeln, near the town of **Valkenswaard**, a popular holiday centre close to attractive countryside. North-east of Valkenswaard is **Heeze**, another holiday centre with a castle, Kasteel Heeze, containing many works of art and antique furnishings.

North-west of Eindhoven is the little town of **Oirschot**, whose centre is a conservation area with typical Noord-Brabant farmhouses, many with reed-thatched roofs. A unusual monument in the town is an enormous wooden chair symbolising the thriving furniture industry here. To the east, at **Best**, is the Netherlands Klompenmuseum, where demonstrations are given of the art of making a pair of wooden shoes from a block of poplar. East again is **Son en Breugel**, a busy commuter town for Eindhoven, where the painter Pieter Breughel was born in 1515.

To the south of the town is a memorial to the American Airborne forces who were dropped here in 1944. From here the road runs south again to **Nuenen**, best known as the family home of Vincent van Gogh, whose father was the pastor of the little church. In a former coach house is a permanent collection of the painter's papers and letters, while a monument to him stands on De Berg.

East along the motorway from Nuenen is **Helmond**, where there are some extraordinary buildings, including 'Het Speelhuis', a theatre which looks like huge cubes each standing on a corner and grouped together on brick pillars.

South of Helmond is **Asten**, home of the Eijsbouts Bell Foundry and the National Beiaardmuseum, illustrating the history and use of bells round the world. Exhibits and films show the moulding, casting, finishing, hanging and ringing of bells. Also here is the nature study centre and museum, Jan Vriends, devoted to the natural history of the Peel. About 10km south of Asten, reached by the village of Heusden and small country roads is the Mijl op Zeven Visitor Centre. Here is an interesting display of photographs and artifacts devoted to peat cutting and the natural history of the Groote Peel. There are many waymarked walks in the reserve.

From Asten the best route to **Venray**, in northern Limburg, is via the main road through Deurne. Venray is one of the largest municipalities, by area, in Holland, more than one third of it being fenland and forest, mostly freely accessible on foot or by cycle. The town was badly damaged during World War II, but most of the treasures of the fifteenth-century St Petruskerk were saved from destruction. The church, popularly called the 'Cathedral of the Peel' and one of the largest in Holland, has outstanding fifteenth- and sixteenth-century woodcarvings, in particular a fine series of statues of the Apostles, and a beautiful pulpit. Nearby is the local museum, 't Freulekeshuus', with prehistoric, Roman and medieval artefacts as well as religious objects, old costumes, guild regalia and livery.

North of Venray is **Overloon**, site of one of the fiercest tank battles of World War II, lasting from 24 September to 16 October 1944 with many casualties on both sides. The full story is told in the Netherlands National War and Resistance Museum on the edge of the town, where much of the fighting took place. Equipment and vehicles used by both sides are on display. Documents, photographs, models and other items show how the Dutch people were overcome and treated during the country's occupation, and how many of them resisted their oppressors. Overloon was one of the main centres of Dutch resistance during the war, and the Onderduikerskapel is a memorial chapel to restance fighters. On the edge of the town is a British war cematary.

East of Overloon is **Vierlingsbeek**, where there is a ferry over the river Maas. Beyond the main road on the other side are large areas of woodland and heath with many recreation areas, including the large water recreation centre 'Leukerheide'. Between the road and the river is the little white St Antoniuskapel at **Ayen**, built in the seventeenth century, and a fifteenth-century castle at **Well**.

The road runs north from Overloon along what was once the old trade route through the Peel. At **Oploo** is an eighteenth-century watermill still in working order, and a windmill. Take the road through Sint Anthonis and continue north to **Wanroij**, where there is the only post mill in Holland with three floors. In the village is the recreation centre De Bergen, lying on the edge of typical Peel landscape. Take the road north again to the villages of **Sint Hubert** and **Mill**, each having a nineteenth-century windmill and a fifteenth-century church. At Mill is Kasteel Alendriel, dating from 1450 and completely surrounded by a moat.

From Mill take the road west towards Uden, and after passing a military airfield turn south towards Boekel and Gemert. At **Boekel** is a small museum with a collection of antique stoves from Holland and other parts of Europe. **Gemert** was once ruled by a German Order of Knights and has a fourteenth-century castle. The windmill in Gemert was originally a papermill in the Zaan area, and was transferred to here in 1907 to be used as a corn mill.

From Gemert the road through Beek-en-Donk and Nuenen leads back to Eindhoven.

The statue of Anton Philips, one of the founding brothers of the Philips Company, in Stationsplein, Eindhoven. In the background is a coach with a trailer for cycles.

Additional Information

Places of Interest

Asten
National Beiaardmuseum (bell museum)
Natuurstudiecentrum Jan Vriends
Ostaderstraat 23
Open: Tues to Fri 10am-5pm. Sat and Sun noon-5pm. Closed 1 January and 25 Dec.

Best
Nederlands Klompenmuseum (clog museum)
De Platijn
Broekdijk 16
Open: Apr to Oct, daily 10am-5pm.

Boekel
Kachelmuseum de Drie Kronen (antique stoves)
Volkelsweg 8
Open: Mon, Wed to Fri 9am-6pm, Sun 12noon-5pm. Public holidays 9am-5pm. Closed Easter Sun, Whit Sun and 25 Dec.

Den Bosch
Noordbrabants Museum
Verwersstraat 41
Open: Tues to Fri 10am-5pm; Sat, Sun and public holidays noon-5pm.

Museum voor Hedendaagse Kunst 'Het Kruithuise' (modern art)
Citadellaan 7
Open: Tues to Sat 11am-5pm. Sun, 1 Jan, Easter Mon, Ascension Day, Whit Mon and 26 Dec 1-5pm. Closed Carnaval, Easter Day, Whit Sun.

Museum Slager
Choorstraat 16
Open: Tues to Fri, Sun, Easter Mon, 30 Apr, 5 May, Whit Mon, 26-7 Dec 2-5pm. Closed Easter Sun, Whit Sun, 25 Dec.

Zwanenbroedershuis (religious art)
Hinthamerstraat 94
Open: daily 11am-5pm. Closed Good Friday, 1 Jan, 25-6 Dec.

Eindhoven
* Museum Kempenland
St Antoniusstraat 5-7
Open: Tues to Sun 1-5pm.

Stedelijk van Abbe Museum (modern art)
Bilderdijklaan 10
Open: Tues to Sun 11am-5pm.

Prehistorische Nederzetting (Iron Age village)
Boutensllan 161B
Open: Mid-Oct to Mar 10am-5pm. April to mid-Oct 10am-6pm.

Heeswijk-Dinther
Stichting Meierische Museumboerderij (farm museum)
Meerstraat 28
Open: May to Sept Wed, Sat, Sun and public holidays 2-5pm.

Kasteel Heeswijk
Due to reopen after restoration, enquire locally for details.

Heeze
Kasteel Heeze
Kapelstraat 25
Open: Mar to Oct, Wed, Sun and public holidays conducted tours at 2pm. and 3pm. Closed 5 May.

Kaatsheuvel
De Efteling Leisure Park
Europaweg
Open: Apr to mid-Oct, daily, 10am-6pm.

Nuenen
Van Gogh Documentatiecentrum
Papenvoort 15
Open: Mon to Fri 9am-noon and 2-4pm. Closed Fri afternoon on first and third Fri of month.

Oisterwijk
Vogelpark (bird park)
Gemullehoekenweg 147
Open: Easter Sun to mid-Oct daily 9am-6pm.

Ospel
Bezoekerscentrum Mijl op Zeven (visitor centre)
Moostdijk 8
Open: Apr to Oct Mon to Fri 9am-5pm, Sat, Sun and public holidays10am-5pm. Closed 1 Jan and 25 Dec.

Overloon
Nationaal Oorlogs en Verzetsmuseum
  (war and resistance museum)
Museumpark 1
Open: June to Aug daily 9.30am-6pm;
Sept to Apr, daily 10am-5pm.

Rosmalen
Autotron Rosmalen
Graafsebaan 133
Open: Mid-April to Sept daily 10am-
5pm. July and Aug 10am-6pm.

Schinjdel
De Pegstukken (windmill)
Pegstukken 32
Open: enquire at VVV.

Sint Oedenrode
* Museum Sint-Paulusgasthuis
Kerkstraat 20
Open: Aprill to Aug Mon to Sat and
public holidays 1-4pm. Sun 1.30-4pm.
Also mid-June to mid-Aug Mon to Sat
10am-12noon.

Venray
* 't Freulekeshuus (local museum)
Eindstraat 8
Open: Wed, Sat, 30Apr, Whit Sun, 31
Dec 2-5pm. Closed second week Aug,
Easter Sun, 25 Dec and Carnaval.

Waalwijk
* Nederlands Leder- en
  Schoenenmuseum
Elzenweg 25
Open: Tues to Fri 10am-5pm; Sat and
Sun noon- 4pm.

Wanroij
De Bergen Recreation Park
Campinglaan 1
Open: Apr to Sept, daily, 9.30am-6pm.

16

NOORD BRABANT — TILBURG, BREDA AND BERGEN OP ZOOM

This chapter deals with the remainder of the Province of Noord Brabant, known as Hart van Brabant (Centre of Brabant) and West-Brabant. Apart from a strip of land along the northern boundary formed by the river Maas, and a corner bordering on Zeeland in the north-west, most of the area is woodland, heath, farmland and old estates, with much being devoted to nature conservation and recreation. There are, however, some busy industrial areas.

Route 39: Tilburg and its Surroundings. Approx 60km

Tilburg, at the centre of Hart van Brabant, became important during the industrial revolution, when a group of rural hamlets became a world textile centre. Since the decline of the textile industry other industries have been established in large estates around the town. Much of Tilburg's 'small-town' character remains, although there are now many modern buildings. The centre is dominated by the twin spires of the nineteenth-century neo-Gothic church. Nearby stands the palace for King Willem II, not completed until after his death. It was later used as the town hall, until the completion of the modern civic centre.

The Netherlands Textile Museum, housed in old mill buildings, describes the history of the industry in Holland with old machines and examples of textiles from all over the world. Another fascinating museum is the Scryption, a massive collection of writing equipment and the written word, from clay tablet and quill pens to typewriters and computers. Tilburg is a centre for wine importers, where a wine museum, the 'Maison du Vin', shows aspects of winemaking and bottling.

Take the road leading from the western ring road to Gilze, the southern part of the town of Gilze-Rijen, which is divided by a large military airfield. From the town centre take the road to Chaam, which leads through Chaambos and Prinsenbos, where there are extensive walking and cycling routes and picnic areas.

From Chaam take the road to **Baarle-Nassau-Hertog**. This complicated name for a small town arises because it lies on a very confusing part of the

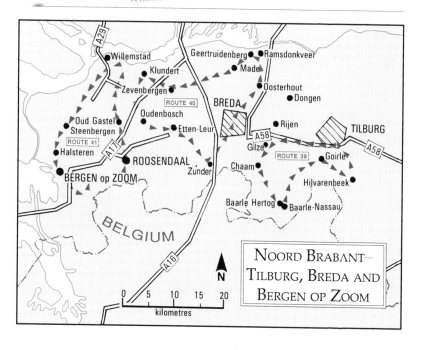

Dutch-Belgian frontier. Part of the town is Dutch and part Belgian. The explanation is that the Dutch municipality of Baarle-Nassau comprises eight Dutch enclaves, seven of which are within Belgian enclaves and one in Belgium. The Belgian municipality of Baarle-Hertog consists of twenty-one Belgian enclaves on Dutch territory. As if that is not enough, there are places where the frontier runs through houses, and in one case through a café. One house has two number plates, one Dutch and one Belgian, because the frontier divides the front door of the house! The area must have been a paradise for smugglers. St Remigiuskerk stands in Belgian territory, and the town hall of Baarle-Nassau was originally in one of the oldest houses in Baarle, bearing the date 1639.

From the town centre, take the road north-east towards **Alphen**, which croses and recrosses the frontier on the way. This is farming country, but in recent years several conservation areas have been opened for walking, cycling and picnics. Alphen has a small local archaeological museum, as old tumuli, or burial mounds, have been found in the hilly heathland of the area. Through Alphen the road bears right to Riel and Goirle.

Goirle is a commuter town for Tilburg. In Kerkstraat is St Janskerk, a new church with an old tower from about 1460. Nearby is a windmill (1896), still in working order, and the museum 'Heemerf De Schutsboom'. This deals with the Catholic Netherlands during the past century and has an eighteenth-century weaver's cottage, nineteenth-century dwelling house, old vegetable and herb gardens and beehives.

From Goirle, take the road across the Beekse Heide to **Hilvarenbeek**. After passing the Jonkers Likeurmuseum and a windmill (1830), the town centre or Vrijthof is reached. This is a unique Frankish market-field which is a conservation area, with an old town pump, several beautiful alleys and small streets, a fourteenth-century church and old houses. The museum, De Doornboom, has a fine collection of medical instruments, books and other items from the eighteenth century to World War II, together with archaeological finds from the district.

The dual-carriageway, and the parallel secondary road run north to Tilburg, past the Beekse Bergen Safari and Recreation Park. Numerous rides, water-amusements and other entertainments can be enjoyed in the Recreation Park, while the Safari Park contains more than 800 wild animals, roaming freely; visitors may drive their own cars or ride through in special buses. There is also a bird park and children's farm. To return to Tilburg, follow the main road and join the ring road.

Route 40: In and Around Breda. Approx 80km

From Tilburg, **Breda** may be reached directly either by motorway or by the parallel main road past Rijen. It is a town with a very stormy history and the town walls were extended in the early sixteenth century to the line of the present Singel. In the same century, Breda saw the start of the line of Orange-Nassau, from which the present Royal Family of the Netherlands is descended. Through the various struggles with French and Spanish invaders, the town was frequently under attack.

In 1879 the old town walls were demolished to allow expansion north- wards. The castle was reconstructed in its present form in 1696. Since 1828 it has housed the Royal Military Academy. Breda has been a garrison town for a long time, and there are other military barracks in the neighbourhood. Breda has a good shopping centre with plenty of pedestrianised streets. Many of the interesting old buildings lie close together around the centre of the town.

Breda makes a good centre for exploring the neighbouring countryside of Noord Brabant, and the following route takes in some of the old towns to the north and west, towards the river Maas. From the station, follow Oranje Singel eastwards, then turn left along Teteringenstraat and Teteringsedijk. Turn left into Kapittelweg, and continue to the ring road (Nieuwe Kadijk). Turn right, and at the next major junction turn left into Oosterhoutseweg. The road leads through **Teteringen**, a suburb of Breda which lies on the border between the higher sandy ground with its woods and sand drifts, and the polder landscape nearer the river Maas. In Teteringen there are still farmhouses from the past two centuries, and the town hall is in a former farmhouse dating from 1750. The road continues to **Oosterhout**, a pleasant residential place, with industrial development on the outskirts. The town has a rather unique group of little castles, built

A Walk in Breda

Starting from the railway station, walk down Willemstraat and cross the former castle moat to the Valkenberg. This public park was once part of the castle gardens. Walk through the park, keeping to the right along the road at the far end to emerge on Kasteelplein, where the National Ethnological Museum is situated. Turn left to Catharinastraat and turn left again to the entrance to the Begijnhof, whose buildings date back to 1535. The beautiful herb garden in the courtyard is worth seeing.

By the Begijnhof is the Waalse Kerk (Walloon church) built in 1438. Continue along Catharinastraat, bearing right into Veemarkt-straat, passing on the right the Lutherse Kerk (1560), then into Grote Markt. Turn left to the Municipal and Episcopal Museum, housed in the former Vleeshal (1617). Turn right along Ridderstraat, and right again along Torenstraat to the most noticeable building in the town centre, the Grote or Onze Lieve Vrouwe Kerk. The present building was commenced in 1410, being completed in 1538. The tower, 97m high, was built during 1468 to 1509, to replace an earlier one which collapsed. Fire damaged it in 1694 after which it was restored with a new set of bells. The church contains many tombs and memorials to the Lords of Breda, the Counts of Nassau, and many other people famous in the country's history. After extensive restoration, the fine pulpit (1640) was placed in position, also the Princes' pew (1663), used by the Barons and Baronesses of Breda (namely the Royal Family of the Netherlands). The fine organ was installed in 1715, but contains parts of the original one from 1533. Fortunately, the church was not damaged during the liberation of Breda in 1944.

around the thirteenth century by members of the Order of St John (Knights Templar). Five of these castles still exist, and the St Jansbasiliek, which dates from the fifteenth century, has a massive but uncompleted tower. At the convent of St Catharinadal the sisters specialise in the restoration of old books and manuscripts.

The old main road from Oosterhout runs parallel with the A27 motorway north to **Raamsdonksveer**, which lies between the river Donge and the river Maas. In the northern part of the town, in the industrial area, is the National Automobile Museum. From the old main road through the town continue towards the industrial area of Dombosch, where signs to the museum will be seen. There are exhibits of all types of carriage and cart, bicycles and motorcycles from the earliest days, as well as motor vehicles from the end of the nineteenth century, including racing cars.

Cross the river Donge south of the industrial area to the town of **Geertruidenberg**. Lying on a point of land between the rivers Donge and

Amer, into which the Maas flows, the town was an early trading centre, until disastrous floods in 1421, when it became a frontier fortress. Although small, the old town is very picturesque. In the Markt are a number of very fine houses, some from the sixteenth century. The town hall dates from the fourteenth century, and a total of five eighteenth-century stone water pumps together with ancient lime trees, make the market square a beautiful sight. Remains of the ramparts and moats can still be seen.

From the town, a minor road runs west to **Drimmelen**, beside the river Amer, the name by which the Maas is known from this point. The town is developing rapidly as a sailing and boating centre, and has a picturesque canal. Across the water lies the area known as the Biesbosch or 'forest of rushes'. This is an area of river creeks, mud flats and marshland created by the disastrous St Elizabeth Flood of 1421, supporting unique bird and waterplant life, which has been declared a national park. Reservoirs in the area supply Rotterdam's drinking water. At the Biesbosch Bezoekerscentrum in Drimmelen visitors may obtain information about the area, and make boat trips into the Biesbosch.

Made is a growing residential town about 2km south, from where the road west via Wagenberg is taken to Zevenbergen. Beyond the town the road continues to **Klundert**, lying on the edge of a large industrial area, but itself strategically placed in the past as a fortress town, whose restored defence works are worth seeing. The town hall is in Flemish-Renaissance style (1621), while a stone near the entrance marks the height of the flood water in February 1953. Turning south from the town centre the road runs to a bridge across the motorway; turn left over this, then right, crossing a second motorway bridge to **Standdaarbuiten** on the river Mark, a town standing in typical polder landscape with dykes and double rows of trees. The church contains a silver communion table dated 1685. A short distance away is **Oudenbosch**, dominated by the Basilica of Sts Agatha and Barbara, built in 1865–80, a small-scale copy of the Church of St Peter in Rome. A memorial stands here to the Dutch soldiers who fought during 1860-70 for the Pope and the Papal States during the formation of modern Italy, and a small museum also deals with this.

From the centre (signpost 1761) the road south crosses the railway and runs towards **Bosschenhoofd**, where signs direct visitors to the Bosbad Hoeven, a recreation park with facilities for swimming, riding and water sports, and with children's playgrounds and amusements of all kinds. Nearby is the Volksterrenwacht Simon Stevin, an observatory open to the public. From here take the road to Hoeven then follow the road east to **Etten-Leur**, whose industrial expansion has left the town centre of Leur untouched. The twin spires of St Petruskerk, and the Trouwkerkje, together with the St Paulushofje (1681) are of interest, part of the latter now used as a museum showing local costumes and crafts. The town also has a museum of printing. To the south of the town a road runs to Rijsbergen, across pleasant rural countryside with soft fruit growing as one of the specialities of the area. About 5km to the south is **Zundert**, birthplace of

Vincent van Gogh, but now famous for the annual flower parade on the first Sunday in September when floats decorated with thousands of flowers, mostly dahlias, parade through the town.

From Rijsbergen follow minor roads via Kaarschot to cross the A16 motorway to the Mastbos, a beautiful area of woods with many walking and cycle paths. Towards the northern end of the woods, approaching the suburb of **Ginneken** on the edge of Breda, is the Kasteel Bouvigne, built in the fifteenth century as a country mansion and hunting lodge, whose fine landscaped gardens are open to the public. The return into Breda is through Ginneken.

Route 41: Roosendaal to Bergen op Zoom. Approx 45km

Originating as a peat-cutting village in the thirteenth century, **Roosendaal** is now an industrial and shopping centre for West Brabant. Its importance is also partly due to its position as a frontier station of the Netherlands railway system, carrying the main line from France through Brussels and Antwerp towards the north. In the former Presbytery of the Abbey of Tongerlo (1762) is the Museum De Ghulden Roos, with collections of West Brabants folklore and costumes.

From Roosendaal, a road runs north along Gastelseweg to Oud Gastel. It then crosses the river Dintel to **Fijnaart**, in polder landscape with high dykes, noted for fruit growing, and numerous eighteenth and nineteenth century farmhouses breaking the apparently endless horizons.

Continue along the road to beyond the A59 to Oude Molen, then turn left, then fork right. The road may be followed across the polder to the dyke road, then turn left to **Willemstad**, one of the best-preserved fortress towns in the Netherlands. The fortress was built in 1565-83 to guard the entrance to the Hollands Diep, leading into the rivers Maas and Waal, and to Dordrecht. The fortifications, comprising ramparts, moats, high dyke walls and gates are all worth seeing. Because of the obvious strategic importance of the fortress it should be no surprise to find, built into the old ramparts, concrete bunkers and gun positions dating from the German occupation of 1940–4. In the town, the Princehof or Mauritshuis was built in 1623 as a hunting lodge for the Prince of Orange, and later it was used as the governor's residence. It has been restored and is now the town hall. The Arsenal (1793) has a fine façade with three stone gateways. The church, built in 1596, was the first in the Netherlands built for the Protestant faith, and is worth seeing for its stained glass windows and organ.

The road out of Willemstad runs via Helwijk, to cross the motorway following signs to **Heijningen**, where there is a memorial to the floods of 1953. Continue on minor roads to cross the river Dintel into **Dinteloord**, established when the Prinslandse Polder was created in 1605. Outside the town the main road south is followed across typical polder landscape to **Steenbergen**, which was a thriving harbour town on the Steenbergse Vliet

The town windmill at Willemstad

The Gevangenpoort which leads into the town of Bergen op Zoom

in the fourteenth century. When the harbour silted up, the inhabitants turned to agriculture and cattle breeding. The main road continues south to **Halsteren**, with its St Antonius windmill, town hall (1633) and St Martinuskerk (fifteenth century). A number of eighteenth-century farmhouses are to be seen in the district, and just to the east of the town, on the edge of an area of woods open to the public, are the remains of Fort de Rovere, part of the old defence line running north from Bergen op Zoom.

❊   The road south leads to **Bergen op Zoom**, an ideal place for a holiday. Lying on the motorway system from the ferry port of Vlissingen, Bergen op Zoom tends to be passed by visitors which is a pity, as the town deserves more attention. The town, with the exception of the harbour area, was enclosed by ramparts, of which the only remaining part is the Lievevrouwepoortor Gevangenpoort (later used as a prison). In the fifteenth century the town grew in importance and the walls were extended to enclose the harbour area. It was an important market town until the sixteenth century, when its trade was taken by Antwerp in Belgium. Subsequent struggles with Spain and France led to the strengthening of the fortifications, but in the eighteenth century industry began to establish itself. Since the opening of the Schelde-Rijn canal in 1975, Bergen op Zoom has once more become a channel for international transport.

▥   The town hall in the Grote Markt comprises several old houses, which were combined with one façade in 1611. Across the market square is the Grote or St Gertrudiskerk. A short distance from the square, in Steenbergsestraat, is the Markiezenhof, built in 1485 to 1512. The buildings are grouped around three inner courts and have been used as a military hospital by the French, and a barracks by the Dutch army. After restoration, it is now a cultural centre and municipal museum. In the town are some fine and elegant houses which were once occupied by English merchants and weavers.

South-east of Bergen op Zoom is pleasant countryside known as the Wouwse Plantage, with quiet roads ideal for cycling. Another interesting excursion is to take the old main road (**not** the motorway) towards Goes and follow the new road alongside the Schelde-Rijnkanaal to Tholen, then back via Halsteren to Bergen op Zoom. This new road, built on a long dyke, leads across the old 'Verdronken land' or drowned land of Zuid Beveland, and several recreation areas, parlicularly for fishing and board sailing, have been created.

Additional Information

Places of Interest

Alphen
Oudheidkundlig Streekmuseum (local archaeology)
Baarleseweg 1
Open: July and Aug Sun 2-5pm. Sept to June every third Sunday in month 11am-1pm.

Bergen op Zoom
* Gemeentemuseum Markiezenhof
Steenbergsestraat 8
Open: June to Aug, Tues to Sun 11am-5pm; Sat, Sun and public holidays 1-5pm. Sept to May, Tues to Sun 2-5pm. Closed public holidays.

Breda
* Rijksmuseum voor Volkenkunde 'Justinus van Nassau ' (ethnology museum)
Kasteelplein 55
Open: Tues to Sat 10am-5pm; Sun and public holidays 1-5pm.

* Stedelijk and Bissehoppelijk Museum (municipal and episcopal museum)
Grote Markt 19
Open: Wed to Sat 10.30-5pm, Tues, Sun and public holidays 1-5pm, closed 1 Jan and 25 Dec.
Tuinen Kasteel Bouvigne (castle gardens)
Bouvignelaan 5
Open: Mon to Fri 9am-4pm.

Drimmelen
Biesbosch Visitor Centre
Dorpstraat 14
Open: All year, Wed to Fri 10am-5pm, Sun 11am-5pm. Also March to Oct Sat 1-5pm and June to Aug Tues 10am-5pm.

Etten-Leur
Drukkerijmuseum (printing museum)
Leeuwerik 8
Open: April to Oct first Sun of month and preceding Sat 1-5pm. Demonstrations on Sun.

Streekmuseum voor Heemkunde 'Jan uten Houte' (costumes and crafts)
Paulushofje
Markt 55-61
Open: Mon to Fri 2-4.30pm and first Sun in month 2-4.30pm. Closed Easter, Whit Sun, Christmas, 1 Jan and Carnaval.

Goirle
Heemerf de Schutsboom (Catholic Holland with old houses and gardens)
Nieuwe Rielseweg 41-43
Open: April to Oct Sun 3-5pm. Nov to Mar first Sun of month 3-5pm.

Hilvarenbeek
De Beekse Bergen Safari and Recreation Park
Beekse Bergen 1
Open: End of Mar to Oct daily, 10am-5pm. July and Aug 10am-6pm.

* Museum de Doornboom
Doelenstraat 53
Open: May to Sept Tues to Fri 10am-12noon, 2-5pm. Sat, Sun and public holidays 2-5pm. Oct to April first Sun in month 2-5pm.

Jonkers Likeurmuseum
Goirisedijk 12
Open: May, Jun and Sept Sat 1-5pm. July and Aug Tues to Thurs, Sat and Sun 1-5pm.

Hoeven
Bosbad Hoeven Recreation Park
Oude Antwerpse Postbaan 81a
Open: Daily end Mar to Apr and Sept to late Oct 1-5pm; May to Aug 10am-8pm.

Volkssterrenwacht Simon Stevin (observatory)
Bovenstraat 89
Open: Sept to April guided tours Sun 1.30pm and 3pm, Wed and Sat 7.30pm. May and June guided tours Sun 1.30pm and 3pm, Wed 3pm and 7.30pm, Sat 7.30pm. July and Aug Mon to Fri 3pm, Wed and Sat 7.30pm, Sun 1.30pm and 3pm. Closed 1 Jan Easter Day, Whit Sun and 25-6 Dec.

Oudenbosch
* Nederlands Zouavenmuseum
Martkt 31
Open: May to Oct Tues, Thurs, first and third Sun in month 2-5pm.

Raamsdonkveer
Nationaal Automobielen Museum
Steurweg 8
Open: Mon to Sat 9am-4.45pm; Sun 11am-4.45pm. Closed 1 Jan and 25 Dec.

Roosendaal
* Museum De Ghulden Roos
Molenstraat 2
Open: Daily except Mon 2-5pm. Closed Easter, Whit Sun, Christmas and 1 Jan.

Tilburg
Maison du Vin (wine museum)
Geminiweg 9
Open: Tues to Sat, 30 April, 5 May and Ascension Day 10am-5pm. Closed first two weeks July and other public holidays.

Nederlands Textielmuseum
Goirkestraat 96
Open: Tues to Fri 10am-5pm; Sat and Sun noon- 5pm.

Scryption, Schrift en
  Schrijfmachinemuseum
Spoorlaan 434a
Open: Tues to Fri 10am-5pm. Sat and Sun 1-5pm.

Boat Trips

Biesbosch
Boat tours of this area start from several places, one example being:

Biesboschtours
Biesboschweg 7
Lage Zwaluwe
☎ 01684 2250

Other tours start from Drimmelen, by Rederij Zilvermeeuw (☎ 01626 2609) and Rondvaartbedrijf 'Avontuur' (☎ 01626 3521).

17

LIMBURG

Although Limburg is part of the Netherlands, the atmosphere is so different that it almost seems you are in another country. Some Dutch people even take their holidays in Limburg because they know it is the one part of the Netherlands where they can feel as if they are in a foreign country without going abroad. Because of the strategic position of the province it has been an arena for battles, sieges and pillaging from Roman times to World War II. Despite this Limburg has managed to preserve a tranquil and unspoilt countryside, dotted with castles, churches, ruins and picturesque villages. The province is some 150km long, and in one place is only about 5km wide. There are some exceptionally attractive routes through varied countryside, ranging from flat peel land in the north, through the central lakes area, to hilly wooded country in the south. Valkenburg was 'discovered' by the British as a tourist resort in the nineteenth century and still attracts 20,000 British visitors. Limburg is a busy industrial area, yet there is still plenty of open space, and even the industrial cities have something of interest for the visitor. The Roman remains at Heerlen, and the mine museum at Kerkrade are just two such places. Limburg is a very cosmopolitan province, with the biggest variation in dialects and a strong French and German influence.

The people of Limburg are described as having the industriousness and precision of the Germans, the *joie de vivre* of the Burgundians, Dutch sobriety and French frivolity. This mixture makes the province quite unique.

Route 42: Around Venlo and Weert. Approx 100km

Venlo, the principal town of North Limburg, is a very busy commercial centre and one of the busiest border crossings in Western Europe. Because it is so close to the Ruhr industrial area, it is an international shopping centre, with more than 80,000 Germans visiting every week. The massive town hall, a great sixteenth-century Renaissance-style building with a double outside staircase and two tall turreted towers, stands in the Markt. Venlo was fortified until the nineteenth century, but the walls and gates were then demolished and the town began to expand. It has developed as the largest market gardening area outside the Westland district of Holland, particularly for salad produce and asparagus.

Apart from the town hall, there are not many old buildings but in Grote Kerkstraat, close to St Martinuskerk, is a seventeenth-century orphanage, and a sixteenth-century nobleman's house with decorated iron wall-plates. The Museum Goltzius is the local history museum, and the Museum van Bommel van Dam exhibits modern art.

North of Venlo, close by the river Maas, are the picturesque ruins of Kasteel Gribben, known as 'Het Gebroken Slot', which has been a ruin for many centuries.and is reputedly haunted by the ghost of a wronged white lady. Further north on the same road is the village of **Lottum**, whose sixteenth-century castle, restored in 1926, miraculously escaped severe damage in World War II.

From Venlo leave via Roermondsestraat, south-west towards **Tegelen**, where the local clay is perfect for bricks and, more especially, floor and roof tiles. They were made here in Roman times, and the industry is still functioning. Tegelen is also famous for its Passion Plays, which are second only to those at Oberammegau, and held every five years in a magnificent open-air theatre, 'De Doolhof'. In the town hall is a small museum of local pottery and a small potters' workshop. In nearby **Steyl**, on the western side of the main road, are two particularly interesting places to visit. The first is the Museum Missiehuis Steyl, dealing with the 'mission' lands of the Far East and Africa, including anything from butterflies and scorpions to Buddhas and African masks. The second is the Botanische Tuin Jochum-Hof, an interesting botanical garden with both indoor and outdoor plants, and a tropical house with cacti, orchids, coffee and banana plants. There are separate herb and heather gardens, a special section devoted to North Limburg flora, and a very interesting 'prehistoric' garden.

From Steyl, follow the road south again, through Belfeld to the N271, and at Reuver bear right towards **Beesel**. The sixteenth-century Kasteel Nieuwenbroek, a white house with wings either side of the main building, has good stepped gables. From here, the road leads south again to join the main road at Swalmen. After about 1km on this road, bear right again to **Asselt**, where, near the river in Pastoor Pinckerstraat, is the oldest church in the Netherlands, known locally as het Rozenkerkje, or the little pink church. In 1915, the ruins were scattered all over the district but were brought together and the church rebuilt in its original state. It is thought that it was once used as a Roman look-out post, and it was a place of worship in the tenth century.

From Asselt rejoin the main road towards Roermond and Weert, crossing the river Maas to **Horn**. Kasteel Hoorn stands on a mound with a high surrounding wall. The castle is not usually open to the public, but the park is freely accessible.

There are two windmills in the village, both situated in Molenweg; one is an old sixteen sided wooden mill, and the other is a brick mill, the smallest in Limburg. Follow the main street through the village to the main N273 road, then turn left and right again in about 500m on to the N68 road leading to Weert. Cyclists will find a parallel road alongside. At **Baexem**, the seventeenth-century Kasteel Baexem can be seen on the left, and shortly after this, on the right, there is a very old windmill, dating from 1599, which originally stood in Haelen and was brought to Baexem in 1845.

Continue along the road to **Weert**, situated on the borders of Holland and Belgium and known to exist in the eleventh century, as 'Weerta', meaning a settlement between the water and the moorland. It became a thriving wool and cloth centre from the early fourteenth century until the Eighty Years' War, when Weert became completely isolated. Things only improved when the Zuid-Willemsevaart was dug in 1825, and with the coming of the railways Weert lost its isolation. Much of the town is now pedestrianised with many covered shopping streets, which although convenient are not in keeping with the older buildings. The old Muntgebouw, or mint, has been restored and stands in the middle of the shopping centre, overshadowed by modern buildings. St Martinuskerk stands in the Mark, its tall tower in Kempen style made even taller in 1960. Inside are fine wall and ceiling painings and carved choir stalls. The remains of the fifteenth-century castle, which was destroyed in the eighteenth century, include an original corner tower and can be seen in the street called Biest, leading off Kasteelsingel. Unfortunately the grounds are now a timber yard, but there are attractive gardens near De Tiend-schuur, by the old moat in nearby Recollectenstraat. De Tiendschuur houses the Gemeentemuseum with dispays of local history and folklore as well as a large natural history department. The Museum of Religious Art is housed in the former town hall opposite St Martinuskerk. Many of the exhibits came from the Franciscan fathers in Weert, whose monastery is in the old Kasteel de Aldeborg in Biest. South of the railway, in Kruisstraat, is the Netherlands Tram Museum, with full-size tramcars and associated objects, situated here because Weert used to be connected by tramline to Maasseik in Belgium.

Leave Weert to the north and follow the road alongside the canal towards Nederweert. This road takes a sharp bend to the left about 1km after passing under the motorway. Turn right after a further kilometre, crossing the canal and following signs towards Meijel. At the crossroads where the road turns left to Meijel, turn right in the direction of Roggel. Continue into the town centre and follow the road towards **Haelen**. After about 1km along this wooded road take the track on the left with the sign 'Leumolen'. Here is a walk along one of the loveliest valleys in Limburg with a restored old water mill, which grinds grain in the summer. A small free visitor centre explains the natural history and archaeology of the area. Walks through the estate lead to the old St Servatuskapel, standing on a hill in a grove of acacia trees.

Drive south to Haelen, then follow the main N273 back towards Venlo.

On reaching **Kessel** (**not** Kessel-Eik) drive into the village centre past the mill. Witches are reputed to have danced in the small square known as De Heksendans. Surrounding the square are old merchants' houses; note particularly the Witte Huis (white house) with decorative wrought iron-work on the door. On a mound beside the river stand the ruins of a massive tenth-century castle, which has been gradually destroyed during many wars over the centuries.

The riverside road leads to **Baarlo**, where Kastel Erp has been restored as the official residence of the Burgemeester. Nearby is an old watermill, in the castle grounds, together with an old public wash house. These have been restored, and the mill can be seen working when there is enough water.

From Baarlo follow the river road again, past the ferry, to the viewpoint at the sharp bend in the road. Turn left and continue past Kasteel de Berckt, now a monastery for both monks and nuns. The castle is not open to the public, except the chapel for Sunday Mass. Continue to the main road, turn right and in 1km turn right again to Venlo.

Route 43: From Roermond to Maastrict. Approx 67km

This route takes the visitor through the narrowest neck of Limburg, along the river Maas and the central lakes area, through beautiful historic villages, and offers fine views over the Maas Valley.

Roermond is an ancient town with a rich history. Once the chief town of the former Gelder district, in the fifteenth century it became a member of the Hanseatic League. This trading association brought much growth and Roermond became famous as a weaving town. The outstanding feature of the town is the huge Munsterkerk, a beautiful twin-towered Romanesque building. The towers were added in the nineteenth century, but they are so much in keeping with the original building that it is difficult to realise this. This lovely abbey church stands in the Munster-plein, a wide open square in the centre of the town, which was once ringed by moats. Now filled in, wide boulevards ring the town in their place.

Despite a number of serious fires over the centuries, many buildings have survived. On the northern corner of the square, behind the Munsterkerk, at the corner of Pollartstraat, is the Prinsenhof, once the governor's palace, but now an almshouse. The building, in Maasland Renaissance style, dates from the seventeenth century. Turn into Pollart-straat, passing the district courts in the old episcopal palace (1666) with an old sundial, turn left into Heilige Geest Straat then right again into Jesuitenstraat. Here are some of the many noblemen's houses in the town, with doorways large enough for coaches to enter. Turn left into Swalmerstraat where there are more of these fine houses then ahead to the Markt, with the large town hall standing at one end of the square. Just across the street to the north is the Kathedraal St Christoffel, its tower

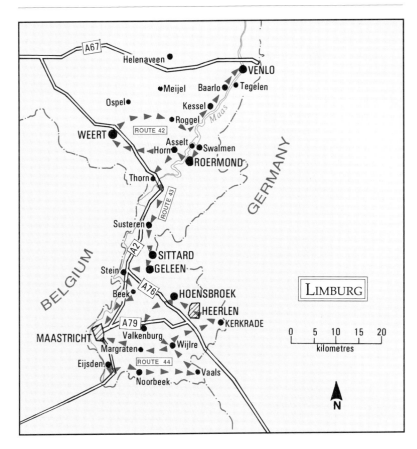

crowned with a gilded statue of the patron saint of the town. Part of the old town defences can be seen at the end of the Buitenop, dating from the mid-fourteenth century. From here return to the town centre via Roerkade, past the eighteenth-century Maria Theresiabrug, then via Brugstraat and Marktstraat to Neerstraat, where there is an attractive nobleman's house known as 'De Steenen Trappen' (stone steps) built in 1666. Further along is the Minderbroederskerk, once belonging to the Franciscans but now a Dutch Reformed Church. Continue along Zwartbroekstraat to Zwartbroekplein then via Kapellerpoort to Andersonweg. At no 4 is the local history museum, which also has the work of local artists.

Leaving Roermond via the bridge (Hornerweg), follow the signposts initially to Horn, then turn left about 1km after entering the village towards Beegden, Heel and Thorn. **Beegden** and **Heel** are known for their characteristic farmhouses, some of which are listed buildings. **Thorn** is a magnificent little town, with a superb church and medieval atmosphere.

The church was founded in AD992, as part of an abbey for both sexes, ruled by a group of noblewomen, whose abbess had almost the power of a sovereign. Because of their wealth, many treasures were obtained for the abbey, and these survive today. Most of the buildings were demolished in 1817, after the French invasion and only the church remains. It has a beautiful baroque interior, with balustraded stairways leading to the sanctuary, once the Canons' choir, and to the 'ladies choir' at the western end. A detailed guide, in English (available on request) gives a clear explanation of all there is to see. On entering the church visitors are shown slides on the history of Thorn. The commentary is in Dutch but they are worth seeing as the church treasures are illustrated.

Thorn is often called the 'White Village' because most of the houses are white-plastered. The old square behind the church, known as the Wijngaard, has cobblestones set in patterns, attractive old lanterns and, in the centre, an enormous old pump. Some of the houses in the square were once homes for the canons and other officials of the abbey and include the treasurer's house. Walking further into Daalstraat, then left at the end into Beekstraat, there is an old watermill. Follow the path alongside the stream back towards the abbey. On the left is a small bridge from where a good view of the houses in the village, backed by the church, can be obtained. Continuing along under the trees, we reach the old gateway into Kloosterberg, one of the original abbey entrances along which is the gate to the old abbey kitchens. The large white house on the right, known as Huis Groenenberg, was the residence of one of the abbesses of Thorn. If you turn left on reaching Hofstraat, the original front of the abbey can be seen and part of the old abbey court. Opposite is a large farmhouse in typical Limburg style with inner courtyard, known as the House with the Three Balls. Leave Thorn via the main N273 road northwards, and on reaching the motorway turn right and continue to the exit signed Sint Joost, where the road to Echt is joined. Cyclists go by way of Wessem and Maasbracht to St Joost. The road crosses the huge lakes area of Central Limburg, formed by the excavation of gravel.

Travel south towards **Susteren** where Limburg is only about 5km wide; there are also large industrial areas in this part of the province. The town has a very old abbey church containing a number of treasures, including a very valuable eleventh-century book, *de Evangelieboek van Susteren*, considered to be one of the earliest books in Holland. Also in the church is some priceless, world-renowned tenth-century silver.

Travel south again towards **Sittard**, another old town with some evidence of its original walls, and a number of interesting half-timbered buildings, including, in the Markt, which is full of small pavement cafés and has a very continental atmosphere, the old town farm. This attractive ochre-coloured house, with its upper floors overhanging the street, seems out of place beside the more modern buildings. Almost next door is the richly decorated baroque façade of the seventeenth-century church of St Michiel. The Grote Kerk, in nearby Kerkplein, contains the original fifteenth-century carved choir stalls and some very fine paintings depicting the life of St Peter, to whom the church is dedicated. The district museum, 'De Tempel', housed in an old Jesuit seminary, has displays of local history, geology and the Limburg Centre for Photography.

Leave Sittard by way of Rijksweg Zuid, leading to the industrial town of **Geleen**, known principally for the Pink Pop Festival held here at Whitsuntide. It should be noted that many areas of the town are sealed off at this time, making it extremely difficult to follow any pre-planned routes.

As you pass through Geleen, it is possible to pick up the ANWB 'Mergelland Route' which takes you to **Stein**. It is worth stopping here to see the old castle ruins by the canal, near the motorway bridge. Also of interest is an archaeological museum, built around the remains of a Neolithic tomb. Continue following the signed route, which diverts away from the canal, but not before there is an opportunity to observe the superb view over the valley from high up beside the motorway bridge. There is plenty of room to park and there is a footpath which can be followed above the canal banks. Through **Elsloo** and **Beek**, passing the seventeenth-century castles of Elsloo and Gebroek, the route crosses under the motorway, and immediately on the right is a good view towards the Maas Valley. The route then descends into Geulle, and down steep winding roads with hairpin bends and very steep hills to the canal. The road passes several castles, at Geulle, Bunde (where the canal is crossed), and Borgharen (where the canal is crosed back again), and the route then joins the N2 motorway. On reaching the junction with the N278, the road is followed into Maastricht city centre.

Route 44: Maastrict and the Far South of Limburg.
Approx 108km

Maastricht is the oldest city of the Netherlands, and the provincial capital of Limburg, with a wealth of old buildings and historic monuments second only to Amsterdam. It has a marvellous international atmosphere, because of its proximity to Belgium and Germany and its excellent communications with other countries. Time is well spent exploring the city, which will take more than a day to see it in any detail.

While in Maastricht, a river trip to St Pietersburg, south of the city, is recommended. It is possible to combine a cruise with a visit to the grottos, which are the result of years of excavation for the local marlstone. There are more than 20,000 passages under the hill which have been used as a refuge during times of war. Old inscriptions and paintings can be seen on some of the walls, and there are remains of the emergency provisions stored here during World War II. From the fort on the top of the hill there is a magnificent view over Maastricht and the Maas valley into Belgium. These labyrinths may only be visited with an official guide, as it would be

A Walk Around Maastricht

Starting in the Markt, notice the seventeenth-century Stadhuis, which has a large twin flight of stairs, said to have been built because there were two authorities controlling the city at that time. The tower contains a carillon of forty-three bells, which are played regularly. The interior contains some very fine Gobelin and Brussels tapestries, painted ceilings and stucco work. From the Markt, walk down Grote Gracht and left into Helmstraat, which brings you to the Vrijthof, a large pleasant square in front of the huge cathedral. Around this square may be seen the Generaalshuis, a neo-classical building constructed in 1809 on the site of a former nunnery, and the 'Spaanse Gouvernement', home of the Dukes of Brabant since the fourteenth century.

On the western side, near the cathedral, stands the Hoofdwacht, or old military guard house, built in 1773. The beautiful St Servaaskerk is well worth visiting. The treasury is open as a museum, and includes the Pectoral Cross and Key of St Servatius himself, and a beautiful reliquary. The lovely south porch is a fine example of early Gothic architecture, richly decorated with carved and gilded columns and figures. Next door to the cathedral is St Janskerk, with a fine tower 70m tall. It has been in use by the Reformed congregation of Maastricht since 1632 and contains a beautiful pulpit and some fine monuments. From the church, walk along St Servatiusklooster into Bouillonstraat, passing the Wachtgebouw, another old military guardhouse, built in 1770. From here, walk down to Ezelmarkt (donkey market) and Bonefantenstraat, with the little 't Huis op de Jeker, built over a stream, on the left, emerging at Heksenhoek or witches' corner. At this point, climb the city walls and walk above the city for a short way; at the end on the left is the fourteenth-century chapel of the Nieuwenhof.

Walk down Zwingelput and Grote Looiersstraat into Lange Grachtje, where some of the original thirteenth-century walls can still be seen. Continue into Begijnenstraat; on the left is the 'Faliezustersklooster', a seventeenth-century convent, and the Patervinktoren, part of the early ramparts. Nearby is access to the later parts of the city walls, with the Vijfkoppen and Haet ende Nijt bastions, and a nineteenth-century gate over the end of Begijnenstraat. The eighteenth-century Pesthuis, once used for plague victims, is next to de Helpoort, or Hell's Gate, and the wall of Our Lady. Continue along St Bernardus straat to OL Vrouweplein, where the twelfth-century Basilica of Our Lady stands, a building of great architectural importance as the western end is unique. This is an enormous wall, flanked by two tall pinnacled towers, much higher than the main roof of the church itself. The treasure-house, open to visitors, contains valuable relics.

Continue along Stokstraat, where there are some good seventeenth and eighteenth-century houses, to St Servaasbrug which was restored to its original state after severe war damage. From the bridge it is possible to look across the river and see some of the other fortifications of the city. Walk back across the bridge into Maastrichterbrugstraat and right into Kleine Staat, at the end of which is the fifteenth-century building known as the Dinghuis, once the home of the Chief Justice but now the VVV offices. From here, walk down Muntstraat back to the Markt, or divert via Grote Staat and Helmstraat to the Bonnefanten Museum, housed in a modern building in 'Entre Deux' shopping centre.

Visitors to Maastricht enjoying the spring sunshine in the many streetside cafés

easy to get lost. Nearby are many country walks including a nature trail, with three different waymarked walks in the very pretty nature reserve known as 'd'n Observant'. The casemates, military store rooms and galleries built into old mine workings may be seen at Tongerseweg, near the Tongerseplein. To reach St Pietersburg and the caves by road, continue eastwards along the ring road from Tongerseplein to Luikerweg, turn right by the police headquarters and follow the road which leads up to fort St Pieter and the grottos.

The countryside south of Maastricht is quite different from anywhere else in Holland There are deep river valleys, hills, many castles, and timber-framed houses, which are rarely seen outside Limburg. By following the ANWB 'Mergelland Route' from Maastricht to Drielandenpunt, near Vaals, you will see some of the loveliest villages and finest views in the province.

Leave Maastricht over the John F. Kennedybrug in the direction of Aachen (Germany) but turn off the road immediately after crossing the bridge, at the first exit, following the signs for Eijsden. Keeping to the road beside the river St Pietersburg is on the right, and just before reaching Eijsden is a large watersports centre. Beautiful castles can be seen along the road towards Sint Geertruid, Mheer and Noorbeek, which twists and turns through the hills and hugs the border with Belgium. There are many views and black-and-white houses, while **Mheer** has a Neo-Gothic-style church.

Continue along the signed route, along small hilly roads towards Epen. By the Hotel 'Ons Krijtland', there is a car park with a superb view into Belgium. A steep hill leads to **Epen**, with more black-and-white houses. It is worth stopping here to look around the village as there are some very fine examples of half-timbered houses, notably the Dorpshof and the Tiendhof near the church. There are some attractive short walks from the village, many of them waymarked. One leads to the Volmolem, a working watermill grinding corn into flour. For a longer walk continue to the Inkelhoes Hotel, on the minor road to Terziet, and take the road to the right, where, in about 500m, are more attractive black and white houses. From Epen the road becomes steeper and twisting, with many viewpoints giving breathtaking views. The road runs through a thickly forested area, 'Boswachterij Vaals', with plenty of parking and picnic areas, and several waymarked paths.

On the approach to the town of **Vaals**, divert to Drielandenpunt, which is signposted from near Vaalsbroek castle. The road twists uphill — watch for one-way circuits — to a parking place near where Belgium, Holland and Germany converge. Unfortunately, the place has become very commercialised, with the Dutch and Belgians each having their own souvenir shops and viewing towers, but it is an experience to be able to stand at the boundary stone.

Return down the hill to Vaals, and leave the marked Mergelland route, taking instead the main road towards Aachen (Aken in Dutch). On reaching the main N278 road turn left and leave the town. About 1km from Vaals is the small village of **Lemiers** with a tiny twelfth-century church. **Mamelis**, further on, is a pretty hamlet, where stone houses are set against a background of trees and the towers of a Benedictine abbey. Turn left here down a narrow road to **Vijlen**, to rejoin the signed Mergelland Route. This village has the highest standing church in the Netherlands, as well as more half-timbered houses.

The next village, **Mechelen**, has an old watermill in the Hoofdstraat, and a little further along the route, at **Wittem**, is a castle which has been converted into a hotel and restaurant. The route turns eastwards now to **Simpelveld**, where the church has a Romanesque tower dating from the twelfth century, and a large convent and monastery of the Loreto sisters and fathers. Continue into **Kerkrade**, via the main road, to visit the Mine Museum which is situated in Rolduc Abbey, close to the German border near **Herzogen**. The museum gives an insight into Holland's coalmining industry, of which Kerkrade was the centre until it ceased after the discovery of natural gas. The abbey itself is one of the most notable Romanesque buildings in Holland, and dates back to the twelfth century. Kerkrade has an attractive town park and botanical gardens.

From Kerkrade drive directly to **Heerlen**, famous for its Roman remains. The Roman baths, excavated in the 1960s and '70s, are now covered with a huge roof and form part of the Thermenuseum, with exhibits such as coins and statuary and also a Roman road map. A granite post, outside the library in nearby Raadhuisplein, marks the spot where two Roman roads crossed. Other interesting buildings include St Pancratiuskerk and the Gevengentoren, both in Kerkplein.

Leave the town via the main Sittard road to the fourteenth-century Kasteel Hoensbroek set on an island surrounded by a lake and moats — the largest castle between the Rhine and the Maas. Some of the buildings are now used as a conference centre, but the most interesting parts of the castle may be visited. It also houses a small museum of guns and a geological collection. Concerts are held here regularly.

Take the road to Nuth and **Hulsberg**, another attractive village with black and white half-timbered houses, a lovely church and beautifully restored monastery. Continue to **Valkenberg**, a place which has made the tourist industry its main source of income. There is a wide variety of ammusements including a casino, surrounded by beautiful countryside. Once the centre of a stone-mining industry, like Maastricht it has many underground passages and grottos, and these are open for tourists. There is a full-scale replica coalmine in one of them. Another has been transformed into Roman-style catacombs. Above the town are the ruins of the highest castle in the Netherlands, complete with a secret passage which leads to one of the grottos. There are many parks offering all kinds of amusements including a bobsleigh run, cable cars, chair lifts and an artificial cross-country ski track. On a hill south of the town is the Thermencentrum, where new thermal springs have been discovered. In the town the Fransche Molen is an old watermill now used as a restaurant. As well as the old castle ruins another castle, more like a small mansion, in the town centre is used as offices. The seventeenth-century Spaanse Leenhof nearby houses the local VVV. The railway station, built in 1853, is the oldest still in use in Holland. The small district museum contains old craft materials and tools, paintings and prints.

Leave Valkenburg and go east, this time along the Geul valley to Gulpen, via Wijlre, where more castles may be seen. From here, turn west to **Margraten**, where, in the American War Cemetery, all the American land forces who were killed in Holland during World War II are buried.

Return to Maastricht along the main N278 road.

Kasteel Den Halder at Valkenburg

Additional Information

Places of Interest

Baarlo
Watermill
In use July and Aug Wed, Fri and Sun 2-4pm, Sat 10am-noon.

Baexem
Auroramolen (windmill)
Rijksweg
Working Sat and Sun afternoon.

Epen
Volmolen (watermill)
Plaatweg 1
May be seen on working days 9am-5pm.

Haelen
St Ursula (watermill and museum)
Leumolen 3
To view if not in use: enquire from SBB
Roermond, ☎ 04750 34251.

Heerlen
* Thermenmuseum
Coriovallumstraat 9
Open: Tues to Fri 10am-5pm; Sat, Sun and public holidays 2-5pm. Closed 1 Jan, Easter, Whitsun, Christmas and 30 Apr.

Hoensbroek
* Kasteel Hoensbroek
Klinkerstraat 118
Open: May-Sept, daily, 10am-5.30pm. Oct-Apr, daily10am-noon,1.30-5.30pm. Open Easter, closed 25 Dec and 1 Jan.

Kerkrade
*Mijn Museum (mine museum)
Rolduc Abbey
Heyendahllaan 82
Open: Tues to Fri 9am-5pm, Sun 1- 5pm; also June to Aug Sat 1-5pm. Closed feast days and public holidays.

Maastricht
* Bonnefanten Museum
Dominicanerplein 5
Open: Tues to Fri 10am-5pm; Sat and Sun 11am-5pm.

Fort St Peter
Tours of the casemates and fort every afternoon at 2.30pm during summer and public holidays. Enquire at VVV office, ☎ 043 252121.

Schatkamer van de Sint Servaas Basiliek (treasury)
Keizer Karelplein 6
Open: daily 10-5pm. Closed 1 Jan< Carnaval and 25 Dec.

St Pietersberg Grottos
Guided tours of two sections of the cave system are provided, the Northern Grotto and the Zonneberg Caves. Generally, the Northern part has daily tours, details from VVV, ☎ 043 252121.

Mechelen
Bovenste Molen (watermill)
Eperweg 21

Roermond
* Gemeentemuseum
Andersonweg 4
Open: Tues to Fri 11am-5pm; Sat and Sun 2-5pm.

Sittard
Museum De Tempel
Gruizenstraat 27
Open: Tues to Fri 10am-5pm. Sat and Sun 2-5pm.

Stein
Archeologisch Museum
Hoppenkampstraat 14a
Open: May to Sept, daily 2-5pm. Oct to Apr, Sun 2-5pm.

Steyl
Botanische Tuin Jochum-Hof
Maashoek 2b
Open: Easter to Oct, daily, 11am-5pm.

* Missiemuseum (mission lands)
St Michaelstraat 7
Open: Apr to Oct, Mon to Sat 10am-5pm. Sun and public holidays 1-5pm.

Tegelen
Pottenbakkersmuseum (pottery)
Kasteellaan 8b
Open: Tues to Sun 2-5pm. Closed 1 Jan Ascension Day, 25-6 Dec.

Valkenburg

Fransche Molen (watermill)
Lindelaan 32
Now a restaurant.

Kasteel van Valkenburg
Grendelplein
Open: Ruins on view, Easter to Sept,
10am-5pm.

Municipal and Fluwelen Grottos.
Guided tours throughout the year,
details obtainable from VVV
☎ 04406 13364.

Pretpark de Valkenier (pleasure park)
Koningswinkelstraat 49-53
Open: Apr to first week Sept daily
10am-6pm.

Skelterbaan Couberg (recreation park)
Couberg 30
Open: Daily Mar to Nov 10am-6pm, July
and Aug 10am-10pm.

Streekmuseum 't Oud Stadhoes
Grotestraat 31
Open: Easter to Oct Mon to Fri and Sun
2-6pm.

Venlo
* Museum van Bommel van Dam
   (modern art)
Deken van Oppensingel 8
Open: Tues to Fri 10am-4.30pm; Sat, Sun
and public holidays 2-5pm.

*Goltziusmuseum (local history)
Goltziusstraat 21
Open: Tues to Fri 10am-4.30pm, Sat, Sun
and public holidays2-5pm. Closed 25
Dec, Easter Sun and Whit Fri.

Weert
Gemeentemuseum De Tiendschuur
Recollectenstraat 5-5a
Open: Tues to Sun 2-5pm.

*Kerkelijk Museum Jacob van Horne
   (religious art)
Markt
Open: Tues to Sun 2-5pm.

Nederlands Tram Museum
Kruisstraat 6
Open: Mid-Apr to Oct, daily 2-6pm.

Boat Trips

Maastricht
Rederij Stiphout
Maaspromenade 27
6211HS Maastricht
☎ 043 254151
Various cruises including a round trip
on the river Maas; daily from Apr to
Sept.

HOLLAND FACT FILE

Accommodation

Bed and Breakfast
Local VVV offices can supply information on local establishments. During holiday times advance booking is usually essential.

Booking Accommodation
Booking may be done direct, through a travel agent, through the *Netherlands Reservation Centre* (NRC) or through local VVV offices. The NBT cannot make bookings.

The NRC will handle reservations for hotels, bungalows, apartments and *Trekkershutten*. The office is open Monday to Friday from 8am to 8pm and Saturdays from 8am to 2pm. The booking will be confirmed in writing and there is no charge to the customer. Either write or telephone to Netherlands Reservations Centre (NRC), PO Box 404, 2260AK Leidschendam, ☎ 070 3202500.

VVV offices offer a joint hotel reservation system for people already in Holland wishing to book for the same or future nights. Offices in the scheme are those displaying the '*i*' sign, but telephone bookings are not accepted. A small fee is charged.

Bungalows and Summer Houses
A wide choice is available. Holiday centres such as those operated by Center Parcs, and some known as a *Recreatiecentrum* provide everything the holidaymaker may wish for, including sport and recreation facilities on site. They can be expensive but details are available from NBT.

Camp Sites
An international camping carnet is advisable. Issued by the national organisation to which you belong, it proves you hold third party insurance and is accepted by most camp sites in lieu of a passport.

The wide variety of sites in Holland range from simple quiet sites to large luxury camping parks. A list of about 400 sites is available from NBT, showing grading according to facilities. A book, *Campings Nederland*, published annually by ANWB, gives details of over 800 sites. Holders of an international camping carnet may purchase a camping permit (*Kampeerbewijs*) from any ANWB office. This allows the holder to use any of about 100 quiet sites, details of which are given in the booklet issued with the permit. Some of these sites belong to the State Forestry Service, which also publishes guides and maps, organises guided walks and establishes information centres. These include sites with all facilities, and sites with minimum facilities (water and toilets), on which cars may not be parked on the pitches. The latter sites are only available to holders of the *Kampeerbewijs*.

Some sites on estates come under a scheme known as Langoed en Kasteel Campings, an association of nearly twenty estate owners with campsites, and in some cases holiday cottages, in quiet country areas. Some sites require campers to have the *Kampeerbewijs* issued by the ANWB. Further information is available from: Landgoed en Kasteel Campings (LKC), Nevelandsehof 14, 7312E, Apeldoorn, ☎ 055 558844.

Some small farm sites in holiday areas are signed 'Mini-camping'.

Camping Huts

'*Trekkershutten*' or wooden cabins on or near existing camp sites have basic beds and cooking facilities. Water and toilet facilities on the camping site are used. Beds are for four people for a maximum of three nights, but advance booking is necessary. Details from local or provincial VVV offices.

Hotels and Motels

A comprehensive 94-page list of hotels and motels is obtainable free from NBT offices. A voluntary star-rating system ranges from luxury (5-star) through first class, very comfortable and comfortable to plain but comfortable (1-star). A final category is 'hotelette', with no star rating but well-maintained very simple rooms.

Youth Hostels

Over forty hostels are open to holders of International Youth Hostel cards. Normal youth hostel rules apply and some have family accommodation.

Details of hostels are available in *The International Youth Hostels Guide to Budget Accommodation,* volume 1, available from national youth hostel associations and some bookshops.

Youth hostels in the Netherlands are under the control of the *Nederlandse Jeugdherberg Centrale (NJHC)*, whose central office is at Prof Tulpplein 4, 1018GX Amsterdam, ☎ 020 6264433, who can supply their hostel handbook, which may also be bought from hostels in Holland.

Climate

The climate of Holland is very similar to that of Britain; temperate, but with seasonal extremes of temperature due to the continental influence. Strong winds are common, as there is nothing to stop them from sweeping across the flat landscape from the sea. This is particularly noticeable in Zeeland and the northern parts of the country. The prevailing wind is from the south-west, and there are about 150cm (60in) of rainfall in a year. The wettest months tend to be from July to November,

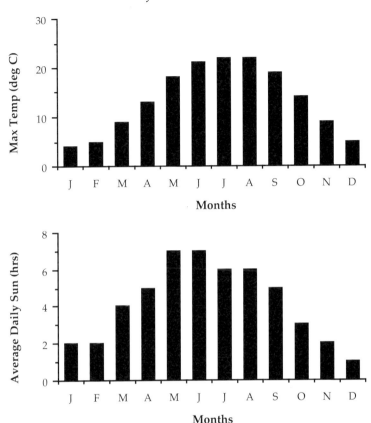

Weather Information: Amsterdam

and the coldest February, when the average temperature is -0.3 °C (30 °F), although, as elsewhere in Northern Europe, there can be no hard and fast rule about this.

Currency and Credit Cards

The unit of currency is the guilder (florin), written Fl (sometimes Hfl or Dfl), sub-divided into 100 cents. Bank notes are f1,000, f250, f100, f50, f25, f10 and f5. Coins are f5, f2.5 (*rijksdaalder*), f1, 25 cents (*kwartje*), 10 cents (*dubbeltje*) and 5 cents (*stuiver*). A 1 cent coin no longer exists and prices are rounded to the nearest 5 cents.

Currency may be changed at any bank or at an exchange office (*wisselkantoor*) of the GWK organisation located in main railway stations, airports, ferry terminals and major frontier crossings. Some major VVV offices may also be used. Other 'change shops' and hotels may be used but usually charge a higher commission.

There is no limit on the amount of cash or travellers' cheques that may be brought into the country. Obtain sufficient Dutch currency, including small change, to cover immediate needs before leaving home. Most banks open from 9am to 4pm Monday to Friday and some have a late opening night. Travellers' cheques should preferably be purchased in Dutch guilders which are widely accepted without surcharge.

Personal cheques (Eurocheques) may be cashed in banks displaying the Eurocheque sign (most branches of the major banks and GWK) on production of a current Eurocheque card. Some branches also require to see your passport.

Holders of National Giro accounts in the UK can draw cash at post offices which handle Dutch Giro business.

Major credit cards are widely accepted by hotels, restaurants and stores, also many petrol stations. Many bank branches have cash dispensers, which may be used with some cards.

Customs

For the private tourist frontier and customs formalities are simple. Normal European customs allowances apply when entering Holland, details of which are available at ports, airports, etc. Provided no prohibited or restricted goods are carried and the allowances are not exceeded, a green 'nothing to declare' label may be displayed on your car windscreen and you will be directed through the 'green' channel in the customs area of ferry ports. You may still be stopped for a spot check. Nationals of EEC countries can display a green card with a letter 'E' on their car windscreens when approaching land frontier controls if allowances are not exceeded, and will usually be allowed through. However, spot checks are always possible.

More thorough checks apply at airports and photographic material should be protected against damage from X-ray examination of luggage.

Similar rules apply when leaving Holland to enter other EEC countries. Dutch flower bulbs must have a health certificate if taken out to other countries. Bulbs bought from a reputable firm will have this supplied on request.

Electricity

220v AC at 50 Hertz (c/s). Adaptors will be needed for use with appliances not fitted with continental European 2-pin plugs.

Food and Shopping

Generally speaking, the cost of food in Holland is about the same as in the UK. Dairy produce and vegetables are normally cheaper, and meat tends to be dearer. Bread is available in an enormous variety, some regions having their own speciality. Spiced bread or cake, known generally as *ontbijtkoek* (breakfast cake) is available in virtually every supermarket.

Shopping from market stalls can be tricky unless you can get a Dutch friend to accompany you. There are, however, a number of supermarket chains in the country, the most well-known being Albert Heijn, whose quality is extremely high. Larger branches of HEMA department stores often have a good food department. Many small towns and villages have shops belonging to the VG or Spar organisation, which provide a fairly standard range of products at reasonable prices. Many of these operate as small supermarkets, often with a surprisingly large range of foods. Butchers and bakers will be found in most villages, and all over the country the *warme-bakker* provides freshly-baked bread in various forms. Unwrapped loaves can be sliced on request.

Insurance and Medical Cover

Personal travel insurance should, if applicable, include vehicle recovery in the event of accident or irreparable breakdown, as this is not normally covered by the green card.

Medical treatment can be expensive. All travellers should ensure they have adequate medical cover including repatriation in the event of serious illness or accident. Nationals of countries within the EEC are entitled to treatment on the same basis as Dutch nationals. British travellers can apply for a Form E111 before leaving, obtainable free from any post office, who will validate the form immediately it is completed. Carry it with at least one photocopy and the accompanying booklet. Normally no vaccinations or innoculations are necessary.

The foreign affairs department of the Dutch Health Service handles the arrangements whereby visitors can receive medical assistance. EEC countries have reciprocal arrangements for free health care; visitors from other countries should ensure they have adequate insurance. Users of medicines are advised to have copies of their prescription details, in Latin. In case of difficulty, contact Afdeling Buitenland van het Ziekenfonds ANOZ, PO Box 9069, 3506GB Utrecht, ☎ 030 618881.

Maps

Recommended maps are the *Toeristenkaarten* or tourist map series published by ANWB (Royal Dutch Touring Club), at a scale of 1:100,000. The country is covered in fourteen sheets, clearly showing all roads, railways, cycle paths and other details, with gazetteer of place names and other information. Explanations are in Dutch.

For motorists the *Wegenkaarten* or road maps by ANWB at a scale of 1:200,000 are recommended. The three sheets, with a good overlap, are designated *Noord*, *Midden* and *Zuid* and include gazetteers and small street plans of major towns. They are probably the most up-to-date information on major roads. All the above are cheaper bought in Holland from any ANWB office, most VVV offices and many bookshops.

Cheap but useful maps by Michelin can be bought widely worldwide. Sheet 408 (1:400,000) with gazetteer, large-scale inserts of Amsterdam and Rotterdam areas and explanations in English, French, Dutch and German is an ideal general map. Michelin Sheets 1, 5 and 6 (1:200,000) are good value and are revised frequently. None of these show cycle path information.

Measurements

The metric system is used in Holland. Conversions are:
1 kilogram (kg) = 2.2lb, 1 litre = $1^3/_4$ pints, 4.5 litres = 1 gallon, 8km = 5 miles.

Museums and Places to Visit

Entry fees for museums vary; a few are free. A museum card, available from the VVV and NBT, gives free admission to some museums, castles and gardens. They are indicated with * symbol in the Additional Information at the end of each chapter of this book. If you plan to visit many museums it is well worth the cost. For instance, the Rijksmuseum in Amsterdam and the open-air museums at Enkhuizen, Arnhem, and Barger Compascuum are all in the scheme, and money is saved even if you only visit these. Since there are hundreds of museums in Holland, only a selection can be listed in this guide, but a useful book listing nearly 600 museums is available from major VVV offices.

Unless otherwise stated, most castles and country houses open to the public are closed on feastdays, such as Easter, Ascension Day and Whitsuntide. Many also close on 30 April (Queen's Day) and 5 May. Many of these buildings are open only for conducted tours, so visitors may have to wait for the next tour to start.

Opening Times

Many shops are closed Monday morning but normal opening Monday to Friday is from 8.30am or 9am to 5.30pm or 6pm, often closing for lunch. Saturday closing is usually at 4pm or 6pm. Nearly all shops close for one morning, afternoon or whole day a week and this can vary from place to place. Late night shopping may be on Thursday or Friday evening after closing for a short break. In recreation and tourist resorts shops may remain open in the evening and weekends. Times are displayed on the door.

Banks open Monday to Friday from 9am to 4pm or 5pm; sometimes also on late night shopping evenings. GWK exchange offices open from 8am to 8pm Monday to Saturday and from 10am to 4pm on Sunday.

Sometimes they open in the evening and 24 hour service is available at Amsterdam Central Station and the border crossings near Breda and Arnhem.

Chemists open Monday to Friday from 8am or 9am to 5.30pm. Cover is provided for evenings, nights and weekends. Pharmacies display a green cross.

Passports and Visas

A valid full passport (or British visitor's passport) is required. For stays of not more than 3 months visas are not necessary.

Post and Telephone Services

Post Offices (*Postkantoor*)
In towns look for the sign 'POST'. Normally open from 8.30am to 5pm on weekdays, often Saturday from 8.30am to 12pm. Larger offices have an outer hall with telephone cubicles and stamp machines, which remain open later in the evening and on Saturday. Pre-stamped letter cards are available from machines but may need extra stamps for posting abroad.

Telephone
The system is fully automatic with direct dialling to most other countries, even from call boxes. Clear instructions are in several languages, including English. The unit of charge is 25 cents and in larger towns boxes will also take larger-denomination coins. The charge is monitored and extra coins can be inserted during the call. Unused money will be returned when the call is terminated, but no change is given. Therefore include some *kwartjes* (25 cent coins). Ensure several coins are inserted before dialling a long distance call. An increasing number of boxes are being equipped with card telephones (*Kaarttelephoon*) which accept telephone cards bought from post offices, VVV and a number of shops. The cards are available in 20 units, 40 units or 100 units.

Public Holidays

New Year's Day, Good Friday, Easter Sunday and Monday, Queen's Birthday (30 April), Ascension Day, Whit Sunday and Monday, Christmas and Boxing Day. With the exception of Good Friday, most shops are closed on the above days.

Remembrance days are 4 May (World War II) and 5 May (Liberation Day). These are not generally public holidays and shops remain open.

Queueing

No-one seems to queue for buses or trams, as tickets can be bought in advance and there is usually more than one entrance. However, in banks, busy VVV offices and many shops, including the meat, bread and delicatessen counters in supermarkets, it is usual to find a ticket machine, from which a numbered ticket is taken on arrival. An indicator above the counter shows the number of the next customer to be served, or the number may be called out, so be prepared for this.

Restaurants and Cafés

The standard of food and service in Dutch cafés and restaurants is usually high. Prices vary widely, but it is usually possible to get a good meal at a reasonable price. Owing to its history of trading overseas, Holland has a large number of establishments specialising in food from Indonesia, China, and other countries.

Over 500 restaurants participate in the 'tourist menu' scheme whereby, for a reasonable set price, a three-course menu created by its own chef is provided. Restaurants in the scheme display a blue sign.

Many of the department stores such as Vroom & Dreesman and HEMA have cafeterias which provide good value hot and cold dishes. Good coffee is normal. Tea will be served in a glass, without milk. However, it is weaker than is common in Britain, and can be very refreshing. Many railway restaurants are excellent, and the sign *Pannekoekhuis* indicates a restaurant which specialises in pancakes, large, either savoury or sweet, and a meal in themselves. A number of restaurant chains or groups exist, the members of which follow similar standards. Examples are Neerlands Dis, with a sign of a red, white and blue soup tureen, a group of about 500 restaurants serving traditional Dutch cuisine based on home-produced ingredients. About thirty restaurants are affiliated to Alliance Gastronomique Neerlandaise. They represent a more upmarket type of restaurant where it is pleasant to linger and where a high level of culinary skills can be expected. Many of the motorways have excellent restaurants and cafeterias, such as the 'Albert's Corner' (AC) group, offering rapid self-service at reasonable prices, and the Smits restaurants. In some towns may be found Noord Zee Quick cafeterias which specialise in sea food dishes, while in major towns are the usual burger-bars such as the Macdonalds chain. If all else fails, and everywhere else is closed, *automatieks* dispense hot and cold snacks, but guilder coins are usually needed. Small cafés remain open all day and to quite late hours at night almost everywhere, and coffee and filled rolls (*broodjes*) are usually available, also *frites* (french fries) with mayonnaise.

Time

The Netherlands uses Central European Time, one hour ahead of the UK. Clocks go forward one hour in summer. Check if this occurs at the same time as in the UK. Ferry and air timetables quote departure and arrival in local time.

Tipping

Normally, the bill when presented is inclusive of service change and value added tax (known as BTW in Holland). Extra attention or service may warrant an extra tip, but this is by no means essential or expected. Taxi meter fares include service charge. However, in washrooms and toilets it is usual to give the attendant 25 or 50 cents. Sometimes there is a plate on a table inside for the contribution.

Tourist Boards and Information Offices

Holland Leisure Card
This entitles the holder to considerable discounts on a number of services such as car rental, public transport, purchases in certain large stores and admission to various events and places. The Holland Leisure Card Plus includes free admission to more than 300 museums. The cards may only be purchased from NBT offices abroad. Alternatively a separate museum card can be purchased in Holland from VVV offices, and the Holland Leisure Card gives a 10 per cent discount on this.

Netherlands Board of Tourism (NBT)
NBT has offices in a number of countries. Brochures and leaflets on various subjects are available, many free on request.

Head Office
Vlietweg 15
2266KA Leidschendam
Netherlands
☎ 070 3705705

Australia
6th Floor
5 Elisabeth Street
Sydney, NSW 2000
☎ 02 276921

Canada
Suite 710
25 Adelaide Street East
Toronto
Ontario M5C 1Y2
☎ (416) 3631577

United Kingdom
25-28 Buckingham Gate
London SW1E 6LD
☎ 071 630 0451

USA
21st Floor
355 Lexington Avenue
New York, NY10017
☎ (212) 370 7367

Suite 305
90 New Montgomery St
San Francisco, Cal 94105
☎ (415) 543 6772

225N Michigan Avenue, Suite 326
Chicago, Ill 60601
☎ (312) 819 0300

VVV Tourist Information Offices in Holland
Vereniging Voor Vreemdelingsverkeer, always referred to as VVV (pronounced 'Fay-Fay-Fay') provids detailed information on local sights, events and attractions, public transport and a booking service for accommodation and local events. Publications in various languages, maps and

books, also free leaflets, are normally available. In major towns offices with the sign *i-Nederland* can give information on any region in the Netherlands. Most offices have multi-lingual staff to help visitors.

For advance information it is only necessary to write to 'VVV' followed by the name of the town and 'Holland'.

Tourist Routes and Waymarking

ANWB tourist routes are marked with hexagonal signs with the route name and direction arrow. Routes specifically for cycles (*Toeristische fietsroutes*) carry a cycle symbol and are not normally for mopeds. Booklets describing the routes, with maps, are available from ANWB, VVV and bookshops. Brown signboards with a tree symbol indicate picnic sites, car parks and leisure areas set up by the Forestry Commission (Staatsbosbeheer or SBB) in attractive countryside or dune areas.

A number of footpaths exist, many in woodland controlled by the SBB or on private estates. Many of the latter allow *Vrije Wandelingen* or free rambling on paths and tracks during daylight hours. Long distance footpaths (*Lange-Afstand-Wandelpad* or *LAW*) form a network linking into the European network of long distance paths (GR). Maps and booklets describing waymarked and signed cycle and footpath routes are available from ANWB, VVV and many shops.

Travel

Air Routes

Many international airlines operate services from all over the world direct to the major international airport of Schipol near Amsterdam, or to airports at Rotterdam, Maastricht and Eindhoven. From the UK, including Scotland and Northern Ireland, services operate from around twenty different airports, and others go from Eire and the Channel Islands. Details and timings change rapidly so enquire locally before booking.

From Schipol airport a frequent direct rail link to Amsterdam Central Station takes 17 minutes. A bus service links Rotterdam airport to the city centre in 20 minutes.

ANWB

Algemene Nederlandse Wielrijdersbond (General Dutch Cyclists Union), was founded in 1883 to uphold the interests of cyclists. It now looks after its members' interests in tourism, recreation, environment, traffic and transport — motorised or not, on land, water and in the air. Usually it is known as the Royal Dutch Touring Club, but most Dutch people simply refer to it as the ANWB (pronounced 'Aah-En-Fay-Bay').

Head Office: Wassenaarseweg 220, 2509BA, Den Haag; ☎ 070 3264426. Also here is a shop selling all ANWB publications, including maps, guide books etc. Open Monday to Friday 8.45am-4.45pm, Saturday 8.45am to noon. Closed Sunday.

The ANWB signposts roads, has road patrols, publishes maps, camp site lists, and so on. There is also a day and night service giving up-to-date information on road and traffic conditions, weather and delays to trains or ferries, ☎ 070 3313131.

Visitors from other countries who are members of motoring or touring clubs affiliated to the AIT can receive breakdown assistance from ANWB road patrols The ANWB does not deal with enquiries from overseas.

Bus, Tram and Underground
Buses link railway stations to surrounding towns and villages. In towns there are local buses and trams, while in Amsterdam and Rotterdam the underground (metro) operates. The *Nationale Buswijzer* guide to all bus routes in the country gives information how to reach almost every town and village from the nearest railway station, with route numbers, zones, journey times and frequency of service. Obtainable, with a map, from major railway stations.

Information on city public transport services (bus, tram and metro) can be obtained by telephoning: 070 3824141 for Den Haag, 020 6272727 for Amsterdam, or 010 546890 for Rotterdam.

National 'Strip' Ticket (Nationale Strippenkaart)
This is valid on all buses, trams and metro trains, also for second class rail travel within Den Haag, Amsterdam, Rotterdam, Utrecht and Zoetermeer. Strips are cancelled by the driver or the passenger (in automatic machines) depending on the number of zones crossed on the journey. 15 or 45-strip tickets can be purchased from stations, public transport offices, post offices, tobacconists and some VVV offices, also from the bus driver, although these are more expensive than those bought elsewhere.

Ferries
Services across the Westerschelde in Zeeland and to the Wadden Islands in the north are well appointed car ferries operating to regular schedules. Throughout the country there are many smaller ferries most of which carry cars. Those across the North Sea Canal are free but others charge fares which are usually quite reasonable.

All ferries carry foot passengers and cycles. Where reservation is compulsory, this applies only to cars. A telephone booking made the same day or the previous day is usually sufficient except for peak holiday times, when as much notice as possible is advisable.

Rail Travel
Netherlands Railways (NS) are completely electrified and provide rapid and frequent services over most of the country, with direct links to the rest of Europe including International Express (D-train), Trans-Europe Express (T-E-E) or International Inter-City (IC) services on which a supplement is usually payable. Fares are reasonable and a variety of special cheap tickets are available in addition to normal single (*enkele reis*) and return (*retour*) tickets. Various Rover Tickets range from Day Rover (one day's unlimited travel on all routes) to 7-Day Rover and Multi-Rover for

a family. Information on these and numerous day excursions with combined rail and entry tickets to various events and places of interest are obtainable at any station or from the VVV, also usually from NBT offices abroad, from whom rail tickets may be purchased in advance. Railway timetables (*Spoorboekje*) for the whole country are available from Nederlandse Spoorwegen (NS), PO Box 2025, 3500HA Utrecht, ☎ 030 359111.

All large railway stations in Holland have an information office. Timetables, information, brochures and leaflets (some free) are obtainable in London from Netherlands Railways, 25-28 Buckingham Gate, London SW1E 6LD ☎ 071 630 1735 (the same address as the NBT).

Bicycles by Train
Carriage of cycles is not free. Many trains have restricted or no space for cycles. During summer holidays cycles may be sent in advance in special cycle wagons. Full details are available from NS information offices or at stations.

Steam Train Lines
Full details of steam train services are contained in the free annual booklet *Holland by Steam* in English from the ANWB.

Road Travel
Holland has a good road network which includes an extensive motorway system. There are no toll roads although tolls are payable on the Zeeland Bridge, Prins Willem Alexander Bridge and Kiltunnel. Normal European regulations apply. Vehicles drive on the right and give way to traffic from the right, including bicycles, except at major crossroads and along roads with priority, denoted by white diamond-shaped signs with orange centres. Pedestrians have right of way on crossings. Dipped headlights (not sidelights only) must be used at all times in built-up areas. A warning triangle must be carried and used to warn following traffic of an accident or breakdown.

Car and Bicycle Hire
Most of the internationally-known car hire companies operate in larger towns, airports and ferry ports. It is cheaper to book in advance, before leaving home.

Cycle hire is very common. Details of some eighty railway stations with hiring facilities are contained in a booklet (*Fiets en Spoor*) published by NS. Many places, including stations, have covered cycle parking (*Rijwielstalling*), where cycles may also be hired. Be prepared for the machines to have 'back-pedal' brakes.

Fuel
Leaded super grade (98 octane) and unleaded (regular and super) are freely available. The latter (*loodvrije*) is sometimes known as 'Euro'. Diesel fuel and LP gas for cars is available from larger stations, also 'mix' for mopeds. Credit cards are usually accepted. Signs on major roads give notice of approaching filling stations.

Parking
Do not park on priority roads outside built-up areas, or on roads signed *Stop-verbod*. Do not stop or park on cycle paths or footpaths. Multi-storey car parks have automatic barriers — take ticket on entry and pay at cash machine before leaving. Outdoor 'pay and display' parks have *Parkeer-Automat* machines where a ticket is bought and displayed in the car. The instructions on ticket machines are usually multi-lingual. Many towns use parking meters, or free parking in 'blue zones' for a fixed time. The latter use a *Parkeerschrijf* or parking disc, which is set to the time of arrival and placed so that it is visible from the outside. Discs may often be obtained free from VVV ofices, banks and police stations.

Road Restrictions and Hazards
Non-motorised vehicles are excluded from motorways and trunk roads, the latter being indicated by a square blue sign with a car in white.

In some towns residential streets (*woonerf*), marked by blue signs with a house in white, may have width restrictions and strict speed limits. Be aware of pedestrians and children playing. Circular blue signs with a white bicycle or a lane marked by a solid or interrupted white line and a white bicycle painted on the ground, indicate mandatory cycle paths for both pedal cycles and mopeds. A circular blue sign with a white man and child, or a black sign with the word *Voetpad* in white, indicates a footpath, banned to all vehicles including cycles. Junctions with traffic lights may have separate lights for pedestrians and for cycles, and car drivers should be aware of this. A double line of white dashes on the road surface, accompanied by a blue sign with a white arrow and the words '*Fietsers Oversteken*' (cyclists crossing) shows a cycle crossing. Cycles and mopeds have priority.

Railway level crossings and opening bridges are common. Some crossings only have a warning bell and flashing lights, with no barrier. Allow extra time for delays at opening bridges if driving to catch ferries or trains.

Road Signs
Signing is generally good. White lettering on blue signs apply to all traffic. Local signs and signs in towns are black on white boards. Red or green lettering with a bicycle symbol on white boards refer to cycle routes. If a moped symbol (small motorcycle without rider) with a line through it is shown the route is for pedal cycles only and mopeds are banned. Most of the major signs are mounted on blue and white striped poles, and each carries a serial number, small and not easily visible from the road. This number is shown in the appropriate place on all ANWB tourist maps and road maps, also many other maps. Walking and cycling routes may also have *paddestoelen* or 'toadstools', knee-high square blocks with sloping sides bearing arrows pointing to various destinations, with distances. Here again, a serial number appears on the top which is shown on the maps. Signs marked 'P+R' at approaches to towns indicate park and ride schemes where cars or cycles may be parked and the journey continued into town by bus.

International Road Signs may be supplemented by pictorial signs, most of which are self-explanatory. Other signs include the following:

Alle (Andere) Richtingen: All (other) directions
Behalve, Uitgezonderd: Except
Doorgaand Verkeer: Through traffic
Dus NIET Brommen!: NO mopeds!
Fietsers Afstappen: Cyclists dismount
Fileforming: Queue ahead
Geen: No
Gestremd: Obstructed
Gevaar: Danger
Inhaalverbod: No overtaking
Korte invoegstrook: Short entry lane (used where the entry lane on a motorway is shorter then usual. Take care.)
Langzaam Rijden: Slow down
Pas Op! Let Op!: Take care! Attention!
Opspattend Grind: Loose grit
Rem vast Motor Af: Handbrake on. Switch off (on ferries and at opening bridges)
Slecht Wegdek: Rough or broken road surface
Spoorvorming: Potholes (also used instead of the above)
Tegenliggers: Two-way traffic ahead
Tussen: Between (Usually used with parking times)
Volg or *Richting*: Follow/Go in direction of (used where smaller place does not appear on major road signs, eg Doetinchem *Volg* Emmerich)
Weg Omlegging: Diversion
Werk in Uitvoering: Road work in progress
Zacht Berm: Soft verge
Ontsteek uw Lichten: Switch on your lights
Denk aan uw Lichten: Remember your lights
(These latter two signs often appear before and after road tunnels.)

Speed Limits

Built-up areas: 50km per hour. Outside built-up areas: 80km per hour. On trunk roads: 100km per hour. On motorways: 120km per hour, all unless indicated otherwise. Cars with trailers: 80km per hour everywhere outside built-up areas. On-the-spot fines may be imposed.

Vehicles and Drivers

Drivers of motor vehicles (including motorcycles and mopeds) must have a valid full (not provisional) driving licence and certificate of motor insurance. The minimum age for drivers is 18. A 'green card' insurance certificate is advisable but not essential. Valid registration documents and proof of passing vehicle road safety test (if applicable in country of origin) must also be carried. The vehicle must have an international identity disc (GB, USA, etc) indicating country of origin. Seat belts for drivers and front-seat passengers must be worn. Children under 12 are not allowed in front seats unless using a special safety seat or, if over 4, using a seat belt. Adjust headlights to prevent dazzle on high beam. A red warning triangle must be used in case of breakdown. Trailers and caravans need documentation valid in their country of origin. Motor-cycle riders and passengers must wear crash helmets.

Pedal cycles require no documentation but should comply with the legal requirements of the country of origin. Good front and rear lights, a rear reflector and reflective pedals or wheel discs should be considered essential.

Sea Routes

International shipping lines sail to Rotterdam and Amsterdam but most visitors by sea travel via the UK, then by ferry services, either direct to Holland or via Belgium or France. Facilities and fare structures vary. Cars with or without caravans, motor cycles, mopeds, pedal cycles and foot passengers are carried.

Direct ferry services:

Harwich to Hoek van Holland (Sealink Stena Line). One day and one night crossing each way. Crossing time varies from $6\frac{3}{4}$ to 8 hours. Direct rail connections from Scotland, north of England and London to Harwich, and from Hoek van Holland to all parts of Holland, Belgium and Germany.

Sheerness to Vlissingen (Olau Line). One day and one night crossing each way. Crossing time about 8 hours. Direct coach connection from London (Victoria) to Sheerness and coach connection from Vlissingen terminal to railway station.

Hull to Rotterdam (Europoort) (North Sea Ferries). Night service only. Crossing time about 13 hours. Rail connections from north of England and Scotland. Inconvenient for foot passengers at Rotterdam end.

Great Yarmouth to Scheveningen (Norfolk Line). Freight service with limited accommodation for passengers and cars. Three sailings daily from Monday to Friday and two on Saturday. Crossing time about 8 hours.

Felixstowe to Rotterdam (Europoort) (P & O European Ferries). Freight service with limited passenger accommodation. Two sailings daily from Monday to Friday. Crossing time about 8 hours. Apply direct to P & O freight office in Felixstowe.

Ferry services via Belgium:

Dover to Zeebrugge (P & O European Ferries). Six sailings daily each way. Crossing time about $4\frac{1}{2}$ hours.

Dover to Oostende (Belgian 'Regie voor Maritiem Transport'). Both normal cross-Channel ferry and jetfoil passenger service (no cars). Bookings handled by P & O European Ferries.

Dover to Oostende (P & O European Ferries). Jetfoil service several times daily for foot passengers only. Crossing time under 2 hours.

Felixstowe to Zeebrugge (P & O European Ferries). Up to three sailings each way per day. Crossing time 5-7 hours.

Hull to Zeebrugge (North Sea Ferries). Nightly service. Crossing time about 15 hours.

Ferry services via France avoiding long sea crossing:

Dover to Calais (P & O European Ferries). Frequent sailings. Crossing time 75 minutes.

Ramsgate to Dunkerque (Sally Line). Frequent sailings. Crossing time about $2^1/_2$ hours.

Dover to Calais or Boulogne. Hovercraft service. Crossing time about 35 minutes. Takes cars and foot passengers.

A number of coach and rail services operate from the UK with direct connections to destinations in Holland. Details from NBT, British Rail or travel agents.

INDEX

Note that in Dutch 'ij' is placed in the same alphabetical order as 'y' (see also page 8).

MPC

A Note to the Reader

Thank you for buying this book, we hope it has helped you to enjoy your stay in Holland. We have worked hard to produce a guidebook which is as accurate as possible. With this in mind, any comments, suggestions or useful information you may have would be appreciated. Those who send in the most helpful letters will be credited in future editions.

Please send your letters **Freepost** to:

The Editor
Moorland Publishing Co Ltd
Free Post
Ashbourne
Derbyshire
DE6 9BR

MPC The Travel Specialists